Aston Martin
and Lagonda

CHRIS HARVEY

The Oxford Illustrated Press

© Chris Harvey and The Oxford Illustrated Press Limited, 1979
Set in Monotype Ehrhardt by Santype International Limited
Printed and bound in Great Britain by
A. Wheaton & Co. Limited, Exeter

ISBN 0 902280 68 6

The Oxford Illustrated Press Limited, Shelley Close, Headington, Oxford

Contents

Acknowledgements

IT COULD have taken a lifetime to write this book had it not been for one extra-ordinary source of information: the Register of the Aston Martin Owners' Club. Nobody knows how many hours of research have gone into the Register, compiled over many years from information supplied by thousands of AMOC members. With such a reference work at my elbow, the task of writing this book was made much easier, but it still took more time than I'd care to recall. So my special thanks must go to Cadet Member 4390 James Holland, who lent me his copy of the Register while efforts were being made to reprint this magnificent work for new members of the AMOC, such as myself. It must be a real sacrifice, letting such a book out of your sight.

I must also thank David Holland, James Holland's father, for sacrificing a great deal of time, while general secretary of the AMOC, to help me with this book; to Shaun Magee for telling me even more about the first generation of post-war Aston Martins and lending me much valuable documentation; to Ian Moss for imparting a lot of wisdom on the second generation cars and to Geoff Courtney and Roger Stowers of Aston Martin Lagonda for dedicated assistance with the third generation, and Lagondas. My thanks also to Brian Joscelyne, editor of the excellent *AM* club magazine, and to fellow writer Graham Robson for invaluable help in preparation of the final manuscript. Their knowledge of Aston Martins and Lagondas proved far-reaching.

Clive Aston, Philip Woolfe-Parry, Michael Ottway, Ian Moss and Pete Foster helped with the competition side; Simon Phillips, Bob Rusk and Tommy Blank provided similar help with research into production cars. Adrian Feather, Roy Chambers, Ian Sheppard, David Lintrey, June Creed, John Goate and Don Aylett of the AMOC and Valerie May of the Lagonda Club gave much-needed en-couragement; my thanks to them all and to Geoffrey Marsh (and the AMOC) for allowing me to use extracts from two superb articles on restoring an exotic racing car, the Le Mans-winning DBR1.

Geoffrey Marsh also loaned me excellent pictures as did Brian Joscelyne (at very short notice), Paul Kunkle, Owen Barnes, Shaun Magee, Robert Morris, Tommy Blank, Michael Ottway, Pete Foster and Dennis Edensor. But this book would have been incomplete without the wonderful pictures supplied by Warren Allport of *Autocar*

Acknowledgements

and Jim Lee of *Motor*, so patiently researched in company with the rest of this series by Paul Skilleter; the cover photography of Maurice Rowe of *Motor*, and the drawings of Tim Holder. Paul Skilleter also found time (goodness knows how) to take many of the pictures, as did Roger Stowers of Aston Martin Lagonda, who also lent me priceless historic pictures from their files.

I would also like to express my deep gratitude to Jane Marshall of Oxford Illustrated Press for making sense of the manuscript as editor; to Gloria Callaway for her marvellous index and to Pete Foster and Ian Moss, who, like James Holland, showed so much confidence in me; they let me drive their racing Aston Martin on the road. I'm happy to report that they got both the car and the Register back, although I was sorry to part with either!

Colour Plates

I

Bespoke Motor Cars

SELDOM HAS THERE BEEN a more emotive motor car than the Aston Martin. Since Lionel Martin's first hill climber of 1914, only about nine thousand have been built, yet their following is one of the biggest and most dedicated in the world. Why? Because every one of those nine thousand cars (8400 of which have been built since the war), has been a sporting machine of the highest quality; there has never been an ordinary, nor a compromise, car. That this exclusive breed survived at all when exotic thoroughbreds were falling all around it, was because of the efforts of the enthusiasts who bought them and, more particularly, because of one man: the wealthy industrialist David Brown. He bought Aston Martin for a bit of fun, and Lagonda because he owned the last one made before the war. Throughout his reign, from 1947 to 1972, every car cost far more to make than the sum it sold for. But Brown didn't mind: he was able to drive all the prototypes and always had a bespoke motor car at his disposal. When he could afford to support Aston Martin and Lagonda no longer, the asset strippers moved in.

But once Company Developments had sold the firm's playing fields to cover the purchase price, they, too, fell under the spell of Aston Martin and Lagonda. They poured in more than a million pounds in three years till they too could afford this extraordinary enterprise no longer. Then, once more, the marque's enthusiasts rallied round to save the firm. They plastered their cars with stickers imploring all and sundry to Save Aston Martin; they sent cheques 'to be used in any way the company sees fit'; they ordered what new cars there were from the receiver; they won a moratorium on bills from anxious suppliers. They held the fort until the next owners, an Anglo-American consortium, could take over. These new owners assessed the situation and saw that it was worth saving Aston Martin and Lagonda. One of their number, Alan Curtis, managed to divest himself of enough involvement in his other businesses to breathe new life into the firm as managing director. He reorganized everything and got his sums right. At the time this book was being written, Aston Martin and Lagonda were selling for a decent amount more than they cost to make, with an order book stretching into the 1980s.

David Brown never achieved such commercial success, although Aston Martin and Lagonda did make him a few thousand pounds some years; his success must be measured in terms of the cars that he made, his great win at Le Mans and

The first Aston Martin David Brown sold to the public after the war, later to be called the DB1, combined the slender elegance of the pre-war radiator grille with the flowing curves fashionable in the late 1940s. In the background is a Lagonda saloon.

the other races they won. One of his greatest achievements was one of his earliest. He turned the immediate post-war Aston Martin and the Lagonda into one wonderful machine that was to herald nearly thirty different models in thirty years; some of them, such as the DB4 and the V8, with five distinct series—such is the complexity of bespoke motoring!

Tantalizingly, the Lagondas have nearly always been more advanced on a technical plane than their stablemates. Because of this, plus the fact that their development has been an integral part of Aston Martin (a fact frequently neglected by those dazzled by the more popular car), it is only proper that they should receive the same focus of attention in this book, even though only about a thousand have been made since the war.

What is so special about these Aston Martins and Lagondas? Firstly, they are rewarding cars, with truly exceptional handling qualities. This is true especially of the Astons whose finish has also been in the realms of the fantastic. Hardly any two are exactly the same in every detail, because they are individual cars made for individual people, welded together by a common enthusiasm for what amounts to an *objet d'art*. Aston Martins and Lagondas have always been tremendously strong (and frequently very heavy) cars in the old-fashioned British tradition; yet they have always had the beauty of line and delicacy of feel of an Italian masterpiece. Their performance has seldom been found wanting and has frequently been

in excess of anything imaginable by many. Yet their concept has kept pace with the times, developing from a fairly spartan sports car to a truly luxurious grand tourer; from a two-seater to a proper four-seater that is the fastest accelerating car in the world, still with the option of a hood that goes down all the way. The euphoria that the very name Aston Martin engenders in their enthusiasts has been heightened by an incredibly charismatic racing heritage. Aston Martins not far removed from cars that could be driven on the road, have frequently 'blasted the pants' off far more powerful and impractical machinery and have set this marque in a class of its own.

Of their rivals, only Ferrari has survived with equal appeal, and there is talk of Aston Martin taking Lamborghini under its wing. The Aston Martin has always been the Englishman's Ferrari; the car of English-speaking people. And like Ferrari owners, Aston Martin and Lagonda devotees have needed all their enthusiasm to overcome all the problems that their temperamental, exotic cars have given them over the years. Aston Martins were so underpriced for so long that their customers had to do the development work! That policy has now changed, and it has put Aston Martin and Lagonda in the Ferrari class at last.

To investigate thirty models of motor car and all their different offshoots in one book seems formidable; but the task has been helped by their distinct grouping into three generations: the 'Feltham cars' made between 1947 and 1959, and

The DB2 was the first truly post-war Aston Martin. It featured a development of the DB1 chassis with the Lagonda's twin-overhead-cam engine and an Italian-style body. VMF 63 was one of the three 1950 team cars.

By 1954 the Aston Martin had acquired two rear seats, a 3-litre engine
and smoother styling. This DB2/4
drop-head coupé was a works demonstration model raced at one time by
David Brown's daughter Angela.

named after the factory's location in that period; and the two groups of 'Newport
cars': those made from 1958 until 1970 (more or less at the time production
moved to Newport Pagnell), and the current V8s which have been built there
since 1969.

The Lagonda 2½-litre and the Aston Martin Spa Special were the first of the
Feltham cars, and were introduced at around the same time in the late 1940s. The
Lagonda twin-overhead-camshaft engine quickly went into a short-chassis development of the Spa Special to form the lithe and legendary Aston Martin DB2; a
two-seater of truly Italian appearance and Aston's first real gran turismo car. The
DB2s distinguished themselves in competition, especially at Le Mans, and so David
Brown commissioned the building of the specialized DB3 sports racers. They begat
that incredibly good-looking giant killer, the Aston Martin DB3S. The DB3S
needed a bigger engine than the 2½-litre and as 3 litres was the biggest that could
be fitted with the existing W. O. Bentley-designed engine, this also went into the
Lagonda tourers. Soon after came the world's first hatchback, a body style that
has proved to be a winner in the most popular of cars, the ultra-practical Aston
Martin DB2/4, and the leviathan Lagonda V12 sports racer. The Lagonda was a
12-cylinder version of the DB3S and was one answer to the problem of more power
or less weight for outright wins. The Aston Martin DBR1 that followed was an
altogether different animal; it had less weight but the same power although its
engine was different. It was a great success, and went on to win both Le Mans
and the World Sports Car Championship in 1959. The DBR2 and DBR3 were
other experimental versions on the same theme. At the same time came the last,
and most sophisticated, of the Feltham cars, the DB Mark III—Aston Martin was
beginning to meet the demand for a more luxurious car than the Le Mans-style
DB2s.

The DBR racing cars had special engines, and one of them, the DBR2, led to
the development of the first of the Newport cars, the DB4, with a performance

The DB4 introduced the second generation of post-war Aston Martins.
This is one of the numerous versions
of the model produced between 1958
and 1963; it is the DB4 Vantage built
for the 1962 London Motor Show.

The DBS V8 with single headlights
was the first car produced under
Company Developments at Newport
Pagnell. This car was pictured in May
1972 with DBS V8 badges; soon after
the DBS prefix was deleted but
David Brown's character lived on in
this third generation of post-war Aston
Martins.

The spectacular new Lagonda four-door saloon using similar mechanical components to the Aston Martin V8 showed that the consortium which took over from Company Developments in 1975 meant business. It proved to be good business, filling order books with revised versions of the Aston Martin V8 well into the 1980s.

so high that there was hardly anything that could stay with it on the road. Its Italian-styled body, was comparable to the best Ferrari could produce, and the car was only half the price. The development of these cars took so much time that David Brown's long-awaited grand prix cars, the DBR4 and DBR5, came too late; they were too heavy and in 1960 they were three years behind the times.

The win by the DBR1 at Le Mans heralded the end of David Brown's very expensive excursion into racing on a big scale. Although the DB4GT, the Zagato, and Project cars 212, 214 and 215 followed, they were either catering for customers' competitive instincts or were being used to try out the Aston Martin and Lagonda design team's ideas for forthcoming cars. It was at this point that the Lagonda Rapide saloon (named after the legendary pre-war car) made a brief appearance. It was something of a test bed for future Aston Martins; its 4-litre engine was used in more highly-tuned form in the DB5. It also had de Dion rear suspension that was to feature in principle on the third generation of Aston Martins once the bugs had been ironed out.

Economic woes hit Britain almost as soon as David Brown launched the DB6. He had to slash the price even though it was one of their best cars, and the faults of the earlier, second generation machines had been eliminated. It was an Aston Martin that was fully developed and it was the first since the war in which four people could sit without being too cramped. It was fast and stable, but far removed from the sports cars of old. It was the introduction to the third generation of Aston Martins; its mechanical components and much of its chassis being the basis of the DBS series.

The hurriedly produced DBS was designed for the new V8 engine which was then under development. David Brown had been dreaming about it since 1954 although work had not actually started until 1964. When the DBS received this long-awaited engine the third generation was born. Big, solid, and very fast, their ultimate form can be seen today in the V8 Vantage. A four-door Lagonda version was visualized from the start, but by the time the V8 engine made its bow in 1969 (and David Brown had been knighted for his services to industry) there were too many financial problems for it to progress further than the prototype stage.

Company Developments took over in 1972 with the Lagonda as the apple of chairman William Willson's eye. But first he had to get the Aston Martin V8 sorted out and the firm back into profit; he succeeded with the Aston Martin car but not quite with the company. With incredible bravery he launched the Lagonda in the height of an energy crisis. The timing could not have been more difficult. By then, late in 1974, Britain was under a socialist government which did not smile upon such exotic cars as Aston Martins and Lagondas; and America, land of promised exports, was in the middle of a frantic (and in my opinion misguided) safety programme. Once more Aston Martin and Lagonda floundered without the finance to cope with the American safety tests and export their way out of trouble. The receiver moved in and the enthusiasts rallied round to save their favourite car. Eventually Alan Curtis was persuaded to put the firm on a proper footing.

Since then it has been a story of unparalleled success, both in the company's history and in its history of extraordinary technical achievement. Within months of Curtis taking over, a dramatic new model was announced: the new Lagonda, the wedge-shaped saloon of the future. Today, Aston Martins and Lagondas leave the factory two by two (two Aston Martin V8s, two Aston Martin convertibles and two Lagondas every week), and the order book is full.

II

The Feltham Cars

THE FIRST GENERATION of post-war Aston Martins and Lagondas were built at Feltham, Middlesex, mostly with the help of mechanical parts and chassis pressings from the main David Brown works in Huddersfield. Some of the bodies were built at Feltham and some by Mulliners in Birmingham. Later, all the bodies were built by Tickfords at Newport Pagnell after they were taken over by David Brown in 1955. But they are all called Feltham cars, and comprise the two-litre (later called the DB1), the DB2, DB3, DB3S, DB2/4, DB2/4 Mark II, and DB Mark III. The DB3 and DB3S were not really road cars, but were racing machines sold to members of the public (usually racing drivers) who were considered sufficiently skilled to handle them (see Chapter VIII).

Of the cars that anybody could buy, the lovely DB1 had the shortest production run. Only fifteen were made between the start of production in September 1948 and the end of the run in May 1950. They were built with Claude Hill's two-litre pushrod economy engine, and were the first and last Aston Martin to use this type of valve gear. Hill had started designing the engine in 1944 to replace the pre-war Bertelli overhead-camshaft two-litre because Gordon Sutherland, who ran Aston Martin before David Brown, had decided that a more simple unit was needed. Besides having pushrod valve gears, this new four-cylinder 82.55 mm × 92 mm 1970 cc cast-iron unit featured such notable breakaways from previous Aston Martin practice as five main bearings (which set a trend that would be widely followed), a cast-iron crankshaft and alloy connecting rods. It had two valves per cylinder with a large vertical inlet valve and smaller exhaust-valve angled at 20 degrees, à la Bertelli. It also had an unusual combustion chamber shape which promoted a marked 'squish' effect. Siamesed inlet ports were on one side of the head with separate exhausts on the opposite side. With a 7.25:1 compression ratio and poor-quality post-war Pool petrol it produced 90 bhp on twin SU 1.5-inch carburetters. With a higher compression head, flat-top alloy pistons and better fuel it produced 115 bhp with 111 lb/ft of torque. Most cars were fitted with the 7.25:1 head, however, and a couple were fitted with an 8.5:1 'Spa' head. A compression ratio of 10:1 was needed for the 115 bhp output.

Such high compression ratios were rarely used, however, as the engine was meant more for long-term durability, maximum service intervals and minimum

The Spa Special was the first post-war Aston Martin, but it did not go into production. Only one was built, because it was very expensive and the potential buyers who saw it at the 1948 London Motor Show realized that something a good deal better and more civilized was on the way. It is pictured here with a new body after winning the Spa Twenty-Four Hour race.

production and running costs, than for high performance. Even in racing use it was capable of 21 mpg, but it proved to be rather noisy and rough in its running compared to the Lagonda-based six-cylinder that was to replace it. The Hill four-cylinder was mated through a Borg and Beck single dry-plate clutch to a David Brown gearbox with synchromesh on the top three ratios of 4.1 : 1 top; 5.17 third; 7.7 second and 12 first and reverse to a hypoid bevel rear axle using a 4.1 : 1 ratio as standard with a 3.9 option. Normally 16-inch wheels with 5.75-inch Dunlop tyres were fitted, but on the Spa replica, 19-inch wheels with 5.50 covers (18 ins by 5.50 at the front) were used. The 3.9 rear axle was also fitted to this car to give 100 mph at 4300 rpm on long straights. Standard cars were geared for 19.2 mph at 1000 rpm.

The chassis was Hill's *pièce de resistance*. It had been developed from the wartime Atom saloon which was built entirely from square or rectangular section tubes, right up to roof level. Sutherland liked rigid roofs and David Brown didn't, so Hill compromised when Brown decreed that the DB1 should have a soft top. He made up for not being able to extend the new chassis up to the roofline by duplicating the main longitudinal members and generally strengthening the structure.

He chose rectangular or square tubing because it was easier to handle than round tubing. All these spider web tubes were steel, and were of 13 gauge for lower members, and 18 gauge for the superstructure; they were gas welded or arc welded according to position. The main tubes were 3 inches deep with 2.5-inch extensions (cunningly grafted on with equal length diagonal cuts rather than crude squared-end butting), and they ended in 2-inch deep tubes at the back of the frame. A bulkhead in the scuttle position was arranged as a main cross-member and the superstructure was made wide enough for three-abreast seating. Body panels were carried on outriggers. This immensely rigid frame with a 9-foot wheelbase and (for the day) soft suspension was to set new standards in roadholding for more than a decade.

Like the engine and the new frame (which replaced an old-style whippy channel section chassis) the suspension was a complete breakthrough from normal pre-war practice. Again it was based on the Atom saloon with an improved version of its trailing-link independent front suspension, the 7-inch links being pivoted on hefty needle roller and ball bearings, mounted in a tubular light-alloy chassis

The first post-war Aston Martin actually sold to a member of the public was the DB1 chassis number two; number one is believed to have been a works experimental chassis that was broken up. This car is a good representative of the fifteen DB1s that were a tribute to the genius and dedicated work of designer Claude Hill.

The DB2 was the car that made Aston Martin's name after the war; a rapid lightweight two-seater endowed with extraordinarily good roadholding. This is one of the first DB2s produced between 1950 and 1953. The ventilation grilles on the front wings were removed on later models, making them even more attractive.

cross-member filled with oil. This lubricated the suspension bearings and the Marles steering box's bell-crank. Coil springs were located at the top on a cast-alloy upright and an anti-roll bar was fitted. Armstrong lever arm hydraulic dampers formed an upper arm to the suspension parallelogram. Hill's steering geometry was very accurate with two separate tie rods overlapping.

The rear suspension showed some similarities. Coil springs and an anti-roll bar were used in conjunction with trailing radius arms and a Panhard rod to locate the live axle. Hill said that he preferred coil springs to the more commonly used leaf springs because they were neater, they needed less maintenance and because they countered brake reaction better. Armstrong lever arm shock absorbers were again used. Roll centres were arranged at ground level at the front, and at hub level at the back, for ultimate handling. Twelve-inch Girling hydraulic drum brakes with a two-leading shoe pattern at the front were considered adequate. They were

certainly effective on the exposed wheel Spa replica but proved to be prone to fade, despite the fitting of wire wheels, when a full-width body was used. This was a problem that would not really be overcome until disc brakes were adopted; it was a problem that was shared by all other manufacturers.

Twin SU electric fuel pumps and Lucas electrical equipment were fitted throughout. The Spa replica's body was a pretty scanty affair with cycle-type mudguards, whereas the standard car's body was the epitome of luxury. It was a drop-head coupé with three-abreast seating and bulbous front wings which fell in a curve to a point at the base of the two doors; from here rose separate egg-shaped rear wings with bulging spats to clear the knock-on hubs. An elegant, and distinctly pre-war, radiator grille was neatly moulded in at the front. These cars weighed in at 22.5 cwt which was 3 cwt more than the Spa replica. The overall dimensions were: length 14 ft 8 ins; height 4 ft 7.5 ins; ground clearance 6.5 ins and turning circle 35 ft. The price was £3109, including British purchase tax.

A price reduction to £1915 including purchase tax, a more powerful engine and an exciting Italian-style GT body all helped to make the DB2 a more attractive proposition when production started in May 1950. The popularity was reflected in the numbers made: 407 (including around 100 drop-head coupés) were produced in the three years from May 1950.

The new engine was the W. O. Bentley-designed Lagonda 2.6 litres which had first seen the light of day in September 1945. It was a classic four-bearing twin-overhead-camshaft unit with cast-iron block and alloy cylinder head. Its bore and stroke of 78 mm × 90 mm gave it a capacity of 2580 cc; the camshafts were chain-driven and the valves were set at 30 degrees to the vertical in hemispherical combustion chambers. Exhaust valve guides and cylinder liners were both exposed to the cooling water and the liners were seated at the bottom. The engine was unusual, however, in that the combined iron block and crankcase extended well below the bottom of the crankshaft throws and was closed by a pressed-steel sump, which was purely an oil container, instead of the rigid device on most engines. The crankshaft was inserted into the barrel of the crankcase from the rear end

W. O. Bentley's beautifully clean 2.6-litre Lagonda engine pictured in its Aston Martin form with side-mounted air cleaners. Lagonda versions had detail differences, including air cleaners mounted on top of the camshaft covers, because there was more room under the higher bonnet line.

The DB2 development of Claude Hill's chassis combined great rigidity with light weight. The coil spring suspension was relatively soft for the day and its geometry was meticulously worked out. The result was that the car handled much better than its stiffly sprung contemporaries with their heavy, but whippy, chassis.

and each main bearing, apart from that at the front, was housed between two semi-circular alloy 'cheeses', which located the bearings into large circular holes in the crankshaft diaphragms. The idea of this system was to make up a structure strong enough to enable wet liners to be used without weakening the engine. It was effective once problems with the differing rates of expansion between the duralumin cheeses and the cast-iron block had been overcome by meticulous assembly. This form of construction with a counter-balanced crankshaft contributed not only to good power output (105 bhp at 5000 rpm on twin 1.5-inch SU H4 carburettors),

David Brown had a good eye for styling; he even made his tractors look good. He was also one of the few people who could change the shape of the DB2 without detracting from its appearance. This is the 1956 DB2/4 Mark II with a hard top modelled on that of the drop-head coupé. The bonnet lifts at the line marked by the chrome strip on the front wing rather than at the sill line as on earlier models. The idea behind this change was to make the bonnet more rigid.

The tiny rear seats in the DB2/4 (this is a Mark II model) met with mixed reactions. They were based on a pre-war design by Frank Feeley. Harold Beach who had taken over the DB2's development, thought they were 'just like lavatory seats'. But he had to admit that the car sold better with four seats, no matter how austere the design of the rear ones.

but to long life and smooth running. The normal compression ratio was 6.5:1 in deference to Pool petrol (on LB6B series engines), although 123 bhp was available from an optional 'Vantage' head (LB6V engines) with a compression ratio of 8.16:1 and HV6 1.75-inch SU carburetters from January 1951.

Later a VB6B Vantage engine with bigger induction manifolds and valves was available, and a similar export version was numbered VB6E. There was also an earlier LB6E engine fitted to a few cars which had a larger inlet manifold and 1.75-inch SUs; these had a 7.5:1 compression ratio and an output of 116 bhp. One or two other cars had prototype 3-litre engines (DP101) fitted.

There was a choice of two Lagonda gearboxes to be driven through a Borg and Beck single dry plate clutch. One had Lagonda ratios of 3.77 top; 5.02 third, 7.48 second; and 11.03 first and reverse; it featured the big saloon's steering column gearchange. The other gearbox, by far the more popular, had the more sporting Aston Martin ratios of 3.77, 4.75, 7.05 and 11.03, with a floor gearchange. Final drive was by a Salisbury hypoid bevel with a wider variety of ratios: 3.5:1, 3.67, 3.77 (the most popular) and 4.1:1. In conjunction with 16-inch wire wheels, this gave a road speed of 21 mph per 1000 rpm, with the standard engine.

The chassis was similar to the DB1 and the suspension was identical. The only real differences were that the side members in the centre section were 5 inches further apart with twin tubes each side, one 5 inches above the other, and the wheelbase was shortened to 8 ft 3 ins. This meant that the frame remained just as rigid despite its extra width to take the slab-sided coachwork.

At that time, many manufacturers were coming under fire for failing to show proper consideration to engine accessibility when fitting the fashionable new all-enveloping bodywork to replace the old gulls'-wing bonnet cars; a failing that

The DB Mark III was the final development of the first-generation cars. Most were fitted with disc brakes and were more powerful and easier to maintain versions of Bentley's original engine. The nose was restyled on the lines of the successful DB3S racing sports car and the interior changed too.

Saloon versions of the DB Mark III retained the rear door which made the car so practical as a grand tourer. This picture shows the piles of luggage—'enough for a month away from home', salesmen claimed—that could be accommodated with the back seats folded flat in estate car style. It was a significant body style that has since been copied by all manner of popular car makers.

Disc front brakes were optional on the first 100 DB Mark IIIs and were standard after that. They proved to be troublesome to maintain but wonderfully effective at stopping the car.

persists to this day. Aston Martin, maintaining closer links with the people who bought their cars, boldly decided to hinge the entire front portion bodywork from the scuttle on swivel points at the nose, so that it could be lifted for maximum accessibility. They were able to do this because they had such a rigid chassis. The only penalty paid was flexing of the alloy frontal portion as the car was driven, a feature that rapidly became familiar in use. By the standards of the day, the rest of the alloy body was extremely rigidly mounted—on steel rear wheel arches, the sills and the bulkhead. The contours of the body were formed in an outline of Z-shaped steel to which small-diameter tubes were welded for additional stiffness. The panels were then turned round the lip of the channel section to make a light, stiff, structure capable of taking the two wide doors, which were also constructed in similar fashion. Another transverse bulkhead ran between the wheel arches for additional rigidity. The dry weight was listed as 22 cwt.

Prototypes constructed for Le Mans were smaller and lighter than the production DB2s which had a 4-inch higher roofline, deeper screen, repositioned pedals and a more sumptuous interior, with heater. Three people could just sit abreast in the production car if they had the optional steering column change or a cushion behind the two seats, but the car was really a two-seater. The drop-head coupés were just that: as cosy as the fixed-head, with the hood bearing a close resemblance to the hard top, and featuring the same enormous blind spots between the side windows and the small rear window(s). But blind spots or not, the hood fitted well and was quite adequate for the car's maximum speed—a considerable achievement in 1950. Overall dimensions were rather smaller than the DB1 at, length: 13 ft 6.5 ins; height 4 ft 5.5 ins; width 5 ft 5 ins.

The DB2/4 which followed was virtually the same size outwardly (it was listed as 14 ft 1.5 ins long because it had separate bumpers rather than the built-in rubbing strips on the DB2 body) but it was cunningly rearranged inside to make it an occasional four-seater. Five hundred and sixty-five were made, including at least seventy-three drop-heads, in the two years from October 1953. Between October 1953 and April 1954 they used the same running gear as the DB2 Vantage and after that the 2.6-litre VB6E engine was enlarged to 2.9 litres (VB6J) for the drop-head (a change that took place in August 1954 on the saloon). The front and centre section of the DB2/4's chassis was identical to that of the DB2, but changes were made behind the location point of the rear springs. By modifying the tubing and reducing the capacity of the petrol tank from 19 to 17 gallons, it was possible to provide a clear space above the tank, which ran from behind the front seats to the tail. Two tiny seats were provided in this space; they were just big enough for two small children or one transverse adult. Alternatively, with the rear seat folded down, an enormous amount of luggage could be carried, making the car a true GT. Access to this luggage was aided by the world's first hatchback door in the raised roofline and tail section. Visibility was also improved by a bigger window in the third door and the introduction of a modern, curved, one-piece windshield to replace the split screen. The rear quarterlights were reshaped and the headlamps were set higher in the bonnet. One car was built for David Brown with a hardtop similar to that used on later DB2/4s. The price of the standard cars went up to £2622 including British purchase tax.

The revised bodywork raised the weight to 23.5 cwt dry, so the Vantage engine as standard did little to improve performance. Therefore the bore was increased to 83 mm and capacity to 2922 cc in 1954. With a compression ratio of

The instruments were moved from the centre of the car to a binnacle in front of the driver in the DB Mark III, emphasizing that it was a real driver's car.

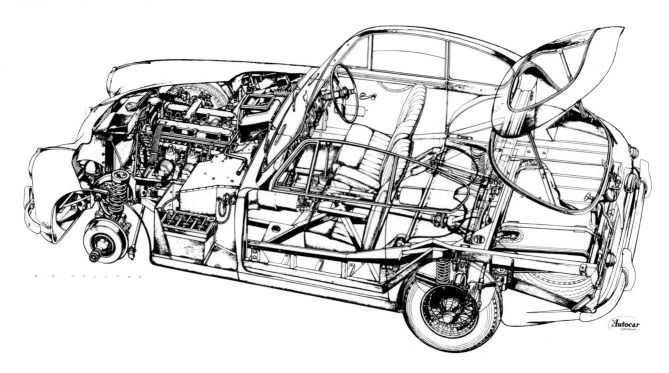

either 8.2 : 1 or 8.6 : 1, with bigger valves and higher lift camshafts, in new Vantage form (VB6J) it was possible to improve the power output to 140 bhp or 165 bhp with a corresponding increase in torque to 178 lb/ft at 3000 rpm from 144 lb/ft at 2400 rpm. Gear ratios were changed first to 3.73 top; 4.96 third; 7.38 second and 10.9 first and reverse, then to 3.77 top, 5.01 third, 7.46 second and 11 first and reverse.

With the acquisition of the Tickford coachworks by David Brown, the DB2/4's body was replaced by Tickford's version. The Newport Pagnell firm followed the same basic outline of the saloon and drop-head, with a fixed-head modelled on the lines of Brown's personal DB2. Three dozen of these fixed heads were built, and about twenty-four drop-heads. The numbers are not absolutely certain, although it is known that 199 DB2/4 Mark IIs were made in the two years from October 1955.

Outwardly, the chief differences between the Mark II and the early DB2/4 were small fins and a revised tail-lamp cluster, a higher roof (with a chrome strip at the front), two small hinged air vents, flashing indicators rather than the old swing-arm semaphore devices, and Tickford badges below chrome strips running horizontally back from the wheel arches to the bonnet's rear edge. These denoted the line at which the bonnet now raised, leaving the lower portions fixed to the main bodywork. The idea was to help alleviate the bonnet shake experienced with the earlier models and did little to hinder the excellent under-bonnet accessibility.

Inside, the seats were reshaped for better location; there were courtesy switches for the roof lights; and a proper fly-off handbrake rather than the awful umbrella handle affair fitted to previous DB2s. The clutch and brakes were improved slightly during the production run to make them last longer, and the price went up to £2788 including purchase tax.

Yet another price rise was on its way with the introduction of the DB Mark III in March 1957, of which 551 were made. They were mostly saloons with some drop-heads and a few fixed-heads. For a time they were produced alongside the Mark II variants, for export only, but when they came on the British market late in 1957, they cost from £3100. Throughout this period, the drop-heads and fixed-heads cost around £300 more than the standard saloons.

However, there were no complaints from the potential purchasers. They were getting a much-improved motor car with a further power boost to 178 bhp in its most popular form; the option of Girling disc brakes at the front (later standard-ized), and overdrive; a nose restyled on the DB3S racing car, plus a general revision of the controls and instruments. The engine (the DBA) had a new, stiffer block, with extra webbing in the crankcase, a stiffer crankshaft, and cylinder liners that seated at the top to make fitting easier. A new Hobourn Eaton oil pump was used with an enlarged sump and a new timing chain. There were further changes at the top of the engine: bigger valves and ports reshaped nearer to the DB3S pattern. Fourteen millimetre sparking plugs replaced the old 10 mm plugs and a new inlet manifold was fitted to take twin 1.75-inch SU carburetters. With a single exhaust system, the revised engine produced 162 bhp and with dual exhausts it produced 178 bhp.

After the first 150 engines had been produced, higher-lift camshafts were fitted and in 1958 a special series engine (the DBB) was listed as giving 195 bhp with three Weber 35 DCO twin choke carburetters (or three SU HV6), the 8.6:1 compression ratio, special camshafts and twin exhausts. Ten cars were fitted with this engine. Forty-seven were fitted with yet another special series engine (the DBD), with two or three SU HV6s, rated at 180 bhp. A special competition 214 bhp engine (the DBC) was also listed in 1959 with numerous modifications and triple 45 DCOE Webers, but it is thought to have been fitted to only one car.

The rest of the DB Mark III was also improved. The flywheel was lightened for better acceleration and the clutch linkage was converted to hydraulic self-adjusting operation. The gearbox was further refined for lighter action and a 2.93:1 optional Laycock overdrive gave 28.4 mph per 1000 rpm on the popular 3.77 rear axle. Girling 12-inch disc front brakes were standardized after being available as an option on the first hundred cars, and the Alfin rear brake drums were increased to 1.75-inch width to balance the additional stopping power on disc-braked cars.

Outwardly the Mark III looked much bigger with its new nose and restyled rear lamps. Inwardly it looked different, too. All the instruments were grouped on a hooded panel facing the driver with a parcel compartment in front of the passenger. There were more detail changes in the trim and the whole car weighed around 2 cwt more than its predecessors. It could also be supplied in rather softer form with Borg Warner automatic transmission on the DBA engines. There was a brake servo for everybody.

The DB Mark III was the last of the Feltham road cars; delightful, durable and sporting. They were at their best on the country roads that abounded before motorways and dual carriageways began to transform Britain and other countries. On such roads, handling was more important than top speed when long, fast journeys had to be made. The cars that were to follow were completely different, and were born in the year that Britain opened its first motorway.

III

The Newport Cars: DB4,
DB5 and DB6

THE SECOND GENERATION of post-war Astons and Lagondas have been dubbed the Newport cars, along with the current third-generation machines. This is something of a misnomer, since they were not all made at Newport Pagnell. Production did not move completely to Newport until 1963, and by then a lot of DB4s had been built at Feltham. However, it has become a convenient, and readily accepted, way to distinguish the old and the new generations. The first of the Newport cars, the DB4, caused a sensation when it was launched in 1958. Not only did it look absolutely right—practically everything about it was right, apart from one or two faults that were cleared up by customers acting as unofficial development engineers. By the time the DB5 was launched in 1963, the Newport cars had become extremely reliable machines providing they had proper maintenance. And when the body shape was modified to launch the DB6 in 1965, they became even more stable at high speed.

The DB4 was a really significant car. It marked the marriage of a lot of engineering principles that were not new in themselves, but that was certainly new to Aston Martin. The Touring-designed body was a classic with a simple, yet aggressive, grace that had defied production before. It not only looked wonderful, but it actually accommodated four people in a surprising degree of comfort. Aston Martin's traditionally high standards of craftsmanship had a lot to do with this. The basic platform chassis was immensely strong and was sufficiently rigid to stand comparison with its multi-tube predecessor; the body, although light (or Superleggera), contributed to this. The suspension, a new design by Harold Beach using the same basic layout as the W. O. Bentley-designed Lagondas at the front, and the Claude Hill-designed DB2s at the back, gave just as good roadholding as that of the Feltham cars, and coped well with the much-increased power.

The new engine was a 3.7-litre twin-overhead-cam straight six, and was technically more advanced than the rival Jaguar XK unit. The four-speed gearbox was all synchromesh and quite adequate in its day; the driving position was superb and the rack and pinion steering felt just right for the sort of tasks facing such a car. It was a real road-burner for the Monte Carlo set; it was a grand tourer even better than the sports cars which had preceded it.

Design work on the DB4 started in 1954 with Beach working on the front suspension and Tadek Marek on the engine; his all-alloy six-cylinder first ran in 1956 and was raced (much against his will) in 1957; the new suspension was also tried on works racing cars. The body, designed by Touring, was an Italian inspiration that somehow accommodated the symbolic race-winning Aston nose, and four people. Tickfords built it at Newport Pagnell using the Italian firm's Superleggera system in which alloy panels are fixed to a tubular frame fitted to the massive steel platform chassis. This form of construction was so strong that the two doors could be made very wide, and were. The third door was abandoned in favour of a reasonably large conventional luggage boot with deep parcel shelf above it, inside the car. The floor, scuttle, wheel arches and suspension support points were all part of the platform; intensive testing showed that this constructional combination could take an extraordinary amount of punishment.

The 3670 cc engine with alloy block and head had a bore and stroke of 92 mm and valves inclined at 80 degrees to give better breathing than the 60 degrees of the earlier engines. Two valves per cylinder were retained as was the two-stage chain drive for the camshaft, although there was a difference here. On the earlier engine the second stage included a tensioner sprocket and a centre sprocket to increase the chain constant on the tensioner. There was, however, no tensioner between the camshafts and the chain ran horizontally from one to the other. On the new engine, the tensioner was placed midway between the camshafts and the chain ran straight between the cams and the second-stage jackshaft. On the DB4 engine the chain from the crank had a tensioner that could be adjusted manually, and the oil pump was driven by a chain directly from the crank with a hydraulic tensioner. With a compression ratio of 8.25:1 and twin SU HD8 2-inch carburetters, power was quoted as 240 bhp at 5500 rpm, remarkably similar to the Jaguar output. Torque was given as 240 lb/ft at 4250 rpm.

There was only one problem. Aston Martin had concentrated on designing a stiff engine with a stiff crankcase and a stiff crankshaft; they did not realize that when the engine ran hot the clearances could practically triple. The result was that the early DB4 engine was loath to hold its oil pressure, a condition that was not helped by the fact that there was hardly room for more than a 15-pint sump.

There were five series of DB4 cars and later series one machines (made until February 1960) had revised bearing clearances to help combat the oil pressure tolerances. There was a limit to how far the tolerances could be reduced, however. If they were reduced too far it was impossible to start the engine on a cold morning; if they were not reduced sufficiently, the oil pressure suffered when the engine was hot.

Originally transmission was by a 10-inch Borg and Beck single dry-plate clutch through a David Brown gearbox to a Salisbury hypoid bevel rear axle, with a 3.54:1 ratio as the favourite combination. This gave overall ratios of 3.54 top; 4.42 third; 6.16 second; 8.82 first and 8.92 reverse. Alternative ratios of 3.31 and 2.93 were available. On the 3.54 axle, and 16-inch wheels, 1000 rpm in top gave 22.6 mph.

The front suspension was made up of unequal length transverse wishbones with coil springs and an anti-roll bar, plus Armstrong telescopic shock absorbers.

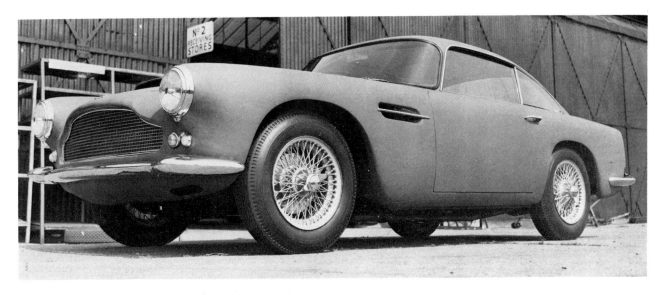

The rakish lines of the series one DB4 are shown to advantage in this picture of a car awaiting its final coat of paint and road test—possibly the first production DB4 built. These very early DB4s had their bonnets hinged at the back and on the first fifty, there were no chrome window surrounds and slim-line bumpers without overriders.

On the series two DB4, pictured here, the bonnet was re-hinged at the front to guard against wind pressure lifting it at speed should it have been incorrectly fastened, heavier bumpers were fitted to help sell the car in America, and chrome window surrounds were added to hold the windows more rigidly and reduce wind noise.

Tadek Marek's six-cylinder all-alloy engine as fitted to the early DB4s. In this case it was fitted with twin SU carburetters.

Superleggera means superlight! Massive as it might have been in relation to the complete car, six Aston Martin employees make light work of transporting this DB4 chassis and body structure.

The rear suspension was also by coils, set behind the axle for better traction, with parallel trailing links and a Watt linkage for lateral location instead of the DB2 Panhard rod, which could have a tendency to 'jack up' the car on cornering. Armstrong telescopic shock absorbers were used again at the front with lever arm shock absorbers at the back. Dunlop disc brakes, like those on the rival Jaguar XK 150, were fitted all round and a David Brown steering rack gave a turning circle of 34 feet.

The DB4 was lower and only slightly longer and wider than the DB Mark III: its length was 14 ft 8.375 ins; width 5 ft 6 ins; front track 4 ft 6 ins, rear 4 ft 5.5 ins; height 4 ft 4 ins; wheelbase 8 ft 2 ins; but it was heavier, at 26.5 cwt. The series one is easily distinguished by having its bonnet hinged at the back. There were no chromium surrounds on the windows of the first fifty cars; over-riders and heavy-duty bumpers were fitted after that and an aluminium radiator fan cowl after the first hundred. One hundred and fifty were made altogether.

The individual front seats were fully reclining and the rest of the interior bore a marked resemblance to that of the Mark III. The series two DB4 built between January 1960 and April 1961 had the bonnet rehung with the hinges at the front for safety, and a 17-pint sump. Optional extras included a much needed oil cooler (standard on the first thirty-three), electric windows and an overdrive; it usually had a 3.77 rear axle. Bigger front brake calipers and a radiator blind were fitted. Three hundred and fifty of these cars were made, with a modified chassis frame to accommodate the overdrive whether it was fitted or not.

The series three made between April 1961 and September 1961 looked a bit different. It had separate rear lights on chrome plates, single stalk switches, five (rather than three) demister outlets, courtesy switches, two bonnet stays, an electric rev counter, modified handbrake, covers over the clutch and brake linkages, and an optional 4.09 axle ratio on some overdrive export cars. An uprated GT engine was fitted to three of these cars, and the first fifty-five had an oil cooler as standard.

The DB5 pictured here, a 1963 model, was similar in appearance to the last of the DB4s, the series five. But there were many changes under the skin, including a 4-litre engine and five-speed ZF gearbox.

The series four made between September 1961 and October 1962 was immediately identifiable by a new grille with seven vertical bars and rear lights recessed into the body and a shallower air intake on the bonnet, plus another duct for the oil cooler which had become standard. Although it was officially standard, amazingly, it was left off some cars. A twin-plate 9-inch Borg and Beck clutch was fitted to increase this unit's life and a wide-ratio gearbox (1, 1.25, 1.85, 2.92 against 1, 1.25, 1.74, 2.49) was fitted to all but nine cars after chassis DB4/943/R; this was intended to help increase clutch life. A Vantage, or Special Series engine (suffix SS) with three SU HD8 carburetters, 9:1 compression ratio and larger valves, quoted at 266 bhp at 5700 rpm, was available as an optional extra. Most cars fitted with this engine had a restyled front with sloping headlight covers as used on the then-current DB4GT and were known as DB4 Vantages. Five of these cars were fitted with a GT engine.

The DB4 was lengthened to 15 feet for the series five, which was built between September 1962 and June 1963, and which resulted in a longer boot. The roof height remained the same and so did the roof line, but the boot lid was longer. There were a number of changes beneath the skin, too. The carburetters had a cold air box, the distributor had a vacuum advance and they were mostly fitted with an electric fan in front of the radiator, although this was subsequently deleted when it was found not to be a great success. Fifteen-inch wheels were fitted with 6.70 tyres instead of 6.00 × 16-inch—on 5.5-inch rims instead of 4.5 inches. This meant that the roof height remained the same at 4 ft 4 ins and the wingline was raised slightly to retain the original proportions. Detail changes included smaller front brake pads and a GT instrument panel with separate water temperature, oil pressure, fuel gauge and ammeter instead of two twin instruments. Seven cars in the previous series also had this panel. Some of the first fifty series five cars were of standard specifications, some were Vantages and after that all were built to Vantage specifications. But, of these, six were fitted with the GT engine and became known as the DB4 Vantage GTs, and some later series five DB4s were fitted with twin filler caps which made them exactly like the DB5 in appearance. Three of these late series DB4s were fitted with automatic gearboxes.

A convertible, the DB4C, was built from October 1961. The first thirty were series four cars (eleven with Vantage engines). There were two batches in series five, twenty-one of them with Vantage engines, two of which had the revised front. One convertible was fitted with a GT engine, but only seventy convertibles, out of the total number of 1110 DB4s, were built.

To add to the confusion over defining DB4 variants, two further series were built between 1959 and 1963. These were the short wheelbase (7 ft 9 ins) DB4GTs, only about eighty-five of which were made. Of these seventy-five were fitted with fairly conventional coachwork, and the remainder were fitted with either Zagato coachwork or were works projects cars (see Chapter VI).

Apart from the wheelbase and shorter overall length of 14 ft 3.375 ins, the most obvious differences are in the engine. It had a twelve-plug, twin distributor (or magneto) head with triple 45 DCOE Weber carburetters, 9:1 compression, large inlet valves, high-lift camshaft and higher compression pistons which put up the

The DB5 convertible was offered with an optional hard top. This was not one of the prettiest made, but had the virtue of having an exceptionally large rear window.

The DB6 Volante was one of the best-looking convertibles made by any-body, using a DB5 chassis at first—as in the car pictured here—and later the longer DB6 chassis.

One of the DB6 saloon's most dramatic features was the spoiler on the tail, to improve stability at high speeds.

The interior of the DB6 was well up to Aston Martin standards, with some owners still claiming it was the best ever made.

power to a quoted 302 bhp at 6000 rpm. Bore and stroke was usually the same although in some cars the bore was increased to 93 mm to give a capacity of 3749 cc. Oil coolers were normally worn.

Sixteen-inch Borrani alloy-rimmed wire wheels—long beloved of Enzo Ferrari—were fitted with triple-eared hub caps as standard. Girling, rather than Dunlop, disc brakes were fitted to give a larger swept area. The Borg and Beck twin-plate clutch fitted to later DB4s was standard with a David Brown close-ratio all-synchromesh four-speed gearbox and a Salisbury axle with Powr-Lok limited slip differential. Early cars had gear ratios of 1, 1.25, 1.74, 2.49 and 2.43 reverse; later cars had 1, 1.25, 1.85, 2.92 and 2.52 reverse; 3.54 was the favourite axle ratio, although 2.93, 3.31, and 3.77 were available as options. You could also have a 4.09 ratio with pre-wide ratio gearbox cars.

The two-seater bodywork was made from thinner-than-standard aluminium with cowled headlights for drag reduction; no over-riders were fitted. A 30-gallon tank filled most of the boot, with just room for the spare wheel. There were no rear seats and the overall weight was reduced by 1.5 cwt from that of the standard cars. Throughout this period, the price of the standard DB4 hardly rose, from £3976 in 1958 to £3989 in 1963; the DB4GT introduced in 1960 cost £4169 and the Zagato at £5470 was considerably more—such was the cost of shipping bits and pieces backwards and forwards from Italy.

The DB5 introduced in 1963 bore a remarkable similarity to the series five DB4 and cost little more: £4175, including British purchase tax. The chief difference was in the engine, from the Lagonda Rapide, which had been bored out to 96 mm, giving it a capacity of 3995 cc; and the standardization of the Vantage faired-in headlight body. This Lagonda engine was no more powerful than that of the DB4, but it was much more flexible. With three SU HD8 carburetters it was quoted at the same 240 bhp, but there was five per cent more torque between 3000 and 4000 rpm. The same applied to the Vantage Weber-carburetted version optional from September 1964, which oddly enough, was quoted at a couple of bhp less than that of the 3.7 GT.

Under the skin, there were more significant changes to the DB5. A 9.5-inch Laycock diaphragm clutch was fitted to either the same David Brown four-speed gearbox (with overdrive as standard) or to a five-speed ZF gearbox, which became standard from chassis number 1340. With the ZF box, which relieved much of the earlier box's graunchiness and didn't need an overdrive, the ratios, with a 3.77 rear axle were: top 0.834; fourth 1; third 1.23; second 1.76; first 2.73; reverse 3.31 (overall 3.14, 3.77, 4.64, 6.64, 10.18, 12.48). In top gear, 1000 rpm worked out at 25.5 mph. Optional ratios of 3.31 and 3.54 were available with the four-speed box or you could have a Borg Warner automatic box instead.

Detail changes included the standardization of twin petrol filler caps, different badges, an alternator instead of a dynamo, variable intensity indicator and rear lights' warning lights on the door edges, four silencers instead of two, Sundym glass, electric windows, a hydraulic jack in the toolkit, a handbrake/low fluid level warning light, tandem master cylinder and servos with Girling brakes and Armstrong Selectaride shock absorbers as an option at the back. All of this had a weight penalty of 250 lb, but the car was a lot less fussy to drive. A total of 1018 DB5s were made between July 1963 and September 1965, of which 123 were convertibles (with the option of a steel hard top) and twelve shooting brakes, which pleased David Brown but caused no end of disruption on the production lines.

The last thirty-seven DB5 chassis were used to build the short-wheelbase Volante drop-heads between October 1965 and October 1966. Basically they were the same as the DB5 convertible except that they had the revised oil cooler slot and the two-piece bumpers of the DB6 made between October 1965 to June 1969. They also had a restyled rear light cluster similar to that of the DB6, their own badges and DB6 options.

The DB6 introduced at the same time cost £4998 including tax; Britain was beginning to feel the effects of inflation. It was, however, a proper four-seater with increased wheelbase, height and weight. The roofline was, of necessity, completely altered, giving reasonable headroom over the new rear seats and ending in an upturned spoiler over the tail. The new shape reduced by 60 lb the aerodynamic lift generated over the back of the car at speed. Whether this, or the movement rearward of the aerodynamic centre of pressure, reduced high-speed understeer is uncertain but whichever it was, the car (only 17 lb heavier than the DB5) was now rock-steady right up to its maximum speed. Some extra weight had been saved by using box-section steel in place of the Superleggera tubes, which had the dual

The installation of the AE-Brico electronic fuel injection system in the Aston Martin DB6 Mark 2.

Aston Martin DB6 Mark 2s lined up outside the works at Newport Pagnell, awaiting delivery.

effect of creating better torsional resistance in the lengthened structure.

The DB6 looked a lot bigger although its overall length was only 2 inches greater at 15 ft 2 ins; this was partly due to the 3.75-inch longer wheelbase (8 ft 5.75 ins) and more steeply racked windscreen (53 degrees against 49 for the DB5).

The compression ratio of the Vantage unit was raised to 9.4:1 with quoted power up to 325 bhp and special camshafts were listed as options from 1967 (engines suffixed VC); later the Borg Warner box in the automatic car was updated. Rear axle ratios were standardized at 3.73 on manual cars and 3.54 on automatics. Selectarides were fitted as standard at the rear and power steering, based on a ZF unit, was offered.

A larger rev counter and speedometer were fitted and for the first time since the DB Mark III, quarter lights were fitted; the split bumpers and redesigned oil cooler opening were shared with the short-chassis Volante.

From October 1966 the Volante used the same long-wheelbase chassis; 140 of this model were made. Total DB6 production excluding the Volantes, was 1330; five of them were shooting brakes, a conversion done by coachbuilders Harold Radford, which meant far less trouble for the men at Newport Pagnell.

The final development of the DB4 theme, the Mark 2 version of the DB6, was announced in June 1969. In addition to the existing DB6 engine options, AE Brico fuel injection was fitted to forty-six of the 245 Mark 2s made to November 1970; the chassis numbers on these cars were prefixed DB6Mk2FI, and they used the higher compression Vantage head. The Mark 2s were rationalized with existing DBS production in that they used the same wire wheels (8.15 × 15 tyres on 6-inch rims), bigger hubs, three-eared hub caps (optional on the DB6) and front seats. The wider wheels necessitated flared wheel arches which kept the styling department happy. However they did nothing for the roadholding in the wet although they were some advantage in the dry. They also slowed the car down by about 2 mph with their extra drag! The track was now 4 ft 6.5 ins front and rear; a 10-inch clutch was fitted and a lower bottom gear of 2.97:1. DB6s were getting softer all the time!

The DB6 was the final embodiment of the DB4 which had caused such a sensation in 1958 and to this day many enthusiasts consider it to be the last 'real' Aston.

IV

The Newport Cars: DBS to AM V8

THE THIRD GENERATION of Aston Martins and Lagondas was heralded by a brand new body shape, designed at Newport Pagnell, with an adaptation of existing chassis components and the DB6 engine and gearboxes. This was the DBS that had been designed for the new V8 engine that Tadek Marek had started in 1963. This engine, first mooted in 1955, took five years to develop from 1963 until it was ready, when Aston Martin produced the new, widened, DBS to bolster sales. Later the V8 engine superseded the six-cylinder, and development continued with the DBS reaching in 1978 what must nearly be its ultimate form in its five distinct series.

In 1967, the DB6 chassis was widened by 4.5 inches and lengthened by 1 inch to allow the engine to be lowered behind the front cross-member in the DBS. This seemingly small change had, however, needed extensive alterations to the cross-membering to keep the same standards of torsional rigidity. But, as Dudley Gershon's engineering team had only a couple of months to make the changes (so that the new car could be introduced at the 1967 London Motor Show), the revised chassis that resulted was on the heavy side, a condition that persists to this day.

This was inevitable when such drastic modifications were being introduced. It is relatively easy to widen a chassis quickly, but it takes many months to pare off the last few pounds without compromising on rigidity or strength. Since that time there has been no point, nor, I suspect, sufficient time or money to take off those extra pounds. Such high standards had been achieved with power output and roadholding that if anything the extra weight is a bonus, for the car is so strong. But at the time when the DBS had the less-powerful six-cylinder engine, it was something of a handicap. The only adverse affects felt now are probably that the shock absorbers take something of a hammering from all that weight, increased by a massive steel superstructure which supports the alloy-panelled body.

The front suspension required little development: it came straight off the DB6 and the rear suspension, although quite different, had been under development for years. It was of de Dion layout to minimize wheelspin in anticipation of the extra power from the V8 and to cope better with the new flat-tread tyres that were being introduced at that time. A de Dion system had been used on the

Two DBS prototypes were built by Touring of Milan who had been responsible for the DB4. One car was left-hand-drive and one right-hand-drive—the left-hand-drive example being shown here at the 1966 London Motor Show. They used a short wheelbase version of the DB6 chassis with de Dion rear suspension. The engine was mounted 10.5 inches further back in the chassis for improved weight distribution, but this made servicing difficult (for instance, the cylinder head could not be removed without taking out the whole engine). These cars were exciting and significant, however, in that they were the first of the third generation of post-war Aston Martins and the first two-seaters since the late lamented DB4GT. Engineering Director Dudley Gershon said development was discontinued on these cars when the design staff were switched to the DBS four-seater and Lagonda four-door during the sales crisis of 1967. Now it seems that they will be the only two seaters made in this generation of Aston Martins.

Lagonda Rapide produced between 1961 and 1963 and which had, ironically, been responsible for that car's demise.

The chief problem with the Rapide was that any wear in the drive shaft splines, or in the chassis-mounted final drive's rubber supports, caused bad vibrations. By 1966 new slip joints had been developed for use in the universally jointed shafts needed with a de Dion layout, which meant that the differential could be relocated to get rid of the vibrations.

Location of the coil-sprung de Dion axle on the DBS was virtually the same as that on the DB6 except that the radius arms were revised to counteract roll tendencies. The Salisbury hypoid final drive incorporated a limited slip differential as standard.

The higher weight of the new car (31.25 cwt dry) decreed that power steering should be standardized and braking power increased. In these departments, the DBS was an immediate success. The ZF steering system was so regulated that effort at the driver's wheel never needed to exceed 10 lb pull, although excellent 'feel' was retained—a magnificent achievement. The twin servo-assisted Girling vented rotor discs, on board at the back, with independent front-rear hydraulic circuits were just as good.

The new bodywork and interior was designed by William Towns to fit in well with the Aston Martin's developing image as a fast four-seater rather than a 'hell-for-leather' two-seater. Despite the enlargement of the chassis and much improved leg-room, the body was 1.5 inches shorter and 1.75 inches lower than that of the DB6. Overall dimensions worked out at: length 15 ft 0.5 ins; width 6 ft; height 4 ft 4.25 ins; wheelbase 8 ft 6.75 ins; track 4 ft 11 ins and turning circle 36 ft.

The DBS four-seater that went into production used the six-cylinder engine at first until Marek's new eight-cylinder was ready. It makes a stunningly pretty picture here by a lakeside.

The DBS was also a very wide car as this early picture shows to advantage. Part of this extra width was due to an error during frantic chassis development work!

Far left:

One of the biggest bugbears of a specialist car manufacturer's existence is the constantly changing American safety standards which require tests such as that pictured. In this case a DBS V8 was anchored by handbrake and chocks and rammed by a steel trolley weighing 4000 lb and travelling at 23 mph. The object was to meet Federal Standard 301 in January 1970, which specified that fuel leakage should not exceed $\frac{1}{2}$ oz per minute after a simulated accident. As the tail of this DBS V8 crumpled there was no leakage. The rear structure collapsed in a progressive manner as it was designed to do, and there was no distortion of the passenger compartment. The rear windows did not crack and the doors still opened normally. Aston Martins were proud of their safety record and even prouder of the fact that they designed their cars to avoid accidents rather than merely survive in the event of a collision with some immense object.

Above right:

Under-bonnet view of the DBS six-cylinder, in this case a Vantage version.

Left:

The DBS V8 of 1971 shared similar styling to that of the earlier DBS six-cylinder.

Left:

By 1973 there had been many detail changes to the V8 including a change of name to the Aston Martin V8, carburetters in place of fuel injection, and body alterations such as those evident from this picture: the air extraction louvres which had been incorporated in the rear quarter panel were let into the panel between the rear window and the bootlid, the panels beneath the nose and tail were made deeper for better air penetration, and the stainless steel trim along the sill line was deepened to match.

Naturally this wider body slowed the car down; it created more drag but, thanks to painstaking testing, the aerodynamic lift was never the problem that it had been with the DB4 and DB5. There was just a little lift over the nose at projected speeds of 180 mph (far greater than that achieved by the six-cylinder DBS). However, this speed was too close to the DBS V8's maximum for comfort, and an air dam was fitted to all DBSs beneath the front bumper at the time the V8 was introduced in September 1969. This cured the lift problem and other aerodynamic changes included moving the interior air-extraction louvres in the side panels behind the rear quarter lights to a position under the rear window for added efficiency.

More cosmetic changes included redesigning the gear console and instrument panel. After eight hundred of these six-cylinder DBSs had been built between October 1967 and May 1972, a revised version was introduced, the AM Vantage, of which seventy were built up to July 1973. They were based on the DBS V8 which went into production in April 1970.

Obviously, the chief difference with the DBS V8 was in the engine, although there were other changes. The engine was based on the one used in the ill-fated Lola racing cars of 1967; it had started life as a 4.8-litre 90 degree quad-cam four-Weber unit in 1963. To save weight, aluminium alloy castings were used extensively, in the heads, block, camshaft covers, crankcase, sump, inlet manifolds and throttle housings. Soon the capacity was increased to the current 5-litre limit and with Lucas fuel injection and dry-sump lubrication it produced more than 450 bhp at 6750 rpm; but it was fragile.

As a result, the unit was redesigned with a general strengthening of main-bearing housings and crankshaft bearings; the block was restressed and the cylinder head studs in each bank were relocated at bottom deck level to eliminate all stress at the cylinder head face. The head was also restressed to give more support to the camshaft bearings and reservoirs were incorporated to ensure an ample oil residue for cold starting.

Vigorous testing failed to break anything or reveal any oil leaks so the bore and stroke was stepped up to 100 mm × 85 mm, giving a capacity of 5340 cc; a convenient size which avoided extensive and expensive retooling. The 90-degree two-throw counterbalanced crankshaft ran in five 2.75-inch steel-backed lead bronze main bearings. The two-stage Renold duplex roller chains drove the cams; the exhausts and inlet valves were laterally opposed at 64 degrees in hemispherical combustion chambers with the camshafts working on steel tappets with shim adjustment. Cast-iron valve seats were shrunk into the head and cast-iron wet cylinder liners were used with solid alloy seals on top and O-rings sealing the bottom. Forged steel connecting rods and die-cast alloy pistons were used with a 9:1 compression ratio and coil and distributor ignition. A chain-driven oil pump fed from a 21-pint sump. There were twin oil coolers, one on either side of the crossflow water radiator.

Initially, Aston Martin opted for fuel injection because it was felt that it gave them the best chance of passing US emission standards without substantial loss of power; a Bosch mechanical system was used as the DB6's Brico injection needed

An under-bonnet view of the V8 engine with carburetters in 1973.

Interior and dashboard of the Company Developments Aston Martin V8 automatic.

The rear seat of the Company Developments V8.

too much development to adapt. These systems were to cause many problems in service, Weber carburetters being substituted when it was discovered that they could meet the US regulations and improve torque.

The engine looked massive yet weighed only 530 lb against 588 lb for a 5-litre Chevrolet V8, 600 lb for Rolls-Royce's contemporary 6.2, 608 lb for Buick's 5.7, and around 500 lb for the Aston Martin six-cylinder. This meant that the spring rates needed only marginal adjustment at the front and the ideal roughly even weight distribution was maintained. At the same time a new, more robust and

Head-on view of the latest Aston Martin Vantage showing the deep frontal spoiler and blanked-off air intake.

Detailed styling changes were made to the Aston Martin range in 1978 including a smaller bonnet air intake. This is the standard V8 model, bearing the factory registration number transferred from car to car.

The long, sweeping lines of the 1978 Aston Martin Vantage, showing its rear spoiler to good effect.

quiet, alloy-cased ZF five-speed gearbox was mated to the engine via the DB6 Mark 2 clutch, giving different ratios: top 0.845:1; fourth 1; third 1.22; second 1.78; first 2.9; reverse 2.63 (overall 2.99, 3.54, 4.31, 6.3, 10.27, 9.31) with the normal 3.54 axle; 3.33 was used with a new automatic gearbox, Chrysler's excellent three-speed Torqueflite. The power output of the new engine was not quoted but engineering director Dudley Gershon put it at 345 bhp in his book *Aston Martin 1963–72* (Oxford Illustrated Press).

There was not much point in tuning the engine for more power although it had been redesigned to produce 460 bhp quite happily; its 345 bhp was enough to give it 170 mph and it practically had to wait for the right road tyres to become available. At first there was only one good enough, Pirelli's low-profile CN73 radial which needed new wheels, so Aston Martin designed their current 7-inch wide 15-inch alloy wheels. They were stiffer than the old wire wheels and were shaped to draw a substantial amount of air away from the new, very big, ventilated brakes which were to cope with the greater speed potential. Everything worked very well in this department, including a changeover to an ADWEST power steering rack, leaving only the fuel injection causing unusual problems.

There were detailed changes inside this first series car during its production run to July 1972, which included replacing its traditional wood-rimmed steering wheel with a more modern leather-covered wheel, fitting a glove box into the gear console, pockets in the back of the front seats and a steering lock. Air conditioning was standardized for the 1971 London Motor Show. The weight went up to 34 cwt and higher gear ratios of 3.33 for the manual version and 2.88 for the automatic were offered. Prices started at £6897 including tax in 1969, rising to £8749 in 1972.

Soon after Company Developments took over at Newport Pagnell, the second series (called the AM V8) was introduced with a distinctive two-headlight set-up replacing the four headlights used on the DBS V8; the idea was that although two 7-inch quartz iodine units did not give as good a spread of light on full beam as the four 5.75-inch lights fitted previously, they were superior on the more frequently used dipped beam. Besides, there wasn't the same sudden contrast between full beam and dipped beam that was experienced with the four-headlight arrangement; and auxiliary lights could always be fitted to improve the new system's spread. The restyled front also looked more like the emotive Astons of old, emphasizing Company Developments' desire to carry on making the cars. The length was increased to 15 ft 3.75 ins and the spare wheel was stowed flat in the boot, improving its carrying capacity; transistorized ignition was fitted now that the bugs had been ironed out on Jaguar's V12 E type; bulkhead insulation was improved; the airboxes were revised and the higher axle ratios of 3.33 and 2.88 were standardized.

The DBS V8 badge was replaced by one bearing the message AM V8 and the plain camshaft covers were embellished with the name Aston Martin Lagonda, again emphasizing the change of proprietorship.

Far more significant changes were on the way, however. In August 1973 the 'new Aston Martin V8' (the series three) was unveiled with four twin-choke 42

DCNF Weber carburetters replacing the Bosch fuel injection. Not only did these legendary Italian carburetters improve the performance with a lot of extra torque, but they were good enough to get the car through US emission regulations a year later. Apart from different manifolding, airboxes and so on, the taller carburetters required a deeper bulge on the bonnet; at the same time numerous other small changes were made. The air extraction louvres behind the rear window were replaced by a shallow lip and the car was stretched another three-quarters of an inch.

Water, oil and automatic transmission cooling was improved; optional rear axle ratios of 3.54 and 3.07 were offered; underbonnet insulation was changed yet again; the front seats were improved; the passenger's door was fitted with an electronic lock which could be operated from the driver's door; new US-style switches were fitted; the fuses were moved into the glove compartment for improved accessibility; the fuel tank was redesigned to allow more luggage space; and there was a bigger ashtray. Aston Martins were heading for America again!

British prices of the AM V8 started at £8949 in 1972 rising to £10,910 in 1975. Prices have risen rapidly since then, of course, to £20,000 for the V8 automatic (£1000 more for the manual version) and £25,000 for a Vantage. But, with a maximum of seven cars a week (including Lagondas) being produced, there was a year-long waiting list by the end of 1978. The changes that were rung in the series four cars produced between 1975 and 1977 were considerable: a lower compression ratio (8.3:1) became available for US and Japanese cars in 1975 so that they could run on lead-free two-star petrol, with improvements to the trim and general finish on all cars. There were also detail changes to the chassis and braking system to make production and servicing easier.

The first of the series five V8s was introduced in 1977. This was the incredibly fast V8 Vantage with power increased to somewhere in the region of 485 bhp—at least, that figure has not been denied by the factory. This was achieved by fitting four 48 IDF Webers in place of the normal 42-mm carburetters with different cams to give great inlet overlap, larger, 2.1-inch, inlet valves, pistons relieved to clear these valves, and a bigger exhaust. The suspension was also modified in detail to take even wider tyres, and a stiffer anti-roll bar was fitted at the front. Braking was made even more efficient by using grooved discs.

Following wind tunnel tests, the grille was blanked off, increasing water temperature at idle from 85 to 95 degrees centigrade (the optimum for efficiency, apparently), and a new large air dam and scoop were fitted under the front bumper; the bootlid also received a spoiler. The total effect was far better aerodynamically. At the same time, two large lights were fitted in the grille blanking to increase lighting capacity, and the petrol tank was expanded to 25 gallons from 21 gallons as fuel consumption went up. Every car was changed to Koni telescopic shock absorbers all round as supplies of Armstrongs ran out; the accelerator pedal was changed to the more modern pendant action and a radio and stereo unit fitted as standard. Instruments were updated and more warning lights fitted.

Gradually, in 1978, all cars were changed to Vantage specification—except for the engine and carburetters—and the front end styling was smoothed out. This

The 1978 Aston Martin convertible that set Americans afire with desire, shown with its hood up, and down.

meant that the standard cars were somewhat faster with a fifteen per cent power boost from the Vantage exhaust system to nearly 400 bhp and less drag. Anti-roll bars reverted to the original, softer, setting and the steering was modified with different castor angles for better feel and more power to make it lighter.

The convertible, called the Volante, was introduced in June 1978 using a power-operated hood on the lines of the 1975 Jensen. This fitted in better with the styling of the car than the roll hoop used by Porsche and Triumph on their Stag, with the well-lined hood following similar lines to the standard hard top except for a notchback rear window area. The chassis and bulkheads of these cars were boxed in to retain torsional rigidity, and, in these forms, Aston Martin felt that they had cars good enough to enter the 1980s.

V

The Luxurious Lagondas

THE PRODUCTION HISTORY of the post-war Lagondas dates back even further than that of the equivalent Aston Martins; and almost invariably they have been ahead of the Astons in some aspect of their technical development. For instance, most have had independent rear suspension (although it was not always an advantage), a chassis-mounted final drive, rack and pinion steering and a twin overhead cam engine. The $2\frac{1}{2}$-litre saloon announced in September 1945 had wishbone and coil independent front suspension (which has seen service in redesigned form in every production Aston Martin since the DB4), and had the twin overhead camshaft engine which powered the first generation of post-war Aston Martins, with the exception of the DB1.

The Rapide saloon introduced in 1961 featured de Dion rear suspension although it was, in effect, a stretched DB4. A de Dion system was used on the third generation of Aston Martins, and the Rapide's enlarged 4-litre engine also pre-dated the DB5. The current Lagonda saloon is so advanced that it makes you wonder what the Aston Martins of the future will look like. Certainly the prototype's extensive use of electronics will find its way into Aston Martins and its styling is eminently suitable for the mid-engined Aston which has been under consideration since the late 1960s.

Three prototype Lagonda four-door $2\frac{1}{2}$-litre saloons were built before David Brown took over the ailing company in 1947. They had the twin overhead camshaft engine that was used in the Aston Martin DB2 (see Chapter II) and a Cotal electric gearbox. Their designer, W. O. Bentley, ingeniously modified this box, reducing its length (and thereby its weight) by fitting a separate reverse-gear box in unit with the 4.55:1 final drive, mounted on the chassis to save unsprung weight. David Brown thought about making these gearboxes, but dropped the idea when he found that he could manufacture a lighter, less expensive, box using the same ratios (see Chapter II). This gearbox used a steering column gearchange, which eliminated the complicated push-pull dashboard control needed for the Bentley reverse gear.

Extensive testing and development at Feltham revealed that the prototype chassis was not so rigid as they would have liked, so the Aston Martin men boxed in the two 6.5-inch deep steel beams which made up the cruciform frame built by

Rubery Owen, and used rubber mountings in the suspension to compensate for the additional rigidity. The front suspension was of the same basic layout as that of the DB4: independent by coils and twin wishbones, which had sockets at their ends to take ball-jointed hub carriers (see Chapter III). Following extensive testing on the Continent, the wheels were mounted two inches further out for better brake cooling, although a certain amount of brake fade was always a problem with this heavy car on its 16 inch × 6-inch steel wheels. Bentley liked the steel wheels better than the wires used by Astons because they were lighter and cheaper; Astons retained them because they were far easier for chauffeurs to clean! However, in combination with the new helmet style wings, they effectively shielded the Lockheed two leading shoe drum brakes which led to brake fade, a problem which had not been encountered to such an extent on pre-war, exposed-wheel Lagondas. It is fair to point out that this was a problem experienced by the rest of the motor industry at the time. The rear drum brakes were mounted inboard to lessen unsprung weight and they needed modified mounting points to get more air to them.

The rear suspension was by long torsion bars running parallel with the chassis frame and linked to the rear hubs by short single wishbones. Longer tubular arms, ball-jointed to the final drive mounting, worked in conjunction with the wishbones, giving a modicum of swing-axle geometry to twin universally jointed drive shafts; a suspension set-up that was to gain a reputation for unpredictability in the wet, although this criticism never appeared in road tests. Radius arms provided location and a vertical box limited travel. Armstrong lever arm shock absorbers were used.

With a sumptuous four-door body, the car weighed in at 31 cwt dry for the prototype and 32 cwt for the production car; David Brown's men modified the styling a little for better air penetration and made the interior even more luxurious. Overall dimensions were: length 15 ft 8 ins; width 5 ft 8 ins; wheelbase 9 ft 5.5 ins; track 4 ft 8.75 ins and turning circle 38 ft. The price was the same as that of the spartan Aston Martin Spa special, a hefty £3100, including British purchase tax.

An elegant two-door drop-head coupé version of the 2½-litre four/five seater saloon was introduced in 1951, selling alongside the saloon and retaining the frankly pre-war styling. Then, in 1952, a Mark II version of these cars was announced. The chief difference was that the interior of the body was widened by four inches,

The post-war Lagonda saloons like that pictured here (a 1953 Mark II model) were conceived by W. O. Bentley to fill a gap in the market for luxurious cars somewhere between the SS Jaguar, Rover, Armstrong Siddeley and smaller Daimlers and the Rolls-Royces and Bentleys. Therefore he designed a car that could carry five people and a lot of luggage in great comfort. This necessitated a flat floor and independent suspension at the back, otherwise it would have been possible only to carry four people in the sort of comfort that would make the car comparable to a Rolls or Bentley although it was intended to sell at a lower price. It was an outstandingly good design, but was rather old fashioned in appearance.

although there were many other refinements, notably the standardization of Jackall chassis-mounted hydraulic jacks, a single twelve-volt battery to replace the twin six volts, and a general rearrangement of the dashboard, resulting in the instruments being sited directly in front of the driver.

In 1953, one or two special Lagondas with more modern and aerodynamic coachwork by Tickford were built, rather similar in side appearance to a notchback Aston Martin DB2. These became the forerunners of a new model introduced at the Motor Show that year. Five hundred and fifty of the 2½-litre cars had been made by that same date.

The chassis of the 3-litre was virtually the same as that of the 2½-litre, except

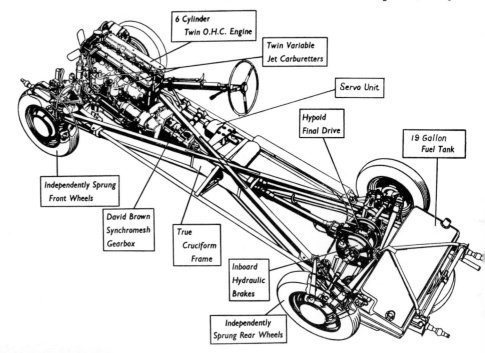

6 Cylinder Twin O.H.C. Engine

Twin Variable Jet Carburetters

Servo Unit

Hypoid Final Drive

19 Gallon Fuel Tank

Independently Sprung Front Wheels

David Brown Synchromesh Gearbox

True Cruciform Frame

Inboard Hydraulic Brakes

Independently Sprung Rear Wheels

for modifications to mount the new body; and its engine predated the fitting of that unit to the DB2/4 by eight months (see Chapter II). At first the 3-litre Tickford Lagonda was made only in two-door form, with a convertible and a four-door saloon following some time after the two-door saloon's introduction. In company with its new-found elegance, the length went up to 16 ft 4 ins and the width to 5 ft 9.5 ins although it was 2 inches lower at 5 ft 2 ins. The weight went up to 34 cwt dry, but with the extra power of the 3-litre engine, the performance was better. Initially the price was £3400 including tax, but by 1955 it had risen to £3600 and by 1956 to £3900—that is before David Brown slashed the price to £3000 to boost sales. Even at the reduced price, cost was a major barrier to sales (Jaguars were far cheaper) and so production ceased in February 1958. Capacity was now needed for the more popular Aston Martin DB Mark III. Production of the drop-head coupé had already stopped in 1956, while limited numbers of a Mark II version of the 3-litre were made throughout 1957. Four hundred and thirty of these 3-litre Lagondas were built, their chief difference being an Aston Martin-style floor gearchange.

There were several experimental Lagondas built between 1958 and 1961, when a new four-door saloon was announced for the Paris Motor Show. This was a stretched Aston Martin DB4 called the Rapide; only fifty-five were produced between 1961 and 1964 and they were all different in detail. Basically, they used a DB4 chassis with a 16-inch longer wheelbase, a bored out 4-litre engine and de Dion rear suspension.

The initial reason for using the de Dion set-up (see Chapter IV) was that a chassis-mounted final drive gave more room in the rear compartment. Transverse torsion bars linked to the lower radius arms provided the suspension medium rather than the coil springs used on the Aston Martin DBS; the improved handling was a bonus. The bored-out engine (see Chapter III) was the same as that used in the Aston Martin DB5 except that it had softer cams and two Solex carburetters for increased flexibility. In this form, torque was improved by ten per cent to 265 lb/ft at 4000 rpm, although power was down 1.5 per cent at a quoted 236 bhp at 5000 rpm; but with the de Dion rear suspension and longer wheelbase, the Rapide was at least the equal of the DB4 through corners!

Borg Warner automatic transmission with a second gear speed hold and first gear lock-up was fitted as standard with a 3.77 or 3.54 rear axle; an Aston Martin DB4 Vantage engine and manual gearbox were optional extras, known to have been fitted to only one Rapide. Four-wheel disc brakes, like those on the DB4, were fitted to the Rapide with distinctive centre-lock pressed-steel racing pattern 15-inch wheels on the same hubs. Tyres, however, were 7.10 Avon Turbospeeds. These tyres, and the extra weight, needed lower-geared steering than the DB4: 3.5 turns lock to lock rather than 2.66; the result was also a very big 41-foot turning circle like that of the current Aston Martin V8! A divided propeller shaft and fuel tanks in both rear wings completed the chassis modifications.

The body, with a distinctive 'Lagonda' front, almost Ford Edsel like, was built on the same principles as the DB4 Superleggera, with an overall length of 16 ft 3.5 ins, giving plenty of room for luggage as well as giving space in the rear seats for people

A.M.—D

Lagonda were always a part of David Brown's planning at Feltham and Newport Pagnell. Here the Rapide, on the left, shares his 1962 London Motor Show stand with the DB4 Vantage saloon and a DB4 convertible.

with normal length legs. In fact, the Rapide reeked of luxury, with electric windows and a filler cap which could be operated without leaving the driver's seat, plus picnic tables in the backs of the front seats and a radio; but then radios were always standard fittings to post-war Lagondas. The Rapide's price was well up to Lagonda standards: £5000 including tax.

David Brown, who loved the name Lagonda, showed great enthusiasm when a new one based on the Aston Martin DBS was visualized in 1966; the go-ahead was given in 1968 when the DBS V8 was under development with a January 1970 target for the prototype. This 11-inch longer fuel-injected DBS V8 with four doors was announced in time and the prototype revealed to the Press, but it was then kept on ice until sufficient engines were available, which, sadly, was not in David Brown's time at Newport Pagnell.

Initially, this car had wire wheels, but they were changed to alloy as soon as these became available. Chassis modifications were few; the extra 11 inches was shared between the boot and the rear passenger seat, with the result that the passengers got an extra 2.5 inches of headroom as the roofline started its drop further back in relation to their seats. The spare wheel was also mounted flat under the boot floor for extra luggage space. Despite its extra length, the chassis needed little modification as it was already very stiff; the propeller shaft was divided as on the Rapide. Again, like the Rapide, it handled at least as well, if not better, than the DBS V8 because of its longer wheelbase! Top speed was comparable because drag was reduced, the extra weight only affecting acceleration. Only the turning circle really suffered; it was an enormous 45 feet.

Eventually, Company Developments took up this design. They called it the Aston Martin Lagonda, and it was given a modified series three V8-style front and a carburetter engine. Seven were made between November 1974 and the time of

Company Development's demise at Newport Pagnell, some being finished while under the receiver. The price was no less than £15,638 including tax—nearly £3000 more than an Aston Martin V8 at that time.

Within eighteen months of buying the factory from the receiver, Aston Martin's new owners were unveiling a new Lagonda which took the 1976 London Motor Show by storm. They were able to do it because William Towns had had the basic design in mind for at least three years. It also proved to be aerodynamically sound as well as aesthetically pleasing. Mechanically it was the same as the standard Aston Martin V8 series four, although chief engineer Mike Loasby had had to revise the suspension geometry and spring rates to cope with the extra wheelbase and weight.

Where this new four-door Lagonda broke new ground, apart from the styling, was in its extraordinary electronics. On the prototypes, all the instruments had digital read-outs, and touch switches, like those found in lifts, worked all sorts of controls such as the wipers, electrically adjusted driver's seat, and even gear-changing.

However, under test conditions, these electrical devices proved to be unreliable and seven months was lost in starting production, which had originally been scheduled for April 1978, before an alternative source of manufacture could be found in America. Even then there had to be some simplification in the operation, although it was hoped that the prototype's full electronic system would be available from 1979. Production cars carried series five V8 mechanical modifications.

Overall dimensions of these latest Lagondas were: length 17 ft 4 ins; width 5 ft 11.5 ins; height 4 ft 3.5 ins; wheelbase 9 ft 6.75 ins; track 4 ft 11 ins and turning circle 38 ft. Dry weight worked out at just under two tons—the biggest and most magnificent Lagonda since the war.

The latest Lagonda is still built very much to W. O. Bentley's post-war concept except that it inhabits the higher price bracket rather than a half-way stage. It has four doors and a large luggage boot, but the styling is thoroughly modern.

VI

The Road Testers' Reports

IT'S A TOUGH JOB, road testing cars for the specialist magazines. Not so much the driving, but the responsibility of it all. Above all, the road tester must be fair to the readers, taking care neither to recommend them to buy a car which will disappoint them, nor to put them off a car which would suit them well. The tester must be absolutely honest and, moreover, if he is one of the old school, like John Bolster of *Autosport*, 'he must remember the effect that a few casual words may have on Britain's export drive'.

Times have changed since Bolster began writing for *Autosport* in 1950. In recent years testers have followed the American trend by placing more emphasis on the consumers' individual interests than on the nation's collective economic welfare. But Bolster's comments on the hundreds of cars that he has tested have held good.

The DB2. It is especially significant therefore that he considered the Aston Martin DB2 to be his ideal car in 1952.

'I have tried nothing that I would rather put in my own garage. The DB2 is a very fast sports car of immense stamina, as a long list of racing successes has proved. What very few people have realized, however, is that this model is remarkable for its comfort and luxury, and is also about the easiest thing there is to drive, outside of the "automatic transmission" carriages.

'As regards performance, one can have the normal engine which gives an easy 110 mph, and never pink on poor petrol. Alternatively, a full 120 mph comes with the Vantage engine, though this prefers a better grade of spirit. In either case, well over 90 mph can be quickly attained in third gear, and the engine is so smooth that this is quite an habitual speed for changing up. The unusually high maxima on the indirects are coupled with a flexible top gear performance. If the 2.6-litre, twin o.h.c. six-cylinder engine merits great praise, the roadholding and steering are no less remarkable. This is the very safest of fast cars, and whether one would go shopping, to the theatre, on a long-distance tour, or even race at Le Mans, one could have no more perfect companion than the Aston Martin.'

Wonderful words that sum up everything Aston Martin stands for today, just as they did in the immediate post-war years. After a blissful twenty years of high octane petrol being readily available, we have to worry again about pinking caused by poor fuel and high compression cylinder heads; and about blanket speed limits. It is sad, therefore, that an Aston Martin's ultimate performance can no longer be used without fear of prosecution outside, perhaps, the Middle East.

The ultimate performance from one of the earlier DB2s in road-going form was extracted in its first test, by *The Motor* in 1950. They wound VMF 63 up to 117.3 mph (116.4 average over four runs) with a 0–60 time of 11.2 seconds, commenting that 'the car has a natural cruising speed that lies anywhere between 70–90 mph. . . .'

The Motor commented in glowing terms on the DB2 they tested in 1950. The car, VMF 63, is pictured here on the notorious Continental pave.

The Autocar tested a similar DB2, VMF 65, in more austere surroundings in the same year. It is seen near their offices in bomb-ravished Stamford Street, South London, after competing in the Tourist Trophy race. Earlier in the year VMF 65 had been crashed on the way to Le Mans. Later, after *The Autocar* test, it was bought by Rob Walker and fitted with the engine from the DB3S team car number six, and tested by John Bolster for *Autosport*, before being returned to standard form in 1955.

'In to the acceleration through the gears, there may be cars which, handled with expertise, can keep level with the Aston Martin up to 30 mph, but there are very few which can match it at the higher speeds. With the close ratio, indirect gears and large rear wheels fitted on the car submitted for test, more than 40, 60 and 90 mph are available in the respective indirect gears, and in the 25 seconds which take a normal high performance production car up to 60 mph, the Aston Martin will reach 90. It follows that when opportunity offers on the road, not only one but a whole row of cars can be passed with safety in the face of oncoming traffic, and within the limits of, say, a 70 mph cruising speed, the top gear performance of the car is unaffected even by a a 1 in 10 gradient.'

The Motor liked the feel of the 'optional' central gear lever, although they recognized it as being 'unfashionable' at the time. They commented in glowing terms and at some length on the handling—it had 'cornering power almost beyond praise'—but said that

'it must be admitted that as the speed of the car rises it becomes appreciably more sensitive to the steering in respect of straight running. It is not hard to hold the car true on its course but it requires more conscious driving than do some modern types. In addition, there is a marked reaction to tram lines or similar ridges.'

Doubtless the fitting of racing tyres had influenced this: VMF 63 was in the same trim as when it had competed in the Silverstone production car event only three days earlier. Its brakes appeared to have been hammered, too.

Under bonnet view of VMF 65 emphasizing engine accessibility.

'It must be recorded that although the brakes give a satisfactorily short stopping distance with moderate pedal pressure, the travel on the pedal increased very noticeably during the 1000 miles of test driving whilst, following a series of stops from high speeds, they developed a fierceness which caused very noticeable shake at the front end of the car under even light applications.'

They also noted a 'small, but distinct chassis shake' on Belgian pave, but they put this down to the racing tyres. It is significant, however, that as the years have gone by, DB2 owners have complained of brake fade, while no other magazine raised this point while the car was current.

The Motor loved the DB2 as a whole.

'Even if this car, like all others, is imperfect, there is nothing available at present which can be compared to it in general character. It is a comfortable saloon which will start instantly from cold, potter quietly around on business and shopping calls, and carry anything from two to five people with varying degrees of comfort. It is also a car which will devour 300 to 500 miles of motoring at a higher average speed in safety than any other of which we have had experience, and this with a fuel consumption which will not fall below 20 mpg. It is in fact a uniquely desirable property and at less than £1500 factory price . . . it represents a really sound economic proposition for many motorists who desire to own a true road express without sacrificing the comfort, convenience, and weather protection which are taken for granted in modern motoring.'

The Autocar tested a DB2, VMF 65, soon after, in the same trim as which it had been raced in the Tourist Trophy three weeks earlier, with the notable exception of the engine: a standard 6.5:1 compression ratio unit had replaced the higher

Left:
Much praise was lavished on the DB2's roadholding and steering. Here is a close-up view of the front suspension.

Right:
A similar shot of the rear suspension showing the locating rods and coil springs.

compression racing engine. The result was that VMF 65 was rather slower than VMF 63, achieving 110 mph with a 0–60 time of 12.4 seconds, although it did manage 96 mph in third gear by using 5750 rpm. 'The recommended rev limit is 5000 rpm, but the engine did not cry for mercy,' said *The Autocar*. VMF 65 was also fitted with road tyres and displayed none of the harsher characteristics of VMF 63, with exception of the braking, which juddered a little during *The Autocar*'s fade test.

'The natural urge is to make not less than a 400-mile run in the day, in which kind of motoring this super car can show its real advantages in putting almost unprecedented miles into the hour, the exact figure depending, naturally, entirely on weather and traffic conditions. Fifty miles in an hour can be achieved on main roads "without trying" and the best recording in this direction, under very far from favourable conditions, and at night, was 62 miles inside 60 minutes. Averages far above the ordinary can be obtained without exceeding 70. This rate is held with supreme ease on part throttle up the slopes, and on all but the more severe bends, 50–60 mph can be the minimum.

'Stability is of the very highest order, no current production surpasses the impression given by the DB2 in this respect. . . !

These were high words of praise when it is realized that they were written before Britain had motorways, and extensive dual carriageway systems, and at a time when the roads were filled with lumbering lorries limited to 20 mph and often senile saloon cars which were capable of little more than an Aston's first-gear maximum.

Bolster tested VMF 65 a few months later in substantially the same trim as had *The Autocar*, and was enchanted. He reported:

'The flexibility of the engine is the first surprise, for the car will trickle along in heavy traffic on its 3.77:1 top gear, and gather speed smoothly at a touch of the accelerator. Its town manners are, in fact, impeccable, and this is an entirely suitable conveyance for business and social purposes. The body is most luxuriously appointed, with every possible comfort, including an efficient heater, and when driven gently this is an exceptionally quiet car, with only a low burble from the exhaust to hint at the other side of its personality.

'On leaving the built-up areas, a sudden metamorphosis takes place, and in spite of the closed body, one feels as though one is at the wheel of a racing car . . . the acceleration is quite out of the ordinary . . . the ratios have been so well chosen that one always seems to have exactly the right gear for the job in hand, and the very wide revolution range of the twin cam engine means that one doesn't have to change up in the middle of a tricky piece of passing.

'Many modern cars are handicapped by having too great a gap between third and top speeds. The Aston Martin had a splendid third gear, on which 90 mph may be easily exceeded, and the central lever is well situated and light to handle; nor could the actual change be simpler. A steering column gear lever is available, but I prefer the present arrangement. The box itself is very quiet on all gears, and thus it is no hardship to stay in third for several miles on end, if the rapid negotiation of a winding piece of road is the object. It is most exhilarating to see the speedometer needle swing round towards the 90 mark on every short straight, and the 60 mph second gear fairly hurls one away from the slower bends.'

Clearly this was an intensely satisfying car to drive and, in the manner of men the world over, Bolster decided to see how far he could go. His logic was disarming. No doubt, he said, the majority of owners will regard the DB2 as a de luxe high-speed touring car in the grand manner.

'Some buyers, however, will wish to take part in speed events, and I therefore thought it proper, for part of my test, to handle the machine in the style of the racing driver. I can say at once that it responds magnificently to the four-wheel-drift technique, and that even the most extreme methods fail to show up any vices or tricks. I remember one particular curve, which was wet and glistening with rain, through which I slid under full control at just over the century. I also attained 110 mph on the road after dark, which should satisfy prospective Le Mans competitors as to the efficacy of the headlights.'

So there you have it, Bolster's answer to magazines such as *The Motor* and *The Autocar*, who had had the temerity to criticize the lights of the car he deemed perfect. (Actually, they had said that they were good only for about 70 mph at night.) What's more, Bolster even liked the brakes.

'A car as fast as this makes altogether exceptional demands on its brakes, and to drive at the speeds I have mentioned calls for frequent powerful applications. I found them entirely adequate at all times, and was quite unable to make them fade.'

Bolster was completely fade free in his summing up, too.

'In an age when vulgarity and ostentation are the order of the day, the plain purity of line of the DB2 gives one great pleasure. No garish decoration mars the functional beauty of the aerodynamic body, and its very low wind resistance makes an important contribution to the high-speed performance. Let the spivs and the wide boys keep their chromium-plated "Wurlitzers", for this is a gentleman's car!'

Thus spoke a true Englishman, noted for his sartorial taste in deerstalkers and county tweed jackets. Neither was Bill Boddy disappointed when he made his Aston Martin DB2 test on the prototype drop-head coupé with steering column gear change for *Motor Sport*:

'In writing of a motor car so superlative, it is distinctly difficult to know where to begin. You see, the DB2 merits praise under so many sub-headings.

It is an exceedingly fast car . . . it is high-geared so that the engine is never very hard pressed, and quite exceptional maximum speeds are realized in the indirect gears . . . the engine is exceptionally smooth, willing and durable . . . the roadholding, steering and handling qualities generally are quite out of the ordinary, the comfort factor high, yet the DB2 will amble along at 10 mph in top gear and has such a foolproof gearchange and such light controls that any "bobby soxer" would get the hang of it in a very few miles . . . in short a superlative machine.'

These were high words of praise, particularly as Boddy tested the drop-head in the most arduous of winter weather while covering the Exeter trial. He covered a lot of miles, too, complaining of the hood only that it drummed at more than 60 mph, considering a leak as the sort of thing that would be confined to the prototype. The severity of the weather penetrated even the test's data panel, with the memorable phrase: 'Brands Hatch flying lap: Cancelled due to snow storm.'

Hail, rain or snow, the drop-head DB2 did 109 mph, with 0–60 in 12.7 seconds, virtually the same speed as the fixed-head.

'Driving the DB2 is an epicurean pleasure', said Boddy, 'which the snow and ice met with all the time we had the car merely served to emphasize.' He had only one grumble, shared with other testers, that 'there is no visual clue as to what the big family of little black switches does'.

Nevertheless, his summing up was typical of everybody who tested the DB2:

'It is no exaggeration to state that it stands out as one of the world's really great cars. That it is selling readily in dollar markets isn't the least surprising.

'Perhaps the best way of summing up the DB2 is to say that it offers the performance, stability and joy-of-handling associated with the sports/racing car while remaining a completely docile, comfortable, practical and withal economical high-grade touring car, allied to which is the unquestionable convenience of the aerodynamic closed coachwork.'

Sadly, *Motor Sport*'s relationship with Aston Martin deteriorated during the 1950s and it was to be eighteen years before the buyers were to read another test in that magazine's pages. They missed some great cars, and the company missed what would have undoubtedly been good publicity. Fortunately, however, other magazines continued to test Astons.

Bolster was lucky enough to try the ultimate DB2, Rob Walker's road car, the faithful VMF 65, now fitted with a DB3S engine.

'On moving off, it was at once obvious that the new engine had added enormously to the already excellent performance of the car. When I tried it in 1951 (it was 1954 when he tested the DB2/3S in *Autosport*) it was capable of an honest 110 mph. Today, it can register a timed speed of 131.5 mph, which is tremendous motoring. Similarly the very good 0–60 figure of 10.8 seconds has been reduced by exactly two whole seconds. It will thus be seen that the performance is now so great that the ordinary man can hardly visualize it. This saloon is, in fact, faster than some of the cars which were competing in Grand Prix races only five years ago!'

Bolster went on to praise the handling, saying it could cope with the extra power without drama, and that he found the fierce racing clutch quite acceptable, even in London traffic.

'Such stupendous motoring is something normally only experienced by tough guys in goggles and helmets. Yet, there I sat in my gents' natty suiting and travelled at racing speeds, without a hair being disturbed. (I refer, of course, to my own hair, for that of my passenger may well have been elevated!) The car cries out to be taken away from Britain's pitifully inadequate highways. With a month's luggage in the back, the seat on one's left suitably occupied, and all the roads of the Continent before one, I can imagine nothing nearer to an earthly paradise!

'After 75,000 of the most hectic miles imaginable, it is of great interest to examine the car to see how it has weathered the storm. It is perfectly true that the new look has gone, but there remains something even finer. Like a well-tailored suit or a craftsman-built pair of shoes, the famous old machine has gained an indefinable something with the passage of years. After a road test, I usually try to find the *mot juste* to describe the vehicle; in this case, I'll call it a *marvellous* car, and leave it at that.

'It remains for me to quarrel with John Wyer! He claims that the engine gives "only" 165 bhp, but if ever I felt a full 180 gee-gees under by boot, this was it. One can but assume that the horses from the Aston Martin stable are of the hairy legged variety, and not like the effeminate creatures from some other factories. . . .'

The 2.6-litre DB2/4. Only *The Autocar* managed to test the 2.6-litre DB2/4 (in September 1953) and found that its performance was virtually the same as that of a standard DB2. The mean average top speed was 111 mph with 120 mph one way and a 12.6 second 0–60 time. The handling and general behaviour of the car were as the DB2. Of the new rear seats, *The Autocar* commented:

'It is, of course, necessary to tilt the backs of the seats in order to gain access to the rear occasional seats. Owing to the low overall height of the car, together with a low-level floor, it is necessary to step down over the side members when getting into the car. This makes entry and exit a little more difficult than with a car of family saloon proportions, but the resultant layout, with the seat cushion a reasonable distance off the floor, is very satisfactory. . . .

'During the test the car was, in fact, driven a hundred miles or so with two passengers at the rear. It must be admitted that both headroom and legroom are a little cramped for adult rear passengers, particularly if the front seats are set well back.'

The Autocar road tested the prototype 2.6-litre DB2/4, YMP 200, in 1953. It differed from the production cars only in details such as the radiator grille which had more widely spaced slats.

Rear quarter view of YMP 200 showing the hatchback door and shorter, separate, bumpers against a rather well-used road test background sheet.

Both *The Motor* and *The Autocar* tested the 1954 London Show car 4 AML, a 2.9-litre version of the DB2/4, which also 'starred' in the film *Checkpoint* in 1956.

The 2.9-litre DB2/4. A year later *The Autocar* tested an identical car with the 2.9-litre engine, and commented of the rear seats:

'They are strictly for occasional use; one long-legged adult can be accommodated here in comparative comfort for short journeys. The view through the rear window from this position can be likened to that of a rear gunner of an aircraft leaving the tarmac, as the road streams away behind the car.'

The performance was becoming increasingly like that of a contemporary aircraft: the same maximum one-way speed of 120 mph was attained as on the previous year's exceptional run, but the average of two runs in opposite directions was much higher at 118.7 mph. Acceleration was a good deal better at 0–60 in 11.1 seconds, too, although fuel consumption was still marginally more than 20 mpg. Obviously the 2.9-litre engine was a considerable improvement.

The Motor were as enthusiastic as ever about Aston Martin when they tested the same car, 4 AML, a month later. Their maximum speed was almost identical to that achieved by *The Autocar*, although they brought the 0–60 time down to 10.5 seconds. 'The roadworthiness of the car is of a quite exceptional order', they reported.

'The springing is soft enough to ensure that typically continental pave causes little discomfort with the tyres inflated to 30 lb for high speed use, yet sufficiently firm to permit cornering in comfort at high fractions of G. What is more, the feeling of security is not illusory and even on wet and slippery roads the car can be driven with the utmost confidence. It may perhaps be added that this feeling of safety is assisted by the remarkable rigidity of the chassis and the solid feel of the body, it being noted at the same time that the latest model is $2\frac{3}{4}$ cwt heavier than the preceding type.'

Rear view of 4 AML showing the interior with rear seats folded flat.

Left:

Interior shot of a DB2 showing the dashboard layout and installation of an optional radio in place of the normal glove box lid. This arrangement was carried over to the DB2/4, the only major difference apparent from the driving seat being a divided windscreen on the earlier car.

Right:

Interior view of the DB2/4 showing how the seats tilted forward at an angle for easier access to the back. The instrument panel on this car is slightly recessed and the glove box is not fitted with a lid.

The Motor went on to praise the baggage space liberated by folding down the children's rear seats ('almost unequalled in European cars') and the extra visibility imparted by the new large rear window, although, surprisingly, neither *The Motor* nor *The Autocar* commented on the ease of access to the luggage area provided by the hinged rear window and surround.

They were quite emphatic about the seats, however. They just did not like them.

'Entry of an elderly person over the high body sides (dictated by the rigid frame) is impeded by doors with a restricted angular opening and no passenger shorter than 6 ft 6 ins could get his separate seat far enough forward to permit him to brace his feet upon the toeboard. This is most unfortunate since neither seat gives any sideways support, the vestige of a centre armrest being used as an accessible tool box and the flat squab being in both cases inclined slightly inwards. The result is that the driver loses much of the merit of the good steering by having to use the wheel as a locating ring, and the passenger, when the car is cornered fast, is thrown around like the proverbial pea in a pod.

'But these are the only criticisms of great consequence in a car of rare quality, unusual performance, exceptional roadworthiness and unrivalled versatility.'

The DB2/4 Mark II. Bolster dubbed the DB2/4 a 'high speed station wagon' when he tested a Mark II version in 1957, adding that the luggage platform was bigger than that of some small estate cars. 'Yet this remains very much the ex-racer', he said. 'All the right noises of a "real Aston" are subdued but definitely there, and in spite of the luxuriously equipped closed body, the DB2/4 remains above all a sports car.'

He noted improvements to the clutch and brakes and welcomed the return of a fly-off handbrake after the often criticized umbrella affair on the earlier DB2s.

'To exploit the Aston to the full, I took it out at dawn one day, and really enjoyed myself while the rest of the world was asleep . . . I found a straight road with a number of islands, between which I was able to achieve about 110 mph. At each island, I braked as hard as possible without actually locking the wheels, but there was no loss of braking power or noticeable increase in pedal travel.'

Strange behaviour? Not likely, Bolster was just doing what Aston owners have been doing for years, driving for the joy of it. And his *mots juste* summed up every car produced since the war: 'If I can describe it as a very sporting car that you can drive in a dinner jacket, perhaps I may make its character clear.'

His performance figures were virtually the same as those obtained with the earlier 2.9-litre DBs, and remarkably like those recorded by *The Autocar* and *Road & Track* in their tests of the Mark III soon after.

The DB Mark III. The Autocar's Mark III, a single exhaust overdrive model, had a mean maximum speed of 119 mph in direct top (118 in overdrive, the same as Bolster's Mark II) with a 9.3-second 0–60 time against the Mark II's 10 seconds. Other acceleration times were virtually the same, with the standing quarter mile being covered in 17.4 seconds by the Mark III and 17 dead by the Mark II.

Obviously, Aston Martin were happy with these performance figures, increasing the engine power of standard models only to compensate for the added weight occasioned by more luxurious fittings. It is a pity that the twin-exhaust Mark III was not tested by the specialist magazines, although it seems unlikely that its performance figures would have been dramatically different from those of the standard Mark III—probably about 4 mph faster and, perhaps, 0.5 seconds quicker up to 60 mph.

The Autocar liked the feel of the Mark III, commenting that it represented a considerable improvement over the previous model, even though the increase in power did little more than offset

'an addition of nearly 1½ cwt to an already heavy design. Very high standards of comparison must be used in judging a car of this character, partly because it is expensive, and also because it has a special appeal to the perfectionist.'

It is therefore significant that they appreciated the overdrive, particularly on the Continent, where much of the testing took place.

'It made cruising between 80 and 100 mph restful, almost to the point of seeming a leisurely form of travel, and the excellent siting of the switch enabled normal top to be regained in an instant. . . .

'Many owners of recent Aston Martins have expressed a wish for an overdrive even though it might be in use less frequently on home roads. Medium-speed cruising becomes more restful with the use of the unit, in part because exhaust noise is much reduced, and there is some gain in fuel economy.'

Some of the journalists employed by the specialist magazines were well-known engineers in their own right. Harry Munday, the Jaguar and Coventry Climax engine man who worked for *The Motor* between 1955 and 1964, is pictured here helping out with tyre testing for Avons in May 1958. The car, 147 MMC, is the works prototype DB Mark III, fitted with disc front brakes and overdrive. Aston Martin were always keen to be involved with Avon testing and the suitability of their cross-ply tyres was given a lot of credit for their cars' good handling.

Interior of a DB Mark III showing the revised dashboard.

They also liked the new fingertip headlamp flasher, a 'system, widely used in one form or another on Continental cars (which) is admirable and well worthy of wider adoption by the industry in the UK'. It took a few years for the rest of the industry to catch up, and just goes to show how quick off the mark Aston Martin could be, even with minor fittings.

Road & Track had the benefit of having read *The Autocar* test when they got their hands on a DB Mark III in December 1958. They agreed with *The Autocar*'s sentiments on the overall effect of the Aston's steering: 'It will be adjudged a near-perfect combination of ratio, precision and lightness', but disagreed vehemently with the comment that 'the ratio does not result in any unreasonable heaviness'.

'We found it to be extremely heavy in parking and in tight manoeuvring at low speeds', said the forthright American magazine, highlighting a basic divergence in opinion that is unresolved to this day on either side of the Atlantic.

Strangely, *Road & Track*'s Mark III did not have overdrive—surely a worthwhile fitting for the wide open spaces of pre-speed limit America. This would indicate that it was probably a privately owned car that they had borrowed, because a US distributor's demonstrator would surely have been equipped with this option. The Americans considered the Aston Martin to be a car for the connoisseur, with many virtues and few faults, the worst of which was the 'astronomical price'. Another drawback, in their estimation, was the continued use of the barrel-type crankcase and only four bearings. 'It also seems paradoxical to continue to build a heavy cast-iron engine when Aston Martin has a racing engine of aluminium alloy with a standard crankcase, and when the company makes so much use of light alloys in other parts of the car,' said *Road & Track*. Little did they know they would have only a short time to wait for the DB4.

Not that they disliked the Mark III. They loved it, even the interior, which was something of a surprise. Ever since the European sports car boom hit the United States in the late 1940s, Americans had been complaining about the lack of space inside imported sports cars. They recognized that an expansive Detroit interior would be out of keeping, if not downright impossible, inside a foreign sports car, but goddam it, couldn't they make just a little bit of room for your elbows? Their comments, therefore, on the 'tiny' Aston Martin's interior are significant:

'Getting into the car is made a little difficult by the high door sills necessitated by the frame design, but practice makes this easier, and with such a delightful car it is so minor a complaint as to be readily overlooked. Once inside, we found the car extremely comfortable. An adjustable steering column and adjustable front bucket seats (with nine inches of travel) mean that a driver of almost any height or girth can find a combination to suit his taste.

'The instruments are located in front of the driver, where they belong, and all controls are conveniently placed. We found the left-hand wind wing, when opened, interfered with the light switch (it got in the way of the ignition/starter switch on right-hand drive cars) and the odometer reset was often hit by the driver's right knee. Aside from a few minor inconveniences like these, the cockpit is excellently laid out and very luxurious.

'We found it to be not only one of the most desirable cars we've driven but one of the easiest to get accustomed to. Driving the Aston has been compared to driving a larger, faster and more comfortable MG. This is fairly accurate. It imparts the same feel as an MG, but on a much higher plane. (No offense to MG. Look at the price differential.)'

With such comments, who could fail to love *Road & Track* for their temerity in summing up such a priceless English institution as Aston Martin? Their performance figures, incidentally, were almost exactly the same as those recorded by every other specialist magazine. The quality control on these cars must have been fantastic, they were so consistent.

A.M.—E

The DB4 road tested by *The Motor* in 1960, 4 XMD, was a series one model fitted with heavy duty bumpers but no chrome surround to the windows. It was also one of the last to have the 3.54 rear axle ratio without overdrive.

The DB4. Only a matter of months later, *Road & Track* were first off the mark with a test of the DB4, written by none other than works driver Roy Salvadori. It might have lacked a little in credibility because Salvadori was not only retained by Aston Martin (and was to win Le Mans the next month) but he was also a car dealer in his own right with premises at Surbiton, Surrey. But these potential compromises of integrity were balanced by the man's reputation! Salvadori, born in Britain of Italian parents, was like so many of the first generation, more English than the English themselves, and by reputation even more honourable; he was also the fastest *road* driver anybody had ever seen. When it appeared impossible that the Aston team could make a television chat show date just before Sebring, they were unanimous in their choice of Salvadori to get them there in one of Briggs Cunningham's limousines. He made it with minutes to spare and it is said that he could have won the Mille Miglia in a Cadillac. Anyway, a DB4 test in May 1959 was a scoop; and Salvadori's piece was certainly well written. It said after a lengthy technical description of the new car:

'Whilst it is perhaps well known that for many years I have driven, as I hope I shall continue to drive, for David Brown, American enthusiasts may not know that I go up in his estimation because of any criticisms that I may make. (He has often said that he had learned more from failure than success in motor racing.) I say this before beginning this test report, which contains barely a word of criticism. The faults generally found in a new car have been sorted out during the rigorous prototype testing period and David Brown has produced a car which will be on top for many a year. . . .

'After only a few miles I realized the DB4 quite definitely had a dual personality. It is a very potent performer and docile family car rolled into one. Let me explain.

'With a good open road ahead, or better, in competition on a circuit, the full use of the remarkable acceleration and speed can be used. Never using more than 6000 rpm, you do about 54 mph in first, 76 in second, 108 in third and 140 in top (with a 3.54 axle ratio). Changing up at over 100 mph,

Rear view of *The Motor*'s road test DB4, 4 XMD, showing its early series rear lights. Later cars had separate lights mounted on a chrome plate.

you still feel a definite kick in the back as you accelerate in fourth. At 70 or 80 mph, when many cars are near their limit, the DB4 is happily cruising at only half the speed for which it has been designed, and you always have ample acceleration, with powerful braking plus the road holding to get you out of almost any difficulty.

'I had read the publicity handout claiming acceleration to 100 mph and back to a stop again in 26.2 seconds, but just to convince myself I decided to have a go. With a sceptical friend operating the stop watch and checking the speed with the speedometer (which was afterwards checked and found to be accurate), I reached 100 mph and stopped dead again in 27.4 seconds. Fair enough, I thought, but immediately repeated this performance in about the same time to see if there was the slightest indication of fade in the brakes, for they had to work really hard in bringing this 2884 lb car to a halt. There was none, a truly magnificent performance.

'The road holding and steering promote confidence, and fast driving on twisting roads is sheer joy; there is just enough feel through the wheel to know what is happening (I hate dead steering). Yet it is light enough not to be tiring, even at low speeds in city traffic. On wet roads one can still use considerable power without any indication of tail breakaway. Naturally care is needed when coming out of a slow corner. . . .

'Very high performance has been achieved without the noise associated with a sports car, and there is space and comfort superior to many family cars—even your grandmother would not object to riding in the DB4!'

The honourable intentions of *Road & Track* and Salvadori were vindicated when *The Motor* tested a DB4 in 1961. They returned virtually identical performance figures plus a 0–60 time of 9.3 seconds and a standing quarter mile figure of 16.8 seconds. Fuel consumption worked out at 17 mpg.

They liked the car. 'Not one major feature of the design is revolutionary,' said *The Motor*, 'but unstinted care over details has produced a remarkable express carriage for those who can afford to travel first class.' Their only criticisms were of a minor nature, such as 'Utterly unexpected simplifications are the absence of door-operated courtesy lights, and of any self-cancelling for the flashers'. Their praise was major:

> 'Using Dunlop RS5 nylon tyres, our test car cornered quite excellently on dry roads, showing a modest but comforting degree of understeer which was not greatly affected by throttle opening until enough power was applied for wheelspin to begin causing an outward drift of the tail. A very little body roll during very fast cornering probably serves a useful purpose of warning against attempts to take bends at utterly impossible speeds. It was a lot easier to slide the tail or induce wheelspin when road surfaces were wet, but bad weather did not show up any vices of the race-bred chassis.'

This car was one of the last to be fitted with the non-overdrive, 3.54:1 axle ratio; the DB4 tested soon after by *The Autocar* was also a non-overdrive model, but with the new clutch and 3.31 final drive. In addition, it had the alternative ratios of 9.67, 6.14 and 4.14 against 8.82, 6.16 and 4.42, which proved to be slightly quicker with a 0–60 time of 8.5 seconds, standing quarter mile time of 16.1 seconds and maximum average speed of 140.6 against 139.3 mph. *The Autocar* noted, however, that the minimum speed in top gear was now 15 mph, against *The Motor*'s figure of 10 mph, and that torque at low engine speeds was

> 'not great, and it is not until 4000 rpm are reached that the power really comes in which it does with a most electrifying effect.
>
> 'The result is that if the excellent performance is to be enjoyed, full use must be made of the gearbox, the ratios of which are very well spaced indeed; second and third speeds will take the car up to 76 and 115 mph respectively, at the recommended limit of 5800 rpm (6000 in top). It is only when one

Interior view of one of the first DB4s made showing its reclining seats and high standard of trimming.

grows accustomed to driving the car that one learns to make full use of second gear. In normal main road traffic, moving at approximately 60 mph, every possible opportunity for overtaking can be used, the car positively leaping forward in this gear. With the lower ratios available, this intermediate gear acceleration would be even more impressive, though at the cost of a small reduction in maximum speed.

'The maximum speed seen during the test runs, 141 mph in one direction, was achieved at an engine speed of 5750 rpm . . . this suggests that the rear axle ratio of 3.31 : 1 is just about right when all-out maximum speed is the owner's prime requirement.'

The Autocar considered that they could have done better with their acceleration figures if the gearchange had not been stiff on their car. The clutch pedal travel was too long for comfort, although the clutch itself was smooth and progressive and showed no signs of slipping. The steering was quick and positive although rather heavy on tight, fast, bends unless the back was helped round with the throttle. The brakes inspired complete confidence although the hard pads fitted gave little bite until the discs were warm. However, they then became 'immensely sure and powerful, pulling the car up quickly in a straight line'. The handbrake could not quite hold the car on a 1-in-4 hill.

'At night, on relatively traffic-free roads, the car is in its element, and it is perhaps in such conditions that one obtains the greatest pleasure from driving it . . . one can put up surprising averages, not by cornering excessively fast, or taking chances through built-up areas, but by using the wonderful indirect gear performance whenever the headlamps reach forward to a stretch of clear straight road.'

Six years later the DB6 looked much the same inside but there was now room (just!) for an average-sized man in the back with the driver's seat at the limit of its rearward travel.

The 3.7-litre twin-overhead-camshaft Special Series engine as fitted to 1963 Aston Martins. This engine featured cold air box induction in conjunction with triple SU carburetters.

That's what Aston Martin motoring is all about.

Eventually *Road & Track* managed to try a DB4 for themselves, in April 1962, and thankfully were just as impressed as Salvadori and the rest of the magazine writers had been. Their car was equipped with a 3.77:1 axle and overdrive, giving it 2.94:1 as the highest ratio, and no less than 148 mph flat out. Nevertheless they reported that the San Francisco distributors considered that the 4.09 axle with overdrive was even better:

'. . . this may be right on San Francisco hills.

'Performance (and we define performance as acceleration, top speed, braking *and* roadholding) can be described as without compromise. Any car that can actually be driven at better than two miles per minute, and yet can accelerate smoothly up a San Francisco hill from a dead stop (thanks to the engine's good torque characteristics and the new twin-plate clutch) is a car anyone can drive. The servo-assisted disc brakes are fully capable of stopping the car from any speed it will attain, smoothly and without swerving.

'A slight trace of understeer is evident, but as the speed increases it becomes more neutral. However, an experienced driver can induce oversteer. He must have the transmission in the correct gear for the desired speed so the curve can be taken at over the 4000 rpm indicated (the point at which the engine really begins to "put out"), allowing him to steer with the rear wheels.

'Only one fault marred the Aston's perfect score for handling, and that was a tendency for the directional stability to be affected when crossing road irregularities roughly paralleling the direction of travel. We've noticed this in a good many cars and we seem to remember the older Aston Martins being less affected in a similar situation. This may be due to the change in front suspension from trailing arms to lateral A-arms.'

The DB4GT. It is difficult to imagine more glowing reports than those on Aston Martin already written until Dennis May tried a DB4GT for the new *Car and Driver* magazine in June 1961. 'If your veins contain anything more viscous than cold tea, the car's attraction is irresistible', reported May from the old country.

'Throw it at a long gradient in third and before you can say David Brown Esquire it's slicing the horizon at 108 mph—with another cog still to come. Harden your heart and button your nose against the thought and smell of a clutch in thermal travail and you can gun 'er from nothing to an authentic century in less than a quarter of a minute. Savour the car's uncanny sidebite under limit-crowding lateral g. . . .'

. . . and so it went on, with May describing the car as an *objet d'art* in its own right.

Vivid as his words might have been, the performance figures were just as good: 0 to 40 mph in 4 seconds; to 60 in 6.8; to 80 in 10.4 and 100 in 14.8.

Rather slow, according to Aston's export manager, Roy Jackson-Moore, but then May had to admit that this test car's clutch had seen better days. . . .

Needless to say, the DB4GT (described by Jackson-Moore as 'the Englishman's car') appealed to Bolster when he tested it in December 1961. For a start he admitted that it was faster than the single-seaters he raced in Grands Prix not so many years before. 'Please may I use some superlatives?' he asked.

'The clutch is absolutely splendid, giving the smoothest possible engagement and yet gripping instantly for a full-blooded racing gearchange. It handles 300 bhp with ease, and adds enormously to the pleasure of driving the car. The gearchange is excellent, being quite light in action though having powerful synchromesh . . . in top gear the acceleration just goes on going on, the car seeming to surge from 120 mph to 140 mph in an incredibly short distance. Even then there is no pause, and in a few seconds 150 mph comes up. When I timed the car at 152.5 mph, the rev counter was nudging the red line at 6000 rpm . . . with a longer run before the timed section one could certainly beat this speed. . . .

'As this is a grand touring car, it is well to consider its suitability for touring in the grand manner. There is ideal accommodation, for such trips are best when two people are involved, but vast luggage space avoids an early return home. The ride is firm at traffic speeds, becoming progressively more comfortable as the car gets into its stride. There is considerable travel on the suspension, both front and rear, which may not at once be apparent because the damping is so effective. At the risk of repeating myself, I must emphasize that the uncanny high-speed stability is a great virtue during long-distance, high-speed travel.'

The DB4GT was easily distinguished from the more standard DB4s by its different frontal treatment. It featured numerous changes under the skin for higher performance besides having a shorter wheelbase—and predictably, it thrilled the road testers.

Jerry Titus in *Sports Car Graphic* preferred to echo Aston Martin's opinion that this was not a car for the average driver, but a high-speed touring car that could be raced. 'Matter of fact, it isn't a car for average transportation use either, unless you live in Arizona and commute daily to Texas', he told fellow Americans. 'It is, in almost every respect, a unique machine.'

He liked the styling, finding the car tasteful and well balanced, creating an impression of solidarity without bulk, while appearing luxurious and functional, 'something not easily captured when the basic function is racing'. As a result he was surprised to find the interior so well furnished and to find that

'around town it's a chore to drive, somewhat heavy steering, the quick clutch, high final drive, and high-lifting camshafts being contributing factors. Out on the highway all these entities come into their own and it takes considerable will-power to hold the velocity within legal limits. *Minimum* speeds in the gears for our test were 60 mph in fourth, 40 mph in third, and 20 mph in second. Going up, you shift into second at 40 mph, third at 65, and fourth at 90. The deceptive quiet helps promote the feeling of loafing at very high speeds, as does the soft ride and inherent stability of the chassis. The gas mileage proved to be a bit luxurious too; something like eleven miles per gallon at cruising speed!'

But those were American gallons, of course. Most Englishmen, even the full-blooded Bolster managed around 15 mpg.

The DB4 Vantage. Next in line to be tested, consigning the DB4GT Zagato to the competition section in the next chapter, was the DB4 Vantage, which effectively combined the virtues of the standard DB4 and DB4GT. *Car and Driver*'s technical editor, Jan Norbye, loved the engine, saying that it reached a superlative level of response and reliability throughout its range of torque and power, but the

'gearbox remains a capricious piece of machinery . . . unfortunately the baulk-ring synchromesh is unpredictable on downshifts into first, especially at stand-still. The usual trick of getting second and then just snicking it into first usually works, but only usually—and the cause of the occasional grinding noise must be a mechanical error, not a human one.

'The clutch deserves top marks, however. . . . Hard springs make high pedal pressures a necessity, but for normal driving this is never objectionable. In heavy traffic, however, it can become annoying; especially in view of the uncertainty of getting first gear on the first try. . . .

'If the Vantage has all the amenities of a town carriage, it still remains an extremely masculine car. The steering tends to be heavy, the gearshift needs considerable muscular effort, and pedal pressures are relatively high. Drivers with a strong sporting sense will derive a great feeling of satisfaction from mastering this car, but the less enthusiastic may begin to talk of power steering and automatic transmissions.'

The DB5 tested by *Autocar* in 1964 showing its revised front end treatment based on that of the earlier DB4GT and DB4 Vantage.

Norbye was a prophet indeed, for he also predicted the coming of a new five-speed gearbox. He also said

> 'it struck us as a little strange that Aston Martin continues to use a rigid rear axle on all models of the DB4 even when the company has developed an excellent de Dion rear suspension for the Lagonda Rapide—a heavier and more luxurious car of little or no sporting appeal—where a rigid axle would matter less than in the very high performance DB4s. We suggest they swap, quite simply, and increase the roadability of the Aston Martin range to the point where it is no longer rivalled by other fast touring cars with well tied-down rear axles such as Ferrari and Maserati.'

The DB5. Norbye's performance figures for the 28.5 cwt DB4 Vantage in July 1963 were significantly faster than those for the 30 cwt DB5 of almost identical appearance tested by the *Autocar* in September 1964: about 150 mph maximum speed against 141 mean; 6.8-seconds 0–60 against 8.1; and a standing quarter mile in 15.4 seconds against 16. Fuel consumption worked out at about the same, however, between 14 and 21 mpg, depending on how the car was driven.

Tyres and gear ratios were roughly comparable, as the DB4 was fitted with a standard 3.31 rear axle and Dunlop RS5s, whereas the DB5 had a 3.77 axle, which in combination with its five-speed ZF gearbox gave a 3.14 highest ratio, and Avon Turbospeeds of significantly smaller rolling radius.

'For out-and-out maximum speed, the Dunlops might prove slightly faster,' said *Autocar*, 'because on our best one-way run at 142.6 mph, the rev counter needle was well into the red danger zone and reading 5800 rpm.' It was clear that Aston Martin were pursuing their old policy of increasing engine power by just enough to make up for the extra weight, as the *Autocar*'s DB5 figures were roughly

Motor tested a DB5, DKX 10B, three months after *Autocar*, in December 1964 and managed to extract 148 mph from it in one direction (6 mph faster than their rivals), with a 0–60 mph time a full one second quicker at 7.1 secs. No doubt they were more liberal with their interpretation of the rev limit!

Close-up shot of the DB5's rear suspension which was well able to cope with the extra torque of the 4-litre engine.

equivalent to those returned by the standard DB4.

Needless to say, techniques employed with the new gearbox warranted a comprehensive description:

'Getting the car away from rest as quickly as possible takes a little practice, for first gear is high and the Aston is no lightweight. The clutch bit firmly at about 2500 rpm; the rear wheels spun for perhaps a yard and a half, and from then on the revs fairly soared up to the limit prescribed. With very powerful synchromesh cones to withstand full engine torque, the gearbox felt stiff in the left-hand, first and second gear plane of the lever. When changing down into second, or from second into first, the loads can be relieved by double-declutching, but when changing up in a hurry some force is required.

'Third gear is very easy to find, with the aid of positive spring assistance towards the middle plane, and the change between all three of the upper ratios is smooth and light. The synchromesh cannot be faulted, and the clutch takes up quickly. A pedal load of only 38 lb is needed to release the diaphragm spring and once past this point only about 20 lb pressure will hold the pedal on the floor—a great boon in dense traffic. When moving off from rest it is possible to induce a little judder until one learns the knack of blipping the throttle to about 2000 rpm and then letting up the clutch as the revs die again. With two-up and a full fuel tank we just got away on a 1-in-4 gradient.'

Other significant points raised, after fullsome praise of the Aston's roadholding and comfort, included a detailed description of how to use the optional dashboard-operated Armstrong Selectaride shock absorbers:

'On the "soft" setting there was bottoming at quite slow speeds over a pave test track and the rear axle could be felt lifting off on the third hump when close-set road waves were taken at 30 mph. With the hard setting, suspension movements were more harsh, but the bump stops were felt far less often and the wheels followed the wave forms much more closely. On the road we preferred to drive with the high speed tyre pressures (35 psi front; 40 psi rear) and the dampers on "2"—one up from "soft".'

Surprisingly, *Road & Track* did not comment on the new Selectarides when they tested the DB5 in October 1964, although they devoted a good deal of space to an appreciation of the car's virtues and a telling comment on the American market for GT cars:

'In European countries where no maximum speed limits are imposed, cars of the calibre of the Aston really come into their own, because the designer has concentrated his energies on the handling and performance at the top end of the speed range. For this reason, 0–60 acceleration times and quarter mile speeds are of little significance and, of course, there are plenty of run-of-the-mill family sedans which will perform better and with less fuss in this part of the test. However, if one were planning a trip from Paris to Rome, a car such as the Aston would be hard to beat for the wide variety of road conditions which one would encounter. This is the essence of GT driving and, in consequence, a true GT car is largely wasted under our own freeway driving conditions.'

Nevertheless, *Road & Track* took performance figures of the DB5 and not surprisingly came up with much the same figures as the *Autocar* had done.

Gregor Grant, editor of *Autosport*, didn't bother to take performance figures when he drove a brand-new, and tight, DB5 for a thousand miles towards the end of 1964, but his comments were no less significant. He took the controversy about the use of the designation GT (Ford's were even using it on their Cortina saloon) a stage further by declaring:

'As befits a car with such a famous name, handling is in the best race-nurtured tradition. Fitted with servo-assisted Girling disc brakes front and rear, safe and smooth stopping is a feature. In point of fact, the DB5 feels an extremely safe machine under all road conditions. It is absolutely effortless to drive and, although it must be classified as a sporting machine, such is the standard of luxury, that one feels that even grand touring is a somewhat inadequate term to describe this new breed of high-performance car. With the performance possible, it is automatically a GT machine: I dislike intensely the term sports-saloon, which to my way of thinking conjures up visions of some really dreadful vehicles which have been described as such. On second thoughts, I feel that the name Aston Martin is self-descriptive.'

The *Motor* scribes, traditionally able to squeeze a little extra performance from a car than their rivals on the *Autocar*, at last managed it with an Aston Martin when they tested a DB5 in February 1965. They extracted 145.2 mph from their car on the mean of four runs with a best flying kilometre at 148.2 mph, with a 0–60 time of 7.1 seconds and standing quarter mile covered in 15.4 seconds. They also produced one of the most enlightened fuel consumption charts with the following figures recorded on various typical journeys: five miles through London rush-hour traffic, average speed 14 mph, 11.2 mpg; fast driving using most of the gears on a twisting country road, average speed 41 mph, 11.8 mpg; fifteen miles of fairly gentle main road cruising (one town) in light traffic, average speed 48 mph, 18.3 mpg; twenty miles fast cruising (80 to 105 mph) on a motorway, average speed 90 mph, 17.3 mpg; with an overall figure for the 1960-mile test of 17.6 mpg. Their summing up was equally impressive:

'"It is respectfully suggested that the car be driven with extra care until the owner has become thoroughly attuned to its high level of performance. . . ." Considering that the DB5 costs nearly £4500 and does 145 mph, Aston Martin's tactful handbook introduction serves as both warning and appetizer of things to come: "When the response of the car has been measured, it will be proved that the car behaves impeccably and safely. . . ." We can confirm the makers' implication that the DB5 is an acquired taste, perhaps even disappointing at first to some people, but once savoured to the full never forgotten, and almost impossible to replace. As with most handbuilt products, the merits do not initially seem to justify the price but familiarity reveals a car of strong, perhaps unique, character and appeal. Less than half the price will buy the same startling performance elsewhere so DB5 owners pay heavily for craftsmen's skill and time. But if money is no object, it is money well spent.

'The DB5 is a very masculine car which responds best to a firm and sometimes strong-armed driver, though this does not mean that it is tiring to drive. Far from it. Like all classic GT cars, it combines enormous speed with comfort and the more you put into your driving, the more the car returns for your entertainment. And the DB5 really is entertaining to any anyone who can exploit its outstanding performance, handling and brakes. It will also carry four people (just) and a fair amount of luggage so the merits of family transport (if need be) have not been entirely sacrificed to speed and elegant looks.'

The DB6 Vantage. None of the specialist magazines seemed to have laid hands on a standard DB6 although six of them tried the DB6 Vantage and *CAR* magazine even had an extended run in a triple SU automatic Volante. *Motor* came nearest to an estimation of the standard DB6's performance in their test of the Vantage model, working out that the new body shape, allied with only about one extra cwt

in weight, was good for an extra 5 mph besides the additional stability. Acceleration figures would obviously have been marginally slower. The factory claimed nearly 160 mph from the DB6 Vantage and *Motor* considered this claim to be 'entirely reasonable' although they managed only 147.6 mph in good conditions. Presumably a considerable distance would have been needed to attain the higher figure, although the factory's claims must be respected, particularly in view of their excellent record on publicity statements. *Motor* put the lack of high-speed urge down to fuel starvation or electrical trouble that manifested itself only after some time at maximum power. It is significant, though, that *Autocar* managed only 148 mph with the same car, registered LBH 8C, and the hard-driving Bolster only 152 mph with another DB6 Vantage. The American magazines never had the opportunity to drive their cars flat out because of speed restrictions.

Motor maintained their high reputation with beautifully succinct comments:

'In an effortless way that few other cars can match, the DB6 makes an overall speed limit of 70 mph look quite ridiculous. At its maximum speed of more than twice this, it is still reassuringly stable, probably more so than many cars struggling to maintain their 70 mph convoy speed. If you need to stop from high speed the brakes are outstandingly powerful, a point which really needs remembering if there is a less well endowed vehicle behind; and the handling in both wet and dry conditions is superior to all but a couple

Both *Motor* and *Autocar* tested the first DB6, a Vantage model registered LBH 8C, in 1966, returning similar performance figures this time. But their 147/8 mph maximum speeds were well below the factory's claims of 160 mph.

The second DB6 made was in station wagon form for David Brown. It was not road tested. It was to become one of his favourite cars, staying in his family for many years.

of the production two-seater sports cars we have tested. . . .

'The DB6 with its longer wheelbase and better headroom makes an Aston Martin available to the far wider four-seater market, and the design is in every way superior to the previous model. A purist might have thought that the longer wheelbase would affect the near-perfect balance of the DB5, but if anything the DB6 is even better.

'The meaning of "balance" is perhaps difficult to convey if you never drive a car so much better than your own. In the Aston it covers driveability— a mixture of handling and the feel of the controls; if you start really to use the tremendous performance on a twisty road it is reassuring that the steering is so sensitive, that the controls are so smooth and the tyres so good in all conditions. In fact, balance or progressive controllability is personified in the DB6 and its shape is entirely advantageous. The tail lip halves the aerodynamic lift around maximum speed and brings in its train greater headroom and more luggage space.'

Their performance figures became the initial yardstick for the DB6 Vantage at 0–60 in 6.1 seconds; the standing quarter mile in 14.9 seconds and 12.5 mpg, a fuel consumption which could be readily improved with gentler driving. *Autocar* produced an almost identical set of figures with the same car, although they estimated that as much as 18 mpg might be possible. In their opinion the handling resembled that of the Zagato they had tested in 1962 (featured in the next chapter), revealing outstanding adhesion and braking ability. They too had the potential owners of standard DB6s in mind when they commented:

'Owners who expect to do a lot of city and traffic driving would do better to take the standard engine with three SU carburetters. The Vantage engine is not very happy in prolonged jams, becoming fluffy to the ear and lumpy in performance.'

However, the rest of what they heard was to their liking:

> 'There is a certain amount of wind hiss around the quarterlight frames and the screen pillars, but no audible transmission or fan noises, and the filtered air intake for the Webers has been silenced effectively. If the accelerator is pressed to the floor a satisfying growl of power is heard from the engine. The exhaust can be picked out only if the windows are open. Aston Martin say that their twin-pipe, four-silencer exhaust system (which has only limited ground clearance) is very effective in keeping down the interior noise.'

Road & Track were more critical of their DB6 Vantage, which had been hurriedly prepared for the 1966 San Francisco show. The coachwork was not quite perfect as a result, but their comments on the car's lines were a more significant reflection of the Americans' reaction to the new model.

> 'Announcement of the DB6 model for the London Auto Show came as a mild surprise to us. We expected there would be an entirely new model before time for another facelift in the existing series . . . now we have the tail-lifted, literally, DB6. . . . In appearance, we think the car suffers a bit from the tail treatment. The "fashionable" Kamm-spoiler rear end may amount to something aerodynamically at high speed, but it seems out of place on the somewhat dated body, expecially from the rear, where the slab section looks awkwardly tall.'

Basically they liked the car as they had liked all Astons before it. But they were critical of details such as the European-style heater (inadequate to Americans), the dashboard that paid only token regard to safety, the shoulder harness which showed similar traits, the lack of a Jaguar-style steering column adjuster knob, and the brakes that could have done with a shade more servo (American cars had long had incredibly powerful servos). They concluded by saying:

> 'Don't get us wrong. The automotive world would be a duller place without Aston Martins. David Brown doesn't build them because he needs the money, but because he wants to build them. It's a dated design, but it's a car of great character, the expression of one man's idea of what a GT car should be at the time of its inception. If it has fallen behind the times, it most definitely hasn't fallen into the rut of being a car designed to satisfy as many people as possible and edify none. We look forward to the DB7.'

Road & Track's test figures were well below the norm for a DB6 Vantage and showed that the car had indeed been hurriedly prepared or that the conservative American magazine was sticking scrupulously to the recommended rev limits, a commendable tendency they had shown in many earlier road tests. The car certainly wasn't brand new however, as the same vehicle, tested in *Sports Car Graphic* in the same month had only fifty miles on the odometer. At that time it returned an

8.6-second 0–60, much the same as in *Road & Track*'s hands, although technical editor Jerry Titus did his best to achieve absolute maximum speed figures with a 17-mile run-up! Despite this extraordinary effort he could extract only 140 mph from the car and *Road & Track* estimated its top speed at only 135 mph. These figures mattered little to the Americans, however, as Titus commented:

> 'Fifth cog is an overdrive and, by the time you engage it, you're already breaking the speed limit in about every state of the union. Seventy is about as low as you want to cruise in that gear, but it will tolerate fifty without lugging too badly.'

Car and Driver, who by July 1966 had established themselves under David E. Davis Jnr and Brock Yates as being the most thoroughly entertaining and out-spoken automotive magazine, excelled themselves with their report on the DB6 Vantage. They declared that it was 'a hard-riding, hard-steering reminder of The Good Old Days . . . for virile purists with an Edwardian turn of mind'; 'It was like Rocky Graziano in a Coldstream Guards' uniform'; and 'Sitting inside a DB6, you can be forgiven if you begin to think that all your wishes have been granted and you've been given some foolproof power over women'.

In glorious, inimitable prose, they said much the same as *Road & Track* about the DB6 Vantage and commented sagely on an alternative Aston:

> 'Before taking delivery on our test car, we spent two days with another DB6, which had the standard engine and the optional Borg-Warner Model 8 automatic transmission. We have never found any car equipped with this transmission to be worth a damn and the Aston was no exception. The shifts were rough and unpredictable, and when we tried to hurry the car, the poor gearbox just got all confused and shifted up and/or down more or less at random.
>
>   'Another thing we learned with this preliminary, "pre-test" car, was that one should resolutely ignore the directions of the owner's manual as to tyre pressures. The manual calls for inflations of 28 psi in the front, and 32 in the rear—evidently in the vain hope that the result will be a silky-smooth ride. It turns out that the resident Aston Martin factory people wouldn't *think* of driving their own cars with less than 35 psi in all four tyres, and this made all the difference in the world.
>
>   'With the official pressures the car was an utter truck. It understeered like mad, required the strength of a hairy mammoth to steer, and wallowed through the corners on loudly protesting tyres. In fact, with the normal pressures and the B-W gearbox it was unable to keep up with our publisher's Plymouth station wagon on a little winding road in Connecticut. We gave it back and began to worry about the advisability of testing a DB6 after all.
>
>   'Fortunately, our worries were for naught. When our test car was delivered, it had the five-speed gearbox, 35 pounds of air in the tyres, and it was an entirely different proposition.'

It also managed more DB6 Vantage-like times of 6.7 seconds for the 0–60 and 15.1 for the standing quarter mile. Top speed was estimated at 140 mph.

Car and Driver is produced in New York, far from the unfettered acres of Nevada where presumably Titus had sought his magic 150 mph.

Bolster was no more inhibited than his American colleagues, although his English remained thoroughly Aston. Somehow, somewhere, he recorded 152 mph in his DB6 Vantage later that year, with a road test record of 6.1 seconds for the 0–60. He recalled:

> 'Everything which this Aston Martin does is done with ease. Though the acceleration is tremendous, it happens inconspicuously while other cars appear to go backwards in the mirror. Incidentally, the curved rear window gives a distorted image so some cars of very curious shape are seen in the mirror which may render it difficult to identify you know who. . . .
>
> 'A cruising speed of 120 mph demands very little throttle and even 140 mph is a quiet and effortless rate of travel, during which the driver may remain quite relaxed. Above 140 mph the needle of the rev counter enters the red section, so such speeds are not for continuous use. Nevertheless it is possible to exceed 150 mph on a suitably long straight, though I did not make a habit of it at such high revolutions.'

Seldom could British roads have seen a faster driver than Bolster, or one who appreciated his Astons more:

> 'I have driven most of the Aston Martin models that have been produced, from the racing twin cam $1\frac{1}{2}$ litre of the 1920s onwards. For years, my favourite has been the DB3S sports-racer [featured in the next chapter], but now my allegiance is wavering. There can be little doubt that the DB6 is the best Aston yet and it is a credit to British engineering.'

The DB6 Volante Automatic. CAR magazine, the nearest British equivalent to *Car and Driver*, were full of good intentions when they set off on the road to Avallon in a DB6 Volante in the autumn of 1967. They arranged everything in the Aston's favour—long Continental highways, the strong hope of sunshine, good food and wine to mellow a scribe's pen—and would brook no criticism of the automatic gearbox till they had tried it, figuring that a drop-head was worth anything; the first tested since Boddy's expedition to Exeter so many years before.

They were full of praise for some aspects of the car, notably the power steering, which 'transmitted plenty of feel right up to breakaway point but never demanded more effort than a healthy female could exert with one hand.' But their initial speed in France was limited to 80 mph, two-up, because of constant grounding by the exhaust system at higher speeds. And once on the autoroute south after picking up a third person speed was limited to 117 mph by the low rear axle ratio dictated by the automatic box. Eventually even this speed had to be reduced to 101 mph (4750 rpm) in deference to the engine's heated attempts to

A.M.—F

All the Volante convertibles introduced in October 1965 looked like a DB6 from the front, although this car, one of the first made, used the shorter DB5 platform chassis.

Close-up of the DB6's rear spoiler developed for improved stability at high speed. The rear light clusters and bumpers were revised in keeping with the changed rear end treatment.

Interior of the DB6 showing the increased amount of leg room available with the passenger's seat fully forward and the driver's seat at its rear-most position.

maintain the higher speed. The noise level at this speed was much reduced and ventilation improved by unzipping the hood's rear window. Citroens, Mercedes and the odd Jaguar sped past, disconcerting in a low-geared Aston. Eventually, when off the autoroute, the shock absorbers had to be set to hard for the benefit of the exhaust and to the further detriment of the rear passenger's comfort, already impinged by the restricted nature of the accommodation shared with the hood and mechanism. Fuel consumption, and as a result range, also suffered dreadfully because of the low axle ratio. All this left *CAR* feeling rather sad and saying:

'All these faults could be eliminated on a higher-geared manual car, and a hardtop version would be both roomier in the back and quieter. What might be done in the way of suspension tuning to improve the ride we don't know, but we are convinced that the ground clearance of the car we tried was too low, in conjunction with the wheelbase and the suspension characteristics, to permit serious motoring in continental Europe. By our reckoning the Volante is hardly a GT car; but it would be unfair to condemn the Vantage out of hand on the strength of this. What we do know is that we would rather have a hardtop DB6, together with manual transmission, and the consequent higher final drive.'

The DBS Six-cylinder. Gregor Grant in *Autosport* was one of the few journalists to report on a drive in a DBS six-cylinder with standard engine, let alone road test one. He did not have time to take performance figures with his manual gearbox version (the 1967 prototype) but said that it cruised as fast as the roads would permit and that a Vantage-engined version was roughly comparable to a DB6 in performance.

His drive took him through the Highlands of Scotland and he said:

'Even on the twists and turns of the roads that lie between Aberfoyle and Crianlarich, it was almost impossible to cause rear end breakaway. This machine always went exactly where it was pointed, with no sign of squealing tyres nor any tendency to hop about on the more bumpy sections. Steering was commendably light (far lighter than on many previous Astons) and even with the tyres inflated above the recommended pressures the ride was most comfortable.

'The de Dion axle layout obviously takes the credit for this inbuilt stability.'

Nearly two years later, in July 1969, Bill Boddy again sat behind the wheel of an Aston (an automatic DBS with standard six-cylinder engine) now that those two thoroughly English institutions, *Motor Sport* and Aston Martin, were back on good terms. Like many other people, he liked the car but was not too keen on the Borg Warner gearbox. It

'lagged a little in pick-up from the lower speeds and possessed a rather distressing pause before anything much happened after kick-down. Once into its stride, however, it proved a good road-burner, accelerating to a hard purposeful sound from its vintage four-litre six-cylinder twin cam engine. It was geared to do 120 mph, indicated at 5000 rpm, and as there was a warning mark on the tachometer dial at 5500 rpm, it was approximately a 130 mph car, which is of only academic interest to we backward but State-protected British. . . .

'We rated the roadholding of a high standard for such a big car, apart from the de Dion back-end hopping sideways a bit on bumps, and matched to a good ride; the steering is excellent, high-geared at three turns, lock-to-lock, light but very quick and precise, although vicious kick-back occurs as the wheels strike pot holes. By engaging "L" and then flicking the gearlever into "D2" it was possible to send the needle more quickly over the calibrations of the 180 mph speedometer.'

Although Boddy did not have time to take comprehensive performance figures, he did calculate the fuel consumption at 13.4 mpg.

Doug Blain of *CAR* magazine managed to borrow a 6000-mile secondhand DBS manual and an automatic, both with standard engines, in November 1969, and saw 125 mph on the speedometers. However, he did not take acceleration figures, in deference to the cars' owners, but wrote some revealing words about them:

'Turning to matters other than performance, we really were most tremendously impressed with the DBS. Thanks to the efforts of young Bill Towns, the freelance designer from whom we commissioned this year's "Car of the Year" trophy, it looks as nearly right as any sports car to emerge from an English stylist's studio since the Lotus Elite. The interior, especially, merits praise not only for its uniquely satisfying aesthetics and superb finish (way, way ahead of any Italian rival in this respect) but also for the thought that has gone into the ergonomic aspects of its layout.'

These cars were, of course, later versions of the DBS with switchgear on the driver's side A posts. Blain went on to describe his impressions of driving the cars:

'We were a little concerned to note during a visit to the factory that some cars in the DBS series are being fitted nowadays with Adwest power-rack steering in place of the original ZF system, which we have always thought the best in the world. Happily, however, our cars had the German set-up and gave us complete satisfaction, with just enough feel of the road while on the move to allow one to forget power assistance altogether. The ZF five-speed box on the manual car, too, felt light and smooth, unlike earlier versions of this box which we have tried in assorted Italian machinery at various times (we have since heard that this is a characteristic of the unit when new, wearing off after a couple of thousand miles). The brakes on both cars we pronounced as just a shade insensitive but undoubtedly efficient, and, of course, there was no sign of fade in the kind of driving we were able to indulge in. Our use of all these thoughtfully laid out and very soundly engineered controls was immeasurably enhanced by the perfect correctness of the DBS driving position, which could hardly be improved on in a car of this size and layout.

'Three things set the DBS body/chassis unit apart from its contemporaries. The first is its quite exceptional rigidity, achieved, albeit at the cost of an alarming weight surplus over the desired minimum, by welding an already chunky steel frame to a body structure made up of liberally stiffened alloy panels. A second factor, analysed last month by an astonished Leonard Setright, is the almost complete absence of compliance anywhere in the suspension. And the third, which cynics may consider to be related to the second, is the makers' continued reliance on crossply tyres of unfashionably small dimensions. Other important features are a weight distribution veering towards a quite strong rearward bias with four occupants and luggage, and suspension settings which are a shade soft by GT standards but are allegedly variable by the use of Selectaride dampers at the rear.

'All of these factors combine to give a car of quite impeccable directional stability, yet with a controlled absorbency, consistency and sheer agreeableness of ride which we consider to be preferable to anything yet achieved by Rolls-Royce even if it cannot quite approach the pinnacle currently occupied jointly by Jaguar's XJ6 and BMW's 2800. Roadholding doesn't come up to the same standard for, although excellent, it is strictly limited by the adhesion of the tyres and any attempt to exceed this will result in the car sliding bodily—nose first with the driver only on board, all of a piece fully laden. The compromise in suspension settings also means that, fully laden and with the dampers on setting four, the car will bottom heavily at the rear if humpback bridges and the like are taken immoderately. Handling remains impeccable until one approaches the tyres' limits, when extreme understeer is apt to give way noisily to the other thing, accompanied by rather a lot of body roll.

'The DBS in its most basic form, tried as it has been by us in circumstances far from the ideal, strikes us as much more of a luxury saloon than an all-out GT car. Its refinement forms the most complete contrast imaginable to its hefty, hearty predecessors, and this holds good in the aesthetic sense as well so that our abiding memories of it centre on a summer day spent cruising with complete disregard for the 70 mph limit on lightly trafficked roads, glorying in the effortlessness, the comfort and the silence with which it gobbled the miles while we sat back—five of us, including a two-year-old—listening to an Aldburgh Festival replay and commenting from time to time on how safe we felt, how slowly everybody else seemed to be travelling and how *nice* it was to be surrounded by fittings and fixtures as beautifully made as they were competently designed.'

The DBS Vantage Six-cylinder. The rest of the DBS six-cylinder tests featured the Vantage-engined model which was hardly surprising, considering that it cost no more. Bolster managed to have two cracks at the car, the first for just one day in Belgium in July 1968 while waiting for his official road test car in September 1969. Initially he said that:

The DBS six-cylinder introduced the third generation of post-war Aston Martins with a bigger and heavier body than that of the DB4, 5 and 6. The car pictured here is a Vantage model on test with *Motor* in December 1968. This car, EPP 8G, which was also tested by *Autocar*, proved to be rather slower than the DB6 Vantage, but received *Motor*'s accolade all the same: 'a rare and worthy car'.

'At the Brighton Speed Trials, it would be handsomely trounced by the earlier model, but after driving all day across the Continent, its occupants would be much fresher and the DBS would probably be well ahead. (This was partly due to the new body.) The extra width gives a great sense of space inside the car, the front passenger seeming very remote from the driver and the rear seats being comfortable for long journeys. Yet, curiously enough, the machine does not feel unusually wide, even when driven fairly briskly through the dense traffic of Brussels. The gear lever, in the centre of the car, seems rather far off to the driver's left, but the pedals are well arranged, the steering wheel is adjustable, and the seats are superb. They embrace the driver and passenger, giving perfect lateral location, and there is full support right up the back of the shoulders. Truly, this is a most sinful luxury! . . .

'It happened that I drove the car during a day of almost unbearable heat. Most front-engined sports cars become intolerable under such conditions, but although this particular DBS lacked air conditioning, no unwanted heat penetrated into the body. I would like to emphasize this point, because I cannot bear being cooked in the driving seat of a car, and in the majority of high-performance coupés, this very real problem has simply not been solved.

'There was a lot of traffic on the roads, and the schedule precluded my usual 4 am session. In consequence I was unable to hold the car flat out for a long enough period in fifth gear to determine the absolute maximum speed, but it should certainly be in the 140 mph bracket. I exceeded 120 mph in fourth gear and 100 mph in third; the gearchange tends to be heavy which is normal with the ZF box. I have driven earlier Aston Martins which had more vivid acceleration, but the DBS picks up speed with deceptive ease, in spite of its considerable weight.'

In his second test, he had time to take comprehensive performance figures, reaching 60 mph from rest in 7.2 seconds, and covering the standing quarter mile in 15.1 with a top speed of 143 mph. Bolster praised the roadholding, paying special tribute to the Avon low-profile radial ply tyres now being used by Aston Martin. He was also happy with the notoriously heavy gearbox, saying:

'The lazy man who uses the synchromesh may find it necessary to exert some force when coming down to second or first, but by adjusting the engine speed correctly it is possible to make these changes with the lever held lightly between thumb and forefinger. When used, the synchromesh is unbeatable.'

Autocar's performance figures were a good deal slower on acceleration: 0–60 in 8.6 seconds and the standing quarter mile in 16.3 but they achieved practically the same maximum speed. Obviously they treated the car in a more restrained manner than Bolster and offered the following advice to readers:

'Sensibly one should always change down before the revs drop below 2000 rpm, and sympathetic drivers will keep the needle swinging nicely between 2500 and 5000. There are no noticeable vibration periods in the rev range, yet somehow it is not completely sweet, probably because of the large (666 cc) cylinder size. . . .

'Unfortunately the clutch is exceedingly heavy, requiring an effort of 60 lb to free it. This is not so bad for occasional use on the open road—the pedal angles are very good—but in a stop-start queue it brings on early leg fatigue and pins and needles in the ball of the left foot.

'The brakes, too, call for unusually heavy pedal loads, although the effort does not feel too great. A normal check stop requires about 50 lb on the pedal and it takes over 15 lb before the twin servos can be felt operating. In an emergency the driver would need to apply nearly 150 lb. Although this sounds a great deal by modern standards it means also that there is a much wider range of sensitivity available.'

This test took place in October 1968, and a couple of months later the rival *Motor* magazine really went to town on their DBS Vantage. They said:

'We were criticized some time ago by a VIP in the industry for not being objective enough in our road tests: too much reliance on subjective opinion, not enough on facts and figures. We didn't—and still don't—agree. The tone of a test report is set not by a stop watch or specification forms, but by people's views; by weighing the plaudits against the laments. If a car gets unanimous assent from anything up to a dozen drivers who covet and acclaim what they find then, by our scoring, it is a rare and worthy car. In the past year the office accolade has been conferred perhaps half a dozen times (it last went to the Ford Escort GT, just to emphasize that price has little to do with the matter); our *corps d'elite* for 1968 is now completed by the Aston Martin DBS which was reviewed with almost lyrical praise by all who drove it here.'

Comprehensive performance figures followed, to satisfy their critics, which surprisingly enough were almost identical to those recorded by Bolster! Obviously they were trying hard . . . and again their petrol consumption figures were illuminating: 'By good fortune (surely it couldn't have been planned?) 70 mph is just about the most economical cruising speed in fifth—economy to the tune of slightly under 18 mpg.' Touring consumption, taken as midway between 30 mph and maximum speed less 5 per cent allowance for acceleration worked out at 14.1 mpg.

The DBS V8. CAR magazine were first off the mark with any sort of test of the DBS V8, as a result of persistent approaches by deputy editor Mike Twite to Newport Pagnell in time for their November 1969 issue. He said:

'Only about four cars had actually been completed at the time . . . two of them being kept virgin clean and undriven because they were show exhibits,

Fast, heavy and expensive is how the *Autocar* described the DBS V8 when they tested this car in 1971—but they had to admit that the performance was tremendous.

one being carefully run in as a demonstrator for shows and the other being the development hack which had led a very hard life and was really rather unrepresentative. But it was this or nothing.'

Apparently engineering director Dudley Gershon spent some time apologizing for the faults in the car because it had just returned from two days' punishing suspension and braking tests at the Motor Industry Research Association's test track 'and it was really rather clapped', said Twite.

'The new ZF five-speed gearbox, too, was not a production example, having been built for prototype testing with hand-filed gears which did not have anywhere near the correct clearances judging from the whining noises emanating from below stairs. The neat gearlever will be three inches farther back on the production cars at the request of the sales people, but both Mr Gershon and I liked it where it was. . . .

'I soon discovered that the lack of rubber in the suspension really does lead to incredible accuracy in positioning on bends, while the springing is supple enough to soak up most bumps. . . .

'It is a pity that sheer lack of time and space prevented me from discovering whether the V8 is capable of 170 mph. . . . Aston Martin did their tests on the Autostrada del Sol in Italy, which must have woken up a few Lamborghini and Ferrari drivers. During their tests, the Aston Martin engineers discovered that the car would do the standing kilometre in 24.5 seconds, a standing quarter in 14 seconds and reach 60 in 5.7 seconds, 70 in 7.1, 100 in 12.5 and 120 in 19.6. Aston Martin instituted the publicity gimmick of accelerating to 100 mph and back to a stop in, I believe, 25 seconds; their latest creation can allegedly do it in 19 seconds time and again. All of these claims have already been doubted in the public prints, and Aston have refuted the doubts. . . .

'In the lower gears the Aston accelerates far more quickly than any of its predecessors, which we have been forced to criticize because of their slothful gait, and although I was unable to prove very much about its performance in my short spell at the wheel I'm sure that this V8 is going to be a far quicker car than any other in Britain. After poodling about in the Buckinghamshire lanes we suddenly appeared on a motorway bridge and I was allowed to descend the slip road and have a quick burst up the M1 before pulling off at the Newport Pagnell exit. Naturally I have no intention of reporting the deliciously illegal speed we reached but it served to prove that one can double the limit in absurd safety.'

The problems associated with the production versions of these DBS V8s were apparent from *Motor*'s full-scale test in March 1971. After commenting on the relatively poor wet-road grip of the Pirelli tyres—the only ones available at the time with a 170 mph rating—*Motor* said:

'These reservations are among several which make our enthusiasm less positive than it was for the earlier car. In traffic, for example, a lack of torque at low rpm becomes evident, the engine surges causing uncomfortable snatch on the overrun, and it exhibits a tendency to stall unnecessarily at traffic lights. As before the minor controls are muddled and the heating and ventilations system is indifferent.'

The fuel-injected V8 proved slow to start, although it never failed, and once started it was smooth right up to the rev limit of 6200. However, said *Motor*:

'. . . in heavy traffic the engine is much less impressive. It lacks torque below 1500 rpm—just where a big V8 should have it—and it tended to surge and snatch at low speeds. The highly retarded ignition settings necessary to achieve an acceptable idling speed with the Bosch fuel injection also made the car very easy to stall when letting in the clutch.'

That apart, the car went well, reaching 60 mph from rest in 5.9 seconds; 100 in 13.9 and 120 in 21.8. The standing quarter mile took 14.3 seconds, and the top speed was an exciting 160 mph.

'Traffic on European motorways normally kept our cruising speed down to about 115 mph, but when the road was clear we were able to cruise at 130–150 mph without any fuss, strain or drama. Using the performance in this way we were able to cover 940 miles in 14 hours including all stops—touring of a very grand kind indeed.'

The handling, brakes and Adwest power steering received high praise, quelling the fears of *CAR* readers. The credit for Aston Martin's adaptation of Adwest's system must go to Gershon, said *Motor*, for his insistence that the steering effort should never drop below 8.5 lb at the wheel.

'The results speak for themselves, for the steering gets detectably heavier during hard cornering and lighter when the front begins to break away on slippery surfaces, but the effort needed at parking speeds should be quite acceptable even for lightly built women.'

The clutch came in for similar praise with a measured 35-lb disengagement pressure.

Autocar backed *Motor* in the comments on the engine in their test in July 1971, adding that towards the end of their days with the car it began to stall and pick up fluffily from low revs 'usually to the accompaniment of two pops through the induction system'. For once they managed to beat *Motor*'s performance figures with a 161.5 mph top speed and 6-second 0–60. Strangely, their car, registered in the same year as that tested by *Motor*, had a much heavier clutch, needing 50 lb of effort to free it. As a result 'by no stretch of the imagination is the V8 a car for city work and it is only when you get away from congested streets and restricting limits that you begin to enjoy the incredible performance available'.

A new wet weather mix for the Pirelli Cinturato GR 70 VR radial ply tyres eliminated previous criticisms of poor traction on slippery surfaces and the tyre thumping normally associated with radials and suspension systems with minimum compliance also seemed to have disappeared. 'Once or twice, when really pushing on through a fast corner and hitting a bump or sudden hollow in the road surface, we noticed an odd kind of diagonal pitching and we think we would prefer the car with stiffer settings for the front dampers', said *Autocar*.

The fuel feed also presented problems.

'The tank holds 21 gallons but due to the peculiar vortex effect of the high-flow rate pick-up for the injection circuit, there is a danger of air getting into the system when down to the last six gallons. We once ran the tank down to four gallons, which caused the engine to cut when moving off in heavy traffic. It took several minutes before it would restart. In practice therefore, the useful capacity is only about 16 gallons, which gives the car a range of barely 200 miles between fill-ups. This, in conjunction with an oil consumption of only 100 miles per pint, meant frequent stops when touring. On the Continent, for example, one needs to look for a filling station about every two hours and it is very easy to run out of working cash in the right currency. . . .'

Such is the price of running an Aston Martin V8.

The AM V8. Another aspect of the cost of running an Aston Martin V8 was revealed in *Motor*'s test of the first carburetter version in September 1973: the much-used test car, UKX 50 L proved somewhat temperamental. Final drive bolts detached themselves, the transistorized ignition amplifier failed and the air conditioning thermostat gave up; swarf was found in a carburetter and the clutch needed attention. All this pointed to poor preparation, but then that was at a time when there were changes in management, and the shopfloor problems associated with that.

Despite these problems the car showed itself to be a considerable improvement over the fuel injection V8. Low-speed running was much better and the car was more tractable. It also used marginally less petrol at 13.2 mpg overall against *Motor*'s previous figure of 12.9. However, some of the troubles with the earlier V8 had not yet been eliminated. The clutch was 'intolerably' heavy needing 65 lb release pressure and the heating and ventilation system was considered to be 'uncontrollable.' Also the gearbox had 'indifferent' action and one of the Avon tyres threw a tread, two points which were not necessarily connected with the car's design.

Once UKX 50 L was running well it was impressive. 'The car will now pull

The Aston Martin V8 with carburetters was a great improvement in the opinion of testers everywhere—and the customers!

The Aston Martin V8 pictured in its natural habitat—a couple of miles from Newport Pagnell on test with the *Autocar*.

without snatch from as low as 600 rpm on part throttle, something it would not do before', said *Motor*. 'Full throttle can be used from 1350 rpm without fear of "drowning" the engine, and the power really starts to surge forth as the needle passes the 1500 rpm mark.' In company with the marginal improvement in the fuel consumption the performance was slightly better: 0–60 in 5.7 seconds, 0–100 in 13.6 and 0–120 in 20.5. The standing quarter mile took 14.1 seconds, but curiously the top speed was a mere 154.8 mph. Subsequent tests of the same car suggest that it was off form in this respect.

Bolster managed to squeeze 162 mph out of it, for instance, with much the same acceleration figures only a month later. However, this was only of academic interest, he said, as the tyres were definitely in danger of throwing treads, such was their temperature afterwards. You had to admire the man's coolheadedness, having survived a broken back in one crash (in an ERA) twenty-five years earlier. As ever, he was enthusiastic about the new Aston, not minding the heavy clutch and obviously hard-used gearbox. He criticized the power of the new single headlights, though, an opinion shared by *Motor*.

No doubt UKX 50 L had received adequate attention by the time Michael Bowler tested it for *Classic Car* (later to change its title to *Thoroughbred and Classic Cars*) in December 1973. It performed faultlessly, once more reproducing its best performance figures. He echoed the previous testers good comments on handling, braking, quality and so on, and added that the lights were adequate only for 100 mph on main beam, providing the road had cat's eye reflectors. As little as 70 mph was the safe cruising speed on dipped beam.

Nearly two years later, *Autocar* intriguingly tested a Canadian de-toxed version of the manual V8, with lowered compression, air pump and large bumpers. Fuel consumption suffered with this emission equipment, at 11 mpg, and performance was also badly affected: it managed only 145 mph, 0–60 in 7.5 seconds; 0–100 in 18.4 and the standing quarter mile in 15.2 seconds. A bonus point was that it would run on low-grade fuel, with its 8.3:1 compression ratio, an effective saving of around 1 mpg in terms of cost, although the already restricted range suffered, of course.

Autocar's test of an automatic V8 (with carburetters) in 1973 found that it was nearly as quick as the manual injection version it had tried earlier, somewhere between the emission car and the unrestricted manual. This car, registered UKX 40 L, reached 60 mph from rest in 6.2 seconds and 100 in 15.7. The standing quarter mile was very fast at 14.7 seconds. Top speed was similar to the emission car at 146 mph with better fuel consumption (12.4 mpg). The Chrysler Torqueflite transmission was altogether more successful than that of earlier automatic Aston Martins. *Autocar* said that when accelerating amid town traffic it was evident that the engine speeded up, but that the car did not respond immediately. However:

> 'This effect is greatly reduced if the manual selector is used to bring in Intermediate. The selector arrangement follows a very logical pattern we have long advocated, with free movement between the two most frequently needed positions: D (or top gear) and intermediate. Stops, cleared by pressing a button in the top of the central selector lever, are positioned on either side of these points, protecting accidental engagement of either Neutral or Low. Because it is so easy just to pull the lever back for Intermediate, this tends to be used more frequently, giving good part-throttle response.
>
> 'Transmission changes both up and down are extremely smooth, even if Intermediate is selected on the over-run for engine braking. Upper limits for the kickdown are at 67 mph into Intermediate, and 30 mph into Low. Maximum automatic upshift speeds in the two gears are 44 and 78 mph respectively on full throttle, but the selector can be used to hold the gears to 64 and no less than 108 mph, corresponding to the start of the red zone on the rev counter at 6000 rpm.
>
> 'Moved fully forward, at rest, the selector locks the transmission in the Park position to supplement the handbrake, which holds reliably on a 1-in-3 gradient.'

When *Motor Sport*'s deputy editor, Clive Richardson, tested the automatic V8 in 1974 he noted that with tickover set rather fast at 1000 rpm, constant use of the brakes was necessary to keep the car down to traffic speeds with no throttle, leaving them slightly rough until the next high-speed application.

> 'Performance of the V8-engined automatic proved in complete contrast to the old four-litre six-cylinder DBS automatic, which would hardly pull the skin off a rice pudding. In spite of power-loss through the Chrysler gearbox, acceleration from 0–100 mph in the region of 15 seconds can be reasonably claimed by the manufacturers, quite shattering when viewed in print, but when

experienced from within the luxurious confines of this huge car, effortless and not at all "mind bending".'

As much as Richardson liked his automatic V8, Leonard Setright in *CAR* magazine was unimpressed in June 1977.

'Perhaps the best recommendation for the car is that it only seems to attract nice people. All the AM people that I have met, from the directors to the Owners' Club, are very pleasant individuals, and if they seem to be imbued with the notion that the V8 represents some sort of amalgamation of a Daytona Ferrari and a Speed-six Bentley, then perhaps I should not argue. The awful suspicion dawns that perhaps I am not nice, because I am left with the lurking doubt that the car is more like a cross between a Camaro and a Bristol—which is probably a better proposition anyway. On the road I had often observed that the AM V8 was always driven very politely, but usually rather slowly and I could never understand why this should be until I came to try the car for myself. In a given set of circumstances I found that I was driving it a good 10 mph slower than I would have driven a Camaro or my Bristol—and it was not until I checked the tyre pressures that I discovered why this should be.'

Setright was of the opinion that the new recommended pressures of 32 lb for the GR 70 VR 15 Avons had been made in an effort to soften the ride of the low compliance suspension; and the car was much better at 40 lb. 'The ride was not significantly harsher', he said, 'but the responses were so much better that I could see no justification for ever lowering the pressures again.'

He also noted a sudden directional instability when the throttle was closed suddenly at 130 mph; a fault which Aston Martin public relations consultant Geoffrey Courtney told me later has since been cured.

Setright was at his most scathing on the changes to the styling. He was of the opinion that the elegant Towns superstructure now lapsed into some grotesque draperies beneath the front and rear bumpers. 'It reminds me of King Lear on women', he said. '"But to the girdle do the Gods inherit, beneath it is all fiends." Poor Lear was wrong, of course, but so was Towns. The Aston Martin is a good car, but the firm are capable of making a much better one without abandoning any of their fundamental ideals.'

The V8 Vantage. They had proved it with the V8 Vantage, of course. Gordon Bruce was wildly enthusiastic over it in the *Motor* early in 1977. 'It has outstanding performance and extraordinarily high levels of handling and adhesion which it combines with the traditional craftsmanship for which British cars were once renowned and after which many still hanker', he said. Astons told him the car was 37 bhp down on power, yet it still returned almost identical figures to the pre-emission car of 1973!

The same car, AMV 8, was evidently on full power when *Autocar* tested it two

Left:

The engine room of the Aston Martin Vantage.

Below:

The latest in a long line of Aston Martins tested by the *Autocar*.

Rear view of the 1978 Aston Martin V8 showing its shapely tail to good effect.

months later, returning consistently quicker times all the way up to 120 mph, with 0–60 in 5.4 seconds, the standing quarter mile in 13.7 and an estimated maximum speed of around 170 mph (Astons claimed 168 mph), with fuel consumption of between 12 and 17 mpg (13.5 mpg overall). The *Autocar* found the AM V8 one of the easiest truly high performance cars to drive, with comfort to match. Their criticisms were confined to the lack of a guard on reverse gear and pendent pedals.

Richardson admitted that he was sceptical about the 'fastest accelerating production car in the world' before he tested the AM V8 for *Motor Sport* in April 1978:

'I have not been the most ardent admirer of modern Astons, although I have nothing but admiration for the craftsmanship involved in their manufacture. Now, after testing the Vantage, I am lost for adequate superlatives. . . .

'It's performance is simply stupendous and relentless. While Boxers, Countachs and Porsches habitually eat their clutches if full-power standing starts are attempted, this Aston simply lays a trail of rubber as the big clutch bites positively, and then takes off like a scalded tiger, the tachometer needle hurtling round the clock so fast that there is hardly time to ram the lever forwards into second. Recommended maximum revs are 6250 rpm but Aston's director of engineering, Mike Loasby, tells me that the engine is safe for 7000 rpm. The performance is such, the torque so massive, that few will be brave

The Aston Martin Vantage featured in the *CAR* road test.

enough, or find the necessity to use high revs. After all, the advisory 6250 rpm limit offers speeds of 45 mph, 73 mph, 107 mph and 130 mph in the gears—or at least the driver runs out of road or bravery first!—and the continuing surge of power as the speedometer needle soars past 120 mph in fifth is a rare experience in a road car. I had that needle as far as 150 mph and even then there was no sign of the acceleration tailing off. . . .

'Not only in performance does this Aston prove that the mid-engined exotica are not the be all and end all. This 35 cwt projectile has leech-like roadholding (almost 0.9-g cornering power, says Loasby), which suffers little on wet roads.'

The specialist magazines' road tests have developed a lot since the immediate post-war years when frequently a passenger with one eye on the speedometer and the other on his stopwatch recorded performance figures. They use all sorts of sophisticated devices now, often in the laboratory-like atmosphere of test tracks rather than on some deserted stretch of public highway at dawn. Throughout the years, however, almost every road tester has loved his Aston, with the notable exception of Leonard Setright of *CAR* magazine. His comments were enough to make Aston Martin enthusiasts howl with rage and point out his well-known delectation of their great rivals, Bristol. One voice of dissent among dozens is a very good record.

VII

The Road Testers and Lagondas

IT IS HARDLY SURPRISING that there have been few real road tests of post-war Lagondas; they are such rare cars and there was hardly ever a problem in selling them. However, we are lucky in that *The Motor* and *The Autocar* tested the 2½-litre in 1949 and Bill Boddy of *Motor Sport* recorded an excellent set of driving impressions; likewise the 3-litre saloon, which was also tested by *The Motor* and *The Autocar* at the time David Brown was having considerable difficulty in selling enough of them. Much later Michael Bowler of *Thoroughbred and Classic Cars* tried a Rapide and the latest model; Edward Francis of *CAR* magazine drove a Company Developments Lagonda and Mel Nichols, also of *CAR*, tried a prototype of the latest Lagonda in 1978.

Despite currency restrictions, *The Motor* managed to take their 2½-litre drop-head to the Continent for a 1000-mile test including the Jabekke autoroute. They recorded performance figures of 90 mph maximum speed, 0–60 mph in 17.6 seconds and the standing quarter mile in 21.7 seconds, with an overall fuel consumption of 17 mpg. They found these figures most impressive for a 30-cwt car, and were even more impressed by the flexibility which gave it a 50–70 mph acceleration time of 12 seconds in third gear. 'No car which has yet been through our hands has equalled the post-war Lagonda in combining superb comfort, particularly in the rear seats, with stability and good handling,' said *The Motor*. 'The ride over rough roads was superior to that achieved in any other car of our experience and on the Belgian pave the occupants of the rear seat could write notes and read small print with no difficulty at 70 mph.' *The Autocar* were no less enthusiastic, returning a slightly better maximum speed of 91 mph.

Boddy was most impressed with his 2.6-litre coupé, using it to visit Raymond Mays at BRM in Bourne, Lincolnshire in 1951; and Mays, a self-confessed Bentley addict, was equally impressed. For a start, Boddy said that the car looked very expensive in an unobtrusive way—just the impression David Brown wanted to give. The engine was as good as it had been found to be in the DB2, and it should be remembered that W. O. Bentley had intended it for this Lagonda in any case. The steering and handling were well up to the high standard set by the more popular and lighter Aston. The only reservations about the steering were that it was rather heavy at low speeds. More serious criticism was levelled at the

Three magazines, *Motor Sport*, *The Autocar* and *The Motor* tested the 3-litre Tickford-bodied Lagonda registered 161 GMC. They all liked the car, *The Autocar* making the most telling comments, such as: 'Few people can afford £3000 for a vehicle to transport at the most four passengers.' Fewer still had been found to buy it at the beginning of that year, 1956, when its price was nearer £4000. Slashing £1000 off the cost of a car improved sales dramatically, however, and it was a ploy that David Brown was to repeat later with the Aston Martin DB6.

brakes. Boddy thought they faded badly from speeds above 85 mph. This was a common complaint with the Aston, and no doubt the Lagonda's considerable extra weight accentuated the problem.

However, the ride was excellent, the independent rear suspension being particularly appreciated by the back-seat passengers in this very luxurious coupé. The drop-head shuddered a little, a tendency which, according to Boddy, would probably have been absent in the more rigid saloon. Much as he liked sports cars (he drove a Morgan 4/4 for normal transport), he said that he preferred the Lagonda coupé for everyday motoring; it returned impressive performance figures of 100 mph maximum speed, with 80–90 mph cruising and an average of 16 mpg.

In 1956 he tried a 3-litre Tickford saloon but this still shuddered a little; however, it was about ten per cent faster than the 2.6-litre with a similar fuel consumption. Boddy preferred its floor gear change to the steering column change fitted to the 2.6, and made similar comments to those of 1951 about the ride, handling and braking. He thought the steering had been improved, although the turning circle was still large.

The Autocar and *The Motor* both tested the same car, 161 GMC, in 1956. *The Autocar* tested it first, early in the year, when it was priced at £3900 (including British purchase tax). *The Motor* tested it later in the year by which time the price had fallen to £2993! *The Motor*'s 'cheaper' car also went considerably faster—about the same speed as when Boddy tested it—giving the impression that Brown was very anxious to sell them! *The Autocar* were well pleased with the car. 'Its character is clear cut and, among today's expensive cars, unusual,' they said.

'Among the aspects which would delight any fast driver are the way in which the engine revs so freely—it will slip up to 6000 rpm without protest if necessary....and the stability.... On corners there is a little "rear wheel steering" effect, but on the straight a slight wiggle is felt occasionally when one of the rear wheels hits a bump and its camber angle changes relative to the other. One quickly gets used to this phenomenon, and is not worried by it. It is preferable in the form experienced on the Lagonda to the rather unpleasant effect that can result on corners from some other swing axle rear suspensions.'

Head-on view of the Aston Martin Lagonda that William Willson launched on an unreceptive and economy-conscious world in 1974: 'A breed apart', said Edward Francis of *CAR* magazine. Note the patriotic flag on the windscreen. Such symbols used to adorn the Bentleys of old.

The latest Lagonda driven by Michael Bowler of *Thoroughbred and Classic Cars* and Mel Nichols of *CAR* magazine: they both spoke highly of it and made many readers wish they could buy one.

The sumptuous interior of the Lagonda Rapide circuit racer tested by Michael Bowler for *Thoroughbred and Classic Cars* magazine—a contrast to most saloon racers!

The Bowler road test Rapide even had a magnificent rear seat.

Engine installation of the Lagonda Rapide tested by Bowler showing what amounted to a DB5 Vantage engine.

Of the car in general, *The Autocar* commented that 'there is in this model a curious mixture of the fast luxury touring car and the out-and-out sports machine.' They managed an average maximum speed of 100 mph with a 0–60 time of 15.8 seconds, figures that were to be considerably improved by *The Motor*. They extracted 104.6 mph with 0–60 in 12.9 seconds, and passed similar comments to *The Autocar* apart from noting that it was a rarity in that it actually oversteered when cornering. Its luggage boot was also a rarity:

'It swallowed a very big cabin trunk merely as a preliminary to ordinary luggage.

'Possibly in the present age the cabin trunk is as rare as the buyer of this kind of car. Few people can afford £3000 for a vehicle to transport at the most four passengers; fewer still are to be found who appreciate qualities in a car for their absolute value, and not according to passing fashion. . . .'

Telling words indeed, summing up what Lagondas were all about.

Michael Bowler of *Thoroughbred and Classic Cars* was given a Rapide to test for a weekend in 1978 and took this luxurious vehicle (and ex-circuit racer!) to Wales with his family which included two children. The boot swallowed a carrycot and lots of luggage; surprising for a car that had been used on the track. In 1968 this 34-cwt, stretched, de Dion-tubed, DB4 Vantage had clocked over 140 mph at the Ghent Speed Trials with a 29.50 second kilometre at Brighton in 1964, and Bowler saw no reason to argue with these performance figures.

The Rapide was fitted with a high-ratio rack and $6\frac{1}{2}$ J Borrani wheels with 225 Avon rubber, which Bowler found tiring. 'A reversion to standard would make it more suitable as an everyday car', he said. Heavy as it was, Bowler felt it was a rewarding car to drive, and he achieved 17.3 mpg.

In his brief trial of the 1976 Show Lagonda, Bowler spent most of the time getting used to the electronic instruments, praising them in general terms but lamenting the lack of conventional readings for town speed limits. 'Figure read-outs for oil, water, voltmeter etc., require more concentration than watching a needle creep nearer the red, as you have to remember danger figures or trust warning lights', he said.

He considered it would take a 250-mile run to get used to the new system; much the same distance as it would require to assess a Citroen SM against the fifty miles or so with most cars. The Lagonda itself felt substantially softer, but just as good as an Aston V8, and he liked the transparent roof panel as an anti-

The long flowing lines of the post-war Lagonda Rapide.

The distinctive frontal view of the Lagonda Rapide, which was, in effect, a stretched DB4 with an early version of the DB5 engine and distinctive de Dion rear suspension.

dote to any claustrophobic feelings in the rear seat. He ended with a plea for electronic anti-lock braking, seeing as the car had a black box for other complex functions; a system which has been under active consideration by a number of manufacturers.

'One of the reasons behind the delay that Mercedes have put forward over the Teldix system is that drivers of their cars would use such a feature so rarely— and I agree—that they would never know if it had actually ceased to function, and perhaps subsequently blame the manufacturer if they had the accident with locked wheels. The Lagonda level of electronic sophistication could surely monitor that one, couldn't it Mr Designer Loasby?'

The sumptuous luxury of the early post-war Lagonda convertible tested by Bill Boddy for *Motor Sport*.

The W. O. Bentley-designed Lagonda drop-head was a real luxury liner.

Mel Nichols's drive in the Lagonda prototype led to a masterpiece of descriptive journalism of the type for which *CAR* magazine has become renowned:

'The speedo and tachometer figures start flicking silently upwards as you ease up the road, not so furiously that they are annoying and you will find that it takes very little time to get used to the system. The car itself is silky. The big V8 pulls it forward with enough ease to provide for 0–60 mph in 7 seconds if you floor the throttle, but progress, even then, is without drama. It feels at once a smooth, balanced, relaxed car—poorly-surfaced backroads will prove the impression correct. Two things will impress you most: the sheer quality of the ride and the remarkable flatness with which the car corners. There is no mistaking its cornering ability, but nor is there any doubting its aplomb. The car is tauter, crisper than a Jaguar XJ 12, but its ride appears to be every bit as impressive and the suppression of road noise excellent. This really is a car in which the backseat passengers can snuggle down amongst the leather and enjoy themselves. They will not be thrown about even when the driver is pressing the car very swiftly along the road, nor even in roundabouts taken really hard; the driver will know he isn't upsetting his passengers too, for the car feels precise, stable and accurate in his hands. The steering is beautifully balanced and properly smooth, and the car responds to it precisely as one would wish; a fine throttle linkage, and when necessary, equally progressive and informative braking, completes the equipment he needs to drive as quickly and smoothly as he might wish. Bumps encountered mid-bend are absorbed without the car being deflected; it just continues going where the driver points it, without real understeer and without oversteer (unless, of course, you cram it into low and stand on it in a really tight bend). What you *will* need to get used to is placing the car properly into the curb or the white line on tight right-hand bends; you need to learn to cock your head around the pillar and once you've picked up your reference point on the road ahead, the car is easy to place and hold through the bend.

'Conditions prevented us travelling much beyond 110 mph; but at that speed the car is stable, easy in the hands, quiet and smooth, with plenty of power left to send it streaking forward if one could unleash it further. Again, it's just as impressive in the rear as in the front. Indeed, that glass panel set into the roof above the rear passengers makes life there especially pleasant, removing any trace of claustrophobia and making the rear like a separate compartment.'

Of the rare early V8 Lagonda, Edward Francis said in *CAR* magazine that it was really a sporting limousine: 'An exalted passenger whose chauffeur was merely on friendly terms with the transport might well have to lift his bushy grey brows from the *Exchange and Mart* to make an offer that brooked no refusal.' Performance figures worked out at six seconds for a 0–60 with the top speed left to the imagination. So there you have it; Lagondas are a breed apart, even if they have been based on Aston Martins since the introduction of the Rapide.

VIII

The Racing Aston Martins

THERE HAVE BEEN more than twenty distinct types of racing Aston Martin since the war and almost without exception they could all be driven on the road. This prodigious output puts the English marque on a par with the great Italians, Ferrari and Maserati, and the fact that they really are race-bred cars goes a long way towards explaining why so much affection has been lavished on them.

Starting with the Spa Special of 1948, the line-up takes in the prototype DB2s of 1949–51, the DB3 of 1951–3, the glorious DB3Ss of the mid-1950s (including a Tasman single seater), the Lagonda V12 of 1954–5 that was really an overgrown Aston, the DBR1 which eventually won Le Mans and the World Sports Car Championship in 1959, the DBR2 and R3, the ill-fated DBR4 and the R5 Grand Prix cars of 1959–60, the Tojeiro and Cooper specials, the DB4GT prototypes, the DB4GT Zagato, the Le Mans Projects 212, 214 and 215 of 1962–3, the Lola T70 Mark III of 1967 which used the prototype V8 engine, today's Thoroughbred racing DB4s and the Hamilton V8s. This does not mean that other Aston Martins have not competed in races, quite the contrary; but these were the cars built specifically for racing. Other more standard road-going Aston Martins have even competed in the Monte Carlo Rally and won the RAC Rally!

The **Spa Special** was the prototype of the DB1 described in Chapter II: the basic difference, apart from its narrower pre-war style body was that the chassis superstructure had to be slimmed down in keeping with the body and the battery could not be located in the front wing as on the road cars; this racing machine's separate wings did little more than keep mud off the driver. The battery, therefore, was located in the tail with the Special's 30-gallon fuel tank. It pulled the highest rear axle ratio available, a 3.9 with 19-inch rear wheels for even higher gearing down the Belgian circuit's long straight. Eighteen-inch front wheels were used and the engine was virtually standard except that it was fitted with oversize SU carburetters and had an eventual compression ratio of 8.5:1, a sort of Vantage 2-litre. The car weighed only 19 cwt and was capable of more than 100 mph with 20 mpg!

Three new cars were built for the 1949 Le Mans race (the first held after the war) and they were the forerunners of the shorter wheelbase **DB2** (see Chapter II). There were many differences, of course, the chief ones being that the roof was

lower, giving four inches less headroom and the interior was far more spartan. Two were fitted with Spa Special 2-litre engines and the third was fitted with the Lagonda 2.6-litre unit. They were followed by the three famous 1950 team cars, VMF 63, 64 and 65 with more standard shape, but lightweight, DB2 bodies and 2.6-litre Vantage engines. They had all the normal long-distance equipment such as 28-gallon fuel tanks but did not use the de Dion axle which was designer Claude Hill's last experiment at the works in 1949; had he stayed longer they might well have received this axle with consequent changes to the DB2's production specification. Various racing brakes and gearboxes were the subject of experiment on those cars. In 1951 both Aston Martin and Jaguar started designing a new chassis for sports car racing and both built lightweight examples of their existing competition cars in case their new machines were not ready for Le Mans. Aston

Three Aston Martin DB2s were built in 1949 with Claude Hill's 2-litre pushrod engine, two of them for the works racing team. This picture shows the engine's installation with its curious high-mounted exhaust manifolding. These cars were also fitted with 19-inch wire wheels and their bodies, although similar in appearance to those of the later production DB2s were smaller, slimmer and lighter.

The works development DB2 built in 1949 and registered UMC 272 had first a 2-litre pushrod engine, then a 2.6-litre Lagonda unit. Its chassis was numbered four and it led an eventful life, being crashed by Lance Macklin in the Targa Florio in 1950 and finishing second in its class in the Inter Europa Cup race at Monza before being raced successfully by John Dalton in the mid-1950s.

Rear view of UMC 272 showing off its lithe lines to good effect. Note the large wire wheels and skinny Dunlop racing tyres.

Martin's team cars were two new ultra-lightweight DB2s, registered XMC 76 and XMC 77, using very thin-gauge aluminium bodies and Weberized engines, with the faithful VMF 64 rebuilt to the same mechanical specification. The XMC cars were about 1 cwt lighter than VMF.

The **DB3** did not make Le Mans in 1951, but made its debut in the Tourist Trophy in September with the same 140 bhp alloy-headed 2.6-litre engine used in one of the XMC cars. The DB3's ladder frame was made up of 4-inch diameter 16-gauge steel tubes with 5-inch diameter cross members. Its rear frame supported the de Dion suspension (a development of Hill's design) which was fabricated from 2-inch tubes and small rectangular tubes. With an overall length of 5 ft 3 ins, the frame weighed 151 lb.

Front and rear suspension was by dual trailing arms, with transverse torsion

The front suspension and steering of the DB3 showing its clever construction and massive Alfin brake drums.

For every person who thought the DB2 was good looking, there was one who shuddered at the stark appearance of the DB3 sports racer introduced late in 1951. This is the first DB3 to be built, later registered TMT 124 and fitted with a hard top for Le Mans in 1952. *Autosport* preferred it in the form pictured here saying it was 'the first genuine open two-seater sports car to appear bearing the famous name since before the Hitler war'. DB3/1 is shown here at Feltham on its way to the Isle of Man for Geoff Duke to drive.

Interior of the Aston Martin DB3, stark and simple with massive chassis tubes running above the floor. The car in this picture is the second built, registered XMY 80, and fitted with touring equipment including a full-width folding windscreen, for use as a demonstrator and for David Brown to drive. It was raced with some success in club meetings later in the 1950s.

The odd-looking DB3 fixed-head coupé (chassis number seven) which proved to be very fast in the hands of Tom Meyer and Philip Fotheringham-Parker during the Goodwood Nine-Hour Race in 1953.

arms running between the lower arms, and an opposite chassis member. At the front, the torsion bars crossed over each other (like a man crossing his arms) to a bronze location block, machined to allow radius movement. A vernier was fitted for ride height adjustment and the shock absorber levers worked in conjunction with the top trailing link to form attachment points for an anti-roll bar. Rack and pinion steering gave two turns from lock to lock. The rear suspension was similar except that the torsion bars ran parallel, one above the other. A Panhard rod located the 3-inch de Dion tube which carried telescopic shock absorbers.

Exceptionally large Alfin drums were used with alloy backplates on the 13-inch two leading shoe brakes at the front, and 11-inch inboard units were used at the back. They were worked by a split hydraulic circuit with up to 8 inches of travel on the pedal to compensate for lining wear in long-distance races. At first the DB3 used a David Brown five-speed gearbox and 4.11:1 final drive, giving overall ratios of 3.41 top; 4.11 fourth; 5.24 third; 7.76 second; 11.91 first and 8.63 reverse, the equivalent of 24.2 mph in top at 1000 rpm. Later, in 1952, the cars used a lower top gear ratio (0.885 against 0.83). By then a more satisfactory four-speed gearbox had been developed for the lightweight DB2s, giving ratios of 1, 1.26, 1.87 and 2.92. This was promptly adopted on the DB3.

The stark and functional slab-sided body with portcullis grille was quickly detachable from the chassis by removing ten bolts after disconnecting instrument drives and the wiring loom. A detachable undertray formed the floor. Overall dimensions were: length 13 ft 2.5 ins; width 5 ft 1.5 ins; height 3 ft 4 ins; wheelbase 7 ft 9 ins; turning circle 32 ft, and weight 18 cwt.

During 1952 the engine capacity was increased to 2922 cc by enlarging the bore to 83 mm, but it wasn't so simple as it sounds. It was only possible to bore out the engine by moving each pair of cylinders slightly further apart, with the result that they were then offset to the crankpin. The small-end bearing was then offset to the gudgeon pin to match, but this overstressed the connecting rods with disastrous results; after that the big end was offset and no more trouble was encountered; power output of the new engine was 163 bhp at 5500 rpm.

Front and rear views of the DB3S Le Mans coupés, pictured at Silverstone in May 1954 before they were registered 62 and 63 EMU. These bodies used the early DB3S front with 'eggbox' grille and lines uncluttered by air scoops. The bodies reduced drag on the long Mulsanne straight but proved to be unstable despite the finned rear wings as used on the DB3S prototype. The car in the background of the second picture is a rather cumbersome Lagonda saloon, a prototype of the elegant Tickford that had been introduced at the London Motor Show in 1953. The two Aston Martins and the Lagonda were both the result of extensive aerodynamic testing.

The first DB3 built was fitted with a hardtop for Le Mans in 1952; another, chassis number two, was fitted with touring equipment for David Brown, and a third, chassis number seven, was fitted with a special coupé body for his daughter Angela to race. Only ten were built because Brown and team manager John Wyer were disappointed by their performance.

The next stage in the development of the Aston Martin competition cars was the introduction of the classic **DB3S** in May 1953. It was easily distinguishable from the DB3 in that it looked far better than its predecessor, which was something of an ugly duckling. Apart from having a curvaceous body and smaller frontal area, it was lighter and the wheelbase was reduced to 7 ft 3 ins, and track to 4 ft 1 in.

The chassis and suspension was basically the same except that the final drive was revised for better cooling after problems with the prototype; on the first three of the line the inboard brakes and final drives had been overheating each other. To cure this, the brakes were moved outboard and a spiral bevel drive replaced the DB3-style hypoid bevel. Not only did the spiral bevel tend to run cooler, but alternative ratios for it cost less. It meant raising the propeller shaft line, but that didn't really matter in a sports/racing car.

The Panhard rod, which had been causing snaking at high speed in the DB3, was replaced by a sliding block location to keep the suspension geometry consistent. The spare wheel was laid flat over the rear axle instead of vertically, as on the DB3, and this was in keeping with the new, lower, body. The engine cooling was revised because of the reduced frontal area. The light alloy radiator, which combined the functions of cooling water and oil as on the DB3, had its header tank mounted on the scuttle; a pipe ran backwards from the cylinder head to this tank, which, in turn, fed the front-mounted radiator. The radiator was shielded so that only a small amount of the air passing through it spilled into the engine compartment and out past the sump. The rest of the considerable airflow passing through the radiator was deflected out through large, elegant cutaways in the front wheelarches, thus reducing overall drag. The six-branch twin-pipe exhaust system was also mounted in this airflow, meaning that it was shielded from the engine compartment. Not only did the front of the DB3S look good, but it was practical, too. An 'eggbox' grille was fitted to the first five cars, built in 1953; and the fifth one had an experimental fibreglass body for David Brown's use. It was to become one of the best-known DB3Ss.

Two more DB3Ss were built in 1954, numbers six and seven. They were fitted with fixed-head coupé bodies to reduce drag and combat driver fatigue in long-distance events. These bodies certainly reduced drag, but proved to be very sensitive to side winds. As a result they were really hard work to drive and lap times were much the same as those returned by open-bodied cars because the drivers daren't go any faster. The experimental alloy twelve-plug head that had been used on one DB3 was further developed and fitted with bigger valves to the 1954 DB3Ss and the prototype, number one.

It was linked to twin distributors, and with new camshafts and three side-draught Weber carburetters instead of the DB3's downdraughts, it produced 225 bhp at 6000 rpm. In furtherance of Aston Martin's belt and braces policy, DB3S/1 also ran at Le Mans with a supercharger and cast iron head (which featured different cooling arrangements) and for one race it was fitted with Girling disc brakes at the front. Astons would have liked to have used the Dunlop discs fitted to Jaguars from 1953, but they had always been faithful to Girling, and as the Dunlop discs were very expensive (£750 a set), and the existing DB3S brakes (13 ins × 2.5 ins Alfin drums at the front and 12 ins × 2.25 ins at the back) worked pretty well it was decided not to fit the Dunlop.

The DB3S was introduced as a production car at the London Motor Show in 1954 with the following specification: a body similar to the first seven team cars, except that it had a nose that was later to be seen on the DB Mark III; a VB6K engine with 8.68:1 compression ratio, six-plug cast iron head, triple 40DCOE3 Weber carburetters, 180 bhp at 5500 rpm, 9-inch single plate clutch, four-speed

An incredible line-up of six DB3S team cars with John Wyer in black on the left supervising operations. This picture shows clearly the two types of tail, one with finned wings and the other with the later, more rounded, wing profile. Two of the cars pictured are 62 and 63 EMU (far left and centre, number fifteen), fitted with new late-style rounded wing bodies after their fixed-head coachwork had been destroyed in crashes at Le Mans in 1954.

Yet another nose for 62 EMU, pictured here with faired-in headlights and oval air intake at the Aston Martin Owners' Club's St John Horsfall meeting in 1962. The car in the background is a Lotus Elite.

The last DB3S team car built, number eleven, went to America as a private entry for Rod Carveth and George Constantine in the Road America 500-mile race in 1957. It finished third in class and raced on in the United States until Carveth took it to Australia for a succession of victories in 1959. The extraordinary hood was not intended for serious use, just to comply with contemporary sports car regulations. It would probably have disappeared at anything like racing speed!

David Brown gearbox with synchromesh on the top three gears and a 3.73 rear axle giving overall ratios of 3.73, 4.69, 6.97 and 10.88. Top gear gave 23 mph at 1000 rpm and alternative ratios of 3.27, 3.54 and 3.91 were available. Outboard Girling brakes with Alfin drums were standard. Overall dimensions were: length 12 ft 10 ins; width 4 ft 11 ins; height including screen 3 ft 5 ins; track 4 ft 1 in; wheelbase 7 ft 3 ins; turning circle 30 ft; weight 17.5 cwt, and price between £3600 and £4800 depending on whether you wanted a roadster or a fixed-head coupé; the DB3 had retailed at £3700 in theory, although so few were built it is difficult to tell what they were sold for. These prices do, however, show that you could buy an Aston Martin for around half the price of a Ferrari or Maserati, and at about the same price as a racing Jaguar. Nineteen 'production' DB3Ss were built between 1954 and 1956. Three of them were coupés based on the 1954 body, and had a higher roofline and more luxurious fittings; they were much more stable in side winds.

John Bolster tested a production DB3S for *Autosport* on the road in 1956, recording 140.6 mph flat out with a spot of over-revving; and a 0–60 time of 6.6 seconds and standing quarter mile of 14.4 with fuel consumption estimated at 10 mpg under racing conditions. He liked its straight-arm driving position, accepted its harsh clutch and found the gearbox easy to use. But his biggest surprise came when he found how tractable it was! His comments on the handling were only to be expected: its cornering power was remarkable and it was extraordinary how much power could be applied coming out of a corner while still under lock.

> 'This Aston Martin does underline one thing,' he said. 'Of recent years, many moderately-priced sports cars have been produced which, by intensive development work, have shown surprisingly good roadholding; this, in spite of having conventional rear axles on homely semi-elliptic springs. But, one has only to drive a thoroughbred such as this to realise that, where a low selling price is not the main objective, a more advanced chassis design can give a standard of roadholding and controllability which is beyond comparison.'

These impressions were echoed by his editor, Gregor Grant, when trying out a similar car a couple of months later: 'Always there seemed to be so much performance, control and roadholding in reserve.'

The fifth, sixth and seventh DB3Ss were rebodied in standard shape during the 1955 season, being fitted with the twelve-plug alloy head and wilder cams to give 210 bhp at 6000 rpm with torque reported as being 210 lb/ft at 4000 rpm. This head, incidentally, had been under development since 1952 and had initially held up work on the 3-litre engine. In one race, a new car, number eight, ran with a modified cast-iron head, giving 200 bhp; in another race it had a new and very expensive fully machined crankshaft with connecting rods to match. When these were fitted the engine produced 236 bhp in alloy-headed form. In yet another race, number five used a short-stroke 2493 cc version of the engine and DB3S/6 used an 84-mm bore engine of 2992 cc capacity: a unit which was used several times later. The 2.5-litre engine was especially attractive at the time because that capacity had just become the Formula One limit.

Petrol injection was used on one car as an experiment in 1956 and several of the works engines had strengthened blocks weighing 50–60 lb more than normal; yet another car, DB3S/10 made in 1956, featured a development of the Lagonda wishbone independent front suspension which later found its way on to the DB4. A third phase of bodywork was also fitted without the compound curves around the radiator opening and with or without headrests.

David McKay tested his 210 bhp Kangaroo Stable DB3S for the Australian magazine *Modern Motor* in 1957, reporting that it was capable of 0–60 mph in 6 seconds and the standing quarter mile in 15.2, with a top speed of 158 mph when fitted with a Perspex bubble canopy over the driver for record breaking. Fuel consumption, he stated, was 18–20 mpg touring, 10–12 mpg racing.

Towards the end of the 1955 season a special single-seater version of the DB3S was built to compete in New Zealand; it had been intended to fit the 3-litre supercharged engine, but this proved troublesome and a 2.5-litre unit was fitted, originally intended for the single-seater DB3 project of 1951. The car did well in its lighter form, but it could have been no match for the contemporary Ferrari and Maserati Formula One cars, as it was still too heavy.

The car which in theory should have won Le Mans for David Brown was the **Lagonda V12** It had been impossible to extract significantly more power from the existing DB3S engine; certainly nothing nearly so much as from Ferrari's fearsome 4.9-litre V12. So it was decided to make a four overhead cam V12 like Ferrari's. It was reasoned that it ought to give more than enough power for the job in hand, even allowing for the fact that a lower output per litre is inevitable with a bigger engine. It could also be detuned slightly for reliability if it had an excess of power. The basic wisdom of the project was supported by the thought that the chassis could be adapted to take the extra weight of the big engine if everything possible was made from alloy; it was the best handling chassis in the world in its DB3S form, far better than those of the rival Ferraris and Jaguars and there appeared to be sufficient reserves to take the extra power. With these thoughts in .nind, David Brown backed the Lagonda V12 project to the hilt, to the expense of DB3S development. He called it a Lagonda, rather than an Aston Martin DB3S V12, after W. O. Bentley's magnificent pre-war Lagonda V12.

The new Lagonda's engine was incredibly complicated, using four overhead camshafts, twenty-four plugs, three down-draught 45-mm Weber 401FC carburetters, each of which had four chokes, and which were mounted Ferrari-style in the middle of the vee. Bore and stroke were 82.55 mm × 69.85 mm, giving 4487 cc. Everything possible was made of alloy to save weight over the front wheels, and there was dry sump lubrication and twin Scintilla magnetos. The power output on a compression ratio of 8.65:1 was 305 bhp at 6000 rpm with 295 lb/ft of torque at 4000 rpm. The crankshaft was still mounted in alloy cheeses, however, and despite two years' development, the team at Feltham could never solve the problems caused by the high rate of linear expansion of the alloy crankcase and cheeses; they were always having crankshaft trouble when the engine got really hot. They also found that there was insufficient travel in the front suspension to cope with the

A.M.—H

The production DB3S with closed bodywork was equipped with drum brakes, conventional wire wheels and six-plug engines and did not need the wing flares and assorted air scoops seen on several team cars. The production DB3Ss also had the pretty DB Mark III-style nose rather than the eggbox or oval air intake used on most team cars.

Northern enthusiast Geoffrey Richardson built an Aston Martin-Jaguar in 1958, named the RRA after previous specials he had raced. It used the chassis from the single-seater DB3S raced by Reg Parnell in 1956 with an ugly version of the body originally fitted to DB3S production model number 105 that had been equipped with a special fixed-head coupé body for Ulster politician Lord O'Neill. The power unit came from a 3.4-litre Jaguar, as did its disc brakes. Recently the car was restored to more normal Aston Martin specification with a twelve-plug Aston Martin engine and DB3S shape body. It was pictured here in the early 1970s.

extra weight, and the whole car weighed too much anyway, despite their attempts at weight-saving.

Practically everything had to be reinforced on this monster, and some of its extra-strong components were eventually to prove useful on DB3Ss. A 7.5-inch triple plate clutch coped well with the extra power, which was conveyed through a strengthened version of the DB3 five-speed gearbox and an equally hefty, David Brown-styled final drive including a ZF limited slip differential (these units quickly found their way on to the DB3S team cars). The 1954 Lagonda's chassis was based on that of the DB3S, with drum brakes increased in size to 13 ins × 3 ins at the front and 12 ins × 2.5 ins at the back. They were servo assisted. The tyres were bigger, too: 7.00 ins × 16 ins. The body looked bigger because of the larger tyres and the distinctive triple-opening eggbox grille front (which was built higher to clear the V12 engine, and featured a massive cold air box scoop on top of the bonnet), but it was in fact based very closely on that of the DB3S. The Lagonda looked very Ferrari-like, however.

Four of these cars were reported to have been built (in Arnold Davey and Anthony May's excellent book, *Lagonda: A History of the Marque*) but one of them is believed to have burned out while testing. Bad luck eliminated the Lagonda at Le Mans in 1954 and the Lagonda for the 1955 race looked much the same from a distance, but was completely different under the skin.

This Lagonda was the forerunner of one of the Aston Martins that was to take over from the DB3S. A spaceframe of small tubes formed a backbone chassis which splayed out at the back and front to take the engine and the rear axle. Girling disc brakes were now available and were fitted all round with special Borrani wire wheels built with an extreme offset to clear the alloy calipers. These wheels, with the outer rows of spokes outboard of the tyre, were also to appear on disc-braked DB3Ss. Although the car was outwardly much the same, the bonnet was different, lifting as a whole like the early DB2s.

The DB3S continued to outpace the Lagonda, however, and it became apparent that an alternative solution would have to be found to produce a faster car capable of winning at Le Mans. The only alternative to increasing the power (which seemed to be beyond Aston Martin's ability at the time) was to reduce the weight. A lighter car should also be able to preserve the excellent balance that was the DB3S's strength.

The **Aston Martin DBR1** of 1956 proved to be the solution. It used a lightweight spaceframe like that of the 1955 Lagonda. It wasn't a backbone, however; it splayed out full width from the rigidly mounted engine and triple-plate clutch housing at the front, to the rear axle, which was mounted in unit with the final drive and five-speed transverse gearbox. In this way the DBR1's frame was reduced to 55 lb in weight which was less than half that of the DB3S, and the balance of the car was even better with the mass of its mechanical components arranged at either end, with the driver in the middle. Suspension was similar to the DB3S except that it was further refined at the back by fitting a split de Dion tube with Watt linkage and longitudinal torsion bars linked to the hub carriers. You had to run

The DBR1 in its most successful form with shrouded wheels, tonneau and head fairing for ultimate speed at Le Mans in 1959. The exhaust pipes exit at the back instead of at the side of the car under the driver's door, apparently in deference to the drivers' wishes; Aston Martins were always among the noisiest cars on the circuits. There was a drawback to this exhaust system, however: it was re-routed close to the pedals with the result that the floor in this area became very hot—racing drivers had to be tough in those days. The car pictured here is DBR1/4, driven by Trintignant and Frere into second place at Le Mans in 1959, a rebuild of the DBR3.

Above:

Powerhouse of the DBR1/4 driven by Salvadori and Maggs at Le Mans in 1961 showing the ultimate development of its RB6 engine. It had an 80-degree cylinder head with inlet and exhaust transposed.

Right:

The DBR1 in its most graceful guise, pictured here in British historic racing leading perennial rivals, a Jaguar D type and a Lister-Jaguar.

them that way because of the transaxle taking up so much room in the middle. The engine was a 2.5-litre at first to meet the then current prototype regulations and happily fit in with David Brown's Formula One ideas. The construction was entirely in alloy to save more weight, although the troublesome cheeses were abandoned for more conventional cap-type main bearings. The engine and chassis saved about 180 lb over the DB3S, and the hefty David Brown transaxle weighed no more than the total of a gearbox and final drive. The wheelbase was increased to 7 ft 6 ins for even better handling and it was all clothed in a body that, although still showing a family resemblance to the DB3S and production cars, was more streamlined.

The engine was quite different in detail from the production-based units that had graced earlier sports racing Astons. It had dry sump lubrication, iron cylinder liners located at the top Lancia-style (at least that was similar to the current production engine), and a crankcase which extended well below the crankshaft line for extra rigidity, and ample internal bracing. At first the head was similar to that of the contemporary DB3S (the works were still racing them in 1956) with a power output of around 220 bhp at 7250 rpm using an 8.5:1 compression ratio, its 83 mm bore and 76.8 mm stroke giving 2493 cc. The stroke was increased to 90 mm for 1957, giving 2922 cc and 240 bhp at 6250 rpm—directly comparable with the hottest DB3S engine, but much lighter.

Later a wider angle (95 degrees) twelve-plug head was developed so that bigger valves could be used, which, with a hotter camshaft and 9.25:1 compression ratio gave 252 bhp at 6000 rpm. A train of gears to drive the camshafts, and oil and water pumps took over at this point. For some races these engines were detuned to 246 bhp for more reliability; for others the bore was increased to 84 mm (it meant risking very thin liners) for 2992 cc and more torque.

For 1959, larger, 50DCO, Weber carburetters were fitted to give an extra couple of bhp. A seven-bearing crankshaft proved more durable at high revs, although the original four-bearing engine usually produced more power. It was a question of building up an engine as well as a chassis for a specific race. In pursuance of this policy, compression ratios rose to 9.8:1 on occasions and larger exhaust valves were sometimes used.

The five-speed gearbox, which gave trouble until wider input spur gears were used, had all indirect ratios of 0.735, 0.818, 1.035, 1.458 and 2.11:1. It was a complete departure from normal Aston practice of a pure racing unit with straight-cut gears howling away, with no synchromesh to shield the clumsy driver, and with its own dry sump lubrication system to trap the unwary. But when its bugs were ironed out, it was the epitome of reliability and strength. Five of these DBR1s were built, bringing Aston Martin the world sports car championship, David Brown his long-awaited Le Mans win, and Britain a lot of glory.

Meanwhile, the Lagonda spaceframe was being put to good use; in 1957 it was incorporated into a new Aston Martin, the fastest raced to that date, and for a long time after. This was the **DBR2** which begat the DB4. Essentially it was the Lagonda chassis fitted with DBR1 suspension and a prototype racing version of the DB4 engine, described in Chapter III. This engine was mated to a magnesium-cased version of the Lagonda's five-speed gearbox (not the DBR1's) with separate final drive, and again a magnesium-cased Lagonda unit to reduce weight. Body-work was similar to that of the DBR1, except that it was bigger because of a 7 ft 9 inch wheelbase resulting in an overall length of 13 ft 5 ins against 13 ft 2 ins, with a track of 4 ft 5 ins rather than 4 ft 3.5 ins. The height was the same, how-ever, at 3 ft 2.5 ins. Really, it was just a slightly longer DBR1 in appearance, with 279 bhp to power it at its best, when it was also fitted with triple 50 DCO Webers. These replaced an earlier experiment with six 48 DOEs and a rather disastrous fuel system, which starved the engine above 5000 rpm. The DBR2 went so well in triple carburetter form that another was built. This car had already proved extremely fast even in six carburetter form at Le Mans in 1957, and would have been a potential winner in 1958 had the regulations not been changed to limit prototypes to three litres (Jaguar suffered in the same way with their race-winning 3.8-litre of 1957). When it became apparent that the DBR2 could compete only outside World Championship events, the second car was bored out to 95 mm to give it 3910 cc. Later the engines were bored out another three millimetres for 4164 cc; they reached 315 bhp in ultimate form.

The **DBR3** was a genuine one-off job, a DBR1 fitted with a short-stroke 75-mm version of the DB4 prototype engine, twelve-plug head and dry sump lubrication. It should have had 300 bhp at 7500 rpm but in the event could produce only 262 bhp with a hundred revs to go. The other chief difference was that it was fitted with a development of the Lagonda 3-litre front suspension that found its way on to the DB4 with coil springs (see Chapters III and IV), before the torsion bar arrangement and the engine were removed and it became a real DBR1; in fact, it was number four.

The **DBR4** and **DBR5**s were totally different beasts: they were the grand prix cars long desired by David Brown. Eberon von Eberhorst had designed a grand prix car for him around the DB3 in 1951, followed by the DB3S in 1955, but neither of these made it to a grand prix because there was so much else happening at Feltham.

Work started on the DBR4 in 1956, but was held up by all the other de-velopments in progress. The DBR4 eventually saw the light of day, at least for the

Complex cockpit of a DBR1, in this case chassis number two used by Brooks and Cunningham-Reid at Le Mans in 1957, showing clearly the frame construction.

The DBR4 as raced by Corner. It was fitted with a 3-litre engine for Australian racing, necessitating bulges on the bonnet to clear the cam covers of its 80-degree head.

public, in 1959, when already mid-engined lightweights, such as the Cooper-Climax, were about to change the face of grand prix racing.

At first the DBR4 was essentially a DBR1 2.5-litre in its hottest form (it was popularly called the DBR1/250), with a slim-line space frame and DBR3 front suspension. Later, the front suspension was revised more in line with the coil-sprung DB4 and four cars were built. These were progressively lightened and ultimately fitted with Maserati five-speed gearboxes, which were lighter than the David Brown transaxle.

The two lightest cars, which had shorter wheelbases than the others, were retained for racing in 1960 in much revised form. These were the DBR5s fitted with a new 80 degree magnesium head based on that used by the then current 350 cc AJS racing motor cycle. Despite experiments with fuel injection and independent rear suspension, they were outdated before they appeared.

Another single-seater Aston-powered racing car was built privately in 1963, with a rear-engined Cooper chassis, to race at Indianapolis. This was basically the Cooper that Jack Brabham had driven into ninth place in the 1961 event with a Coventry Climax engine. San Francisco Aston Martin dealer Kjell Qvale bought the car with the intention of entering it in the 1962 race, but it could not be prepared in time. So he saved the chassis and, in a fit of patriotic zeal for his British Motor Company, fitted a DB4GT engine for the 1963 race. This unit was only a stopgap to enable development to take place until a full-race DB4GT engine could be sent from Newport Pagnell, but when the racing engine arrived it did not propel the car much faster and Pedro Rodriguez failed to qualify at 146.8 mph. The 4.2-litre racing engine's lack of power was caused by the scavenger pump in the dry sump lubrication system failing to clear a build-up of oil from the crank

The beautifully symmetrical power unit of the Aston Martin DB4GT, showing its triple 45DCOE4 Weber carburetters and dual ignition.

case on the long 90-degree turns.

Other attempts at Aston specials included Tony Everard's **Cooper-Aston** of the mid-1950s (HPN 665) and a **Tojeiro-Aston**; in both cases the DB3S engines were no more successful than the Bristol engines that they were designed to replace, in the face of the onslaught from works Aston and Jaguar, and later the very fast Lister-Jaguar. Another attempt at solving the problem of lightening the DB3S, or increasing its power dramatically, was made by Northern enthusiast Geoff Richardson, who campaigned the **RRA**, a Jaguar-powered DB3S special. On paper this might have been a formidable machine, but, like the grand prix Astons, came too late. (Recently this car was restored to standard DB3S trim.)

When the DB4s started to leave Feltham in 1959 it was obvious that lightened versions would stand a good chance of success in GT racing, so the factory built the **DB4GT** for competition-minded customers. They also tried the 3-litre engine from DBR3 in one of their prototype DB4GTs, DP 199/1. But, apart from this prototype and DB4GTs built with lightweight bodies, they were dual purpose road/racing cars. The real racer was the DB4GT Zagato, although, tantalizingly, it also made a good road car if you could tolerate a fairly low level of trim and keep the madding crowds away from its flimsy alloy panels.

About a dozen of these special lightweight-bodied cars were built from October 1960 with higher compression ratio (9.7 : 1) engines quoted as giving 314 bhp. The chassis were virtually the same as the standard DB4GT except that spring rates were modified in keeping with the lighter overall weight.

With a dry weight of 24.5 cwt (more than 3 cwt less than a standard DB4) they performed really well on the road as well as on the track. A Zagato tested by the *Autocar* in 1962 recorded a 0–60 time of 6.1 seconds and the standing quarter

One of the Essex Racing Stable's DB4GT Zagatos pictured at the 1962 Le Mans test day, showing its curvaceous lines to good effect. Unfortunately this car was crashed in the Spa Grand Prix that year and did not reappear until after Le Mans, in the Tourist Trophy.

mile in 14.5 seconds on its way to a top speed of 152 mph, on Dunlop racing tyres. Avon Turbospeeds were more suitable for normal road driving. The *Autocar* gave a good idea of what it was like to drive a Zagato:

'In such a high performance car, driver comfort, field of vision and all the other subtleties of design which combine to give the confidence of full command are of paramount importance; in most respects there is little to criticize on the Zagato. The set of the steering wheel . . . is ideal and the wooden rim does not hinder forward vision; two bulges on the bonnet . . . interfere with some drivers' view of the nearside wing contour and care is required in placing the car in confined spaces. The thin screen pillars are well raked and there is plenty of headroom to the sides of the curved roof, unlike some other Zagato bodies we have experienced. The aluminium-framed Perspex side windows appear rather flimsy, but seated reasonably firmly against their rubber sealing strips at all speeds. Front-hinged rear quarter lights, also made of plastic, assist internal ventilation very materially without producing excessive draught or noise. These have smooth-operating over-centre catches which stay in any selected position regardless of speed.'

Despite the lack of room for luggage—the space in the tail was taken up by a 30-gallon tank and spare wheel—it was obvious that you could use the Zagato on the road, although its tyres, Dunlop R5s, running at 42 psi pressure at the front and 45 rear, could be rather hairy when there were ridges or white lines to be crossed, and were more suited to a race track than a normal road.

'As these GT cars are designed with competition in mind, the front and rear brake hydraulic circuits have separate master cylinders and no servo assistance is provided. In spite of this, the disc brakes are surprisingly good, having a reasonable pedal load at low speeds . . . but do not feel so good when applied at over 100 mph, when the operating pressure becomes very high indeed for maximum efficiency. When thoroughly warmed up they improve in this respect, but most would-be owners would undoubtedly welcome some form of servo assistance for normal road use.'

Car and Driver recorded similar performance figures when they tested a Zagato a few months later and noted that it:

'Understeers throughout the speed range. On a tight circuit, the firmly-sprung car can be a bit of a handful due to the heavy steering, but no car could be more stable. The large wood-rimmed steering wheel affords an excellent grip—a necessity at racing speeds. Unevenness in the road surface is transmitted to the wheel; on a fast bumpy corner, the car rocks gently sideways, with the steering wheel accompanying the movement. The cornering power is amazing and the rear-end behavior nearly perfect.'

As Zagato production ended in 1962, Aston Martin were trying out all their ideas for new production models on three distinct competition versions of the DB4GT. These were the **Project 212, 214** and **215** long-distance racers. Doubtless there would have been a Project 213 had it not been for the racing folk's traditional aversion to the number 13! Although these Project cars were racing two-seaters, they were really rather like stretched Zagatos with room for four. Aston Martin were anxious to get the shapes right because of their projected new generation of cars, which would definitely be four-seaters. The wheelbase of Project 212, built in 1962, was an inch longer than that of the DB4GT at 7 ft 10 ins, with an overall length of 14 ft 6 ins, six inches more than the Zagato, but, then, the legendary Italian coachbuilder liked his cars as short as possible with the minimum of over-hang front or rear. His theory was that if the car looked right, it probably was right—hang all the wind-tunnel theorists. Aston Martin had other ideas; they knew they could make their cars go faster with a more slippery shape. As it turned out, 212 in its 1962 form was a bit too slippery, suffering as it did from rear end lift at high speeds. But it was a good basis for a production car with reasonable headroom and an overall height of 4 ft 2 ins.

Extensive punching of weight-saving holes in the chassis and ultra-light panel-ling reduced 212's dry weight to not much more than 19 cwt. Together with a Lagonda-like capacity of 3996 cc and 9.5:1 DB4GT twin plug 80 degree cylinder head, its engine gave 330 bhp on 50DCOE Weber carburetters. The transmission was by the magnesium-cased gearbox used in DBR2, with suspension following the DB4GT pattern at the front and Lagonda Rapide at the back. Borrani 6 inch wire wheels were used with 6.00 section tyres at the front and 6.50 at the back.

In 1964, Project 212 was given a flat back and spoiler to improve stability.

One of the ultimate DB4GTs, Dr Michael Ottway's Project 214, showing its special body to advantage.

Two more cars had been built in 1963; they were, in effect, logical developments of 212 with more streamlined bodies and DB4GT-style rear suspension now that it was becoming evident that the Rapide rear suspension was giving problems in its production application. The Project 214 cars had 3749 cc versions of the DB4GT engine (with a 93-mm bore rather than the 96-mm of 212) to meet new regulations at Le Mans; they were detuned slightly to give 310 bhp for added reliability. Their suspension was basically the same as the road cars except that it had been modified to make it adjustable for a wide range of suspension tuning. Tyres of up to 7.00 section were used at the back. Four-speed David Brown gearboxes were fitted after the five-speed gave selection troubles, and special rear axles were fitted with additional oil capacity. Their engines were mounted 8.5 inches further back to improve stability. The noses were longer and more streamlined for better penetration, and although they caused some cooling problems, they enabled the 214s to reach nearly 200 mph! The actual speed was just over 300 kph, and they were the first cars to reach that speed at Le Mans.

Later in 1964 the third Project car, 215, was announced. It is believed to have been intended as the first of three for that year which would take the planned V8 engine, but, in the event, only one was built. It contained a dry-sump version of 212's engine, giving 326 bhp: less power but more torque. The chassis was similar to that of Projects 212 and 214, except that it was reinforced with a central cruciform. The engine was mounted only 1.5 inches further back than Project 212's, which was in basically the same position as that of the standard DB4GT. This was because the 214 position was found to be a little too much of a good thing, making the steering very light. The suspension showed evidence of yet another set of theories, ranging from DBR4-style at the front with 214 modifications for adjustment, to something completely new at the back. It was fully independent and adjustable with wide-based uneven wishbones and torsion bars. At first it was built around a DBR1 final drive and gearbox, but when this proved unreliable it was changed to a 212-style transmission, retaining the 215 suspension design intended for the new V8 production car. Project 215's body was similar to that of the 1963 version of 212, except that it was rather lower owing to the use

The ultimate Aston Martin competition V8 in 1978, Robin Hamilton's turbocharged car, pictured at speed at Silverstone.

of a dry sump engine and 15-inch wheels (fitted with 5.5-inch tyres at the front and 6.5-inch at the back).

When John Blunsden tested one of the 214 cars on the track at Brands Hatch for *Motor Racing*, after the 1963 Le Mans, he found that its rear suspension had been changed to the coil springs to be featured in the DBS, and the engine had been detuned to nearer 214 output at 315 bhp. He reported:

'. . . it is difficult to describe the car's handling in a few words. Although the ride was definitely on the hard side, there was quite a lot of body movement at the back end, where the roll stiffness had been kept comparatively low. The Aston has an immensely rigid chassis, so the effect of the rear end movement is for the front of the car to lift an inside wheel on undulating bends.'

A familiar Project car disposition!

'The car was basically an understeerer, despite the fact that the front tyres were getting a little more grip than those at the back, but against this the engine power could be used quite effectively to break away the back end. I was only brave enough to do this coming out of the two second-gear corners, when I found that the breakaway was gradual and indeed of some help in getting the car lined up. I would imagine that this technique in third gear would require a fine degree of judgement for it to be used advantageously.'

Understated in the true English tradition!

At the same time that the factory was carrying out advanced experiments on the Project cars, they were trying to improve the Lagonda Rapide, rebuilding it as a production racing saloon! This car, later to be tested by *Thoroughbred and Classic Cars* (see Chapter V), was basically built to DB5 Vantage mechanical specification, although it pre-dated that model. It also had a high ratio steering rack, improved under-bonnet air extraction, and the final drive unit was moved rearwards to

Sectional drawing of the early DB2
saloon.

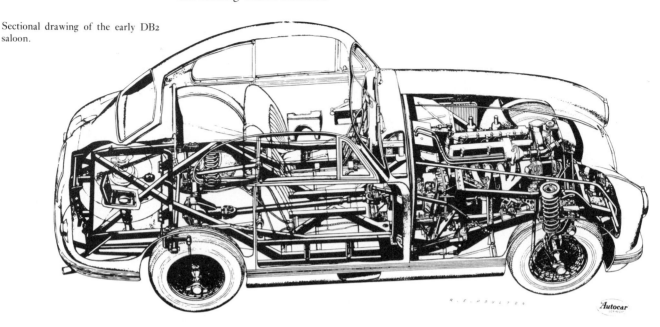

Sectional drawing of the DB3S Aston
Martin.

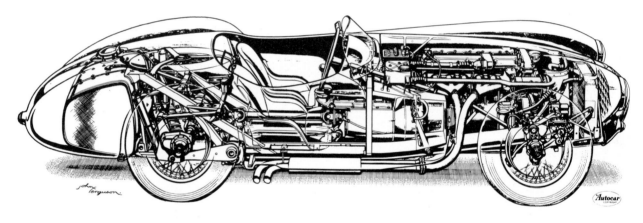

improve the drive-shaft operating angles. Other than that, it was little changed.

The next Aston Martin competition car was more than a little changed: there was nothing Aston Martin about it other than the prototype V8 engine! This was the works **Lola Aston Martin T70 Mark III B** of 1967. Although making extensive use of alloy, the prototype V8 weighed nearly as much as the thinwall cast-iron Chevrolet V8s normally used in the Lola, so there were few development problems with the car itself. And there were few criticisms: with American power it showed itself to be capable of winning races all over the world with its advanced mid-engined concept. Such was the potential of this Lola-Aston Martin that it was bound to give rise to speculation about the form the fourth generation of Aston Martins will take—especially as Lola T70s with American power have been driven on the road and shown themselves to be capable of a performance in excess of that of any road car produced so far.

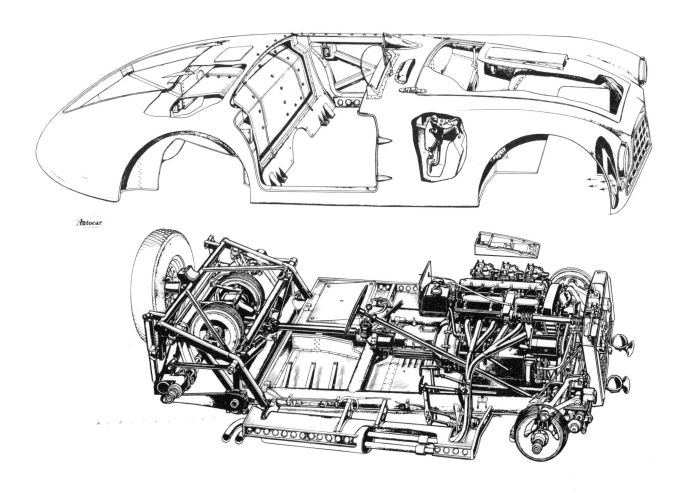

Autocar

The current racing Astons are altogether different machines. Lightened DB4s and Zagatos have put up a brave show in Thoroughbred racing despite the extensive modifications allowed to rival cars which put the former among the also rans. However, recent attempts at racing the V8 have been outstandingly successful at Le Mans and in club events.

The very fastest DB4s are too flimsy to be practical road cars, weighing in at around 20 cwt; other cars weighing around 22.5 cwt have proved themselves to be outstanding dual purpose road/racing cars. I had the good fortune to test the fastest of these cars (affectionately called the 'DLW' after its registration number, 358 DLW) on the road for the British magazine *Cars and Car Conversions* as this book was being written. It showed itself to be capable of around 5.5 seconds 0–60, 15 seconds 0–100 and 135-plus mph on its 3.54 limited slip rear axle (a 3.77 is also used, although wheelspin can be a problem with the 15 inch × 6 inch wheels and low-profile tyres fitted to these cars). Apart from extensive lightening, the car, prepared by its owners, Ian Moss and Pete Foster, was surprisingly standard, modifications being confined to those described in Chapter XIV.

Sectional drawing of the Aston Martin DB3 with its body off.

Allowing for the use of racing tyres, it was outstandingly stable on the road, requiring special consideration only on take-off: actually to leave the mark without undue drama, you had to hold the special Moss-cammed engine at between 1500–2000 rpm, let in the clutch, dip it again as the car lurched forward, then blast the engine as you let the clutch back in again. Easier to do than to read about! The braking was powerful and progressive, the steering heavy but not unmanageably so, and the handling incredibly safe. The car simply did exactly as you told it— still a true Aston. The only drawback to extensive road use was the high sound level inside; it has no interior trim and only Perspex windows to damp the characteristic bark of its big six-cylinder engine and whoosh of the Webers. From the outside, however, this car, fitted with silencers for road use, was not too bad. Other little quirks that needed watching were a tendency for the Bendix fuel pump to flood on the light throttle openings needed on the road (just flick off its switch for a moment when that happens), and the tyres' dislike of bumps and ridges in the road. With better road-going tyres the car feels much softer but lacks the lovely solid feel of a real racer.

The racing V8s present special problems to their owners, because of their great weight and the Salisbury final drive unit which can be something of an Achilles heel under racing conditions. The cars weigh upwards of 30 cwt in racing trim which means that the brakes take a terrible pounding. Consequently the discs heat up to such an extent that the rear ones, being inboard, destroy the final drive's oil seals to the detriment of the differential. Similar problems were experienced on the works racing Jaguar XJ 12 coupés which used the same final drive unit. Ralph Broad, who prepared the Jaguars, solved the problem by a complex oil cooling system, which can be adapted for Aston Martins.

Robin Hamilton overcame the problem on his Le Mans V8 in a similar way with a special sump under the differential feeding an engine-driven pump which circulated the oil through two radiators. He also used Lockheed brakes similar to those used on the works Jaguars, which weigh about the same as his racing V8. The Aston's engine produced around 515 bhp at 6400 rpm for the 1977 Le Mans race in normally aspirated form using special pistons, cams and valves. It was turbocharged for the 1978 race, but sadly lacked development time to enable it to compete. The bodywork featured a variety of aerodynamic devices developed in the Motor Industry Research Association's wind tunnel to meet regulations. These stipulate that the profile above the car's centre line must remain the same as that of the standard vehicle, other than for a rear spoiler or wing. Low profile tyres are used on 19-inch wheels to allow room for the Lockheed brakes. These wheels were developed by Competition Wheels in conjunction with Hamilton who now markets them. The gearbox, specially built by ZF with a closer than normal top ratio, is otherwise virtually standard and has shown itself to be capable of standing all the stress without trouble. In this form the V8 has proved to be competitive with prototypes developed at great expense by firms such as Porsche and has given heart to Aston Martin enthusiasts. The factory shares their enthusiasm and, with the financial situation improved, it has planned for 1979 a full campaign in production sports car racing with the V8 Vantage.

IX

Aston Martin and Lagonda in Competition

THERE'S ONE THING the war didn't change: the spirit that drove on Aston Martin. Both Aston Martin and Lagonda had raced at Le Mans (and a lot of other places) since 1928 and neither needed much encouragement to take up where they had left off, especially when they had Claude Hill's newly developed chassis to build on. Peacetime had released a lot of RAF and Army men who drove Astons and who were looking forward to competition again: Jock Horsfall was one and David Brown and John Wyer were among others. Of these, St John Horsfall was one of the best qualified. He was an Intelligence officer during the war, and after the war he returned to racing Astons with a vengeance winning the Belgian 1946 race (for sports cars that year) with his old black Speed Model which he had first raced eight years earlier.

Horsfall got on very well with Claude Hill, and had spent many months in 1948 with him, developing the DB1. They asked David Brown if they could race the car that year—Brown replied that if they were going to race, they might as well do it properly. So, with only sixty-three days to go, they decided to enter the Spa Twenty-Four Hour race (Le Mans had yet to be revived). That didn't leave much time to build a racing car, but Horsfall and Hill's labours—described as Stakhanovite by the late great Dennis May—were successful. A third chassis was built up to take over from the two prototypes and the car was completed only hours before Horsfall and his erstwhile rival, Leslie Johnson, were due to race it.

In the best traditions of *Boys' Own Paper*, they won convincingly—even after stopping for a while at the end of the first lap to finish work on the car! One of the 'gadgets' that Horsfall had fitted was a windscreen wiper which had worked wonders. As other unfortunates tried to peer through the windscreen during twenty-four hours of non-stop torrential rain, Horsfall and Johnson roared on in relative comfort to win at 72.07 mph, covering a staggering 1729 miles on the car's first outing.

Their triumph was a great send-off for the DB1 production model at London's Motor Show in 1948, but despite this, the spartan Spa Replica that had been built up from Horsfall's winning car and which had been priced at over £3000, drew little interest from anyone with that much money to spend. There was obviously not going to be a market for the car, so no more were made.

Wyer was meanwhile running the 'Red Dragon', a pre-war Aston similar to Horsfall's grand prix winner, for Dudley Folland. It had been as high as second place behind Horsfall at Spa until Folland's co-driver, Ian Connell, crashed in the teeming rain. However, it was obvious to anybody present that Wyer's preparation and team management were second to none.

Sadly, Horsfall and Hill left Aston Martin when David Brown decided to fit the Lagonda engine into their chassis and shorten the chassis as well. In fact only one of the three team cars built for Le Mans in 1949 had a Lagonda engine, although they all looked alike; they were lower, sleeker, forerunners of the DB2. The race did not go well for the Aston Martins: Johnson in his Lagonda-engined car (shared with pre-war Lagonda and Aston ace Charles Brackenbury) was forced to retire with overheating troubles after only six laps, a not uncommon failing with a new, experimental, car. Later Frenchman Pierre Marechal, sharing a 2-litre team car with Lance Macklin, crashed fatally when a brake pipe broke. The third team car, driven by Nick Haines and Arthur Jones, managed to take seventh place, but finished well behind the winning Ferrari driven by Lord Selsdon and Luigi Chinetti. A private entry by Lawrie and Parker in a DB1 finished eleventh.

Disappointing as the race turned out to be for Aston Martin, the Lagonda-engined car had showed itself to be faster than the winning Ferrari on the long Mulsanne straight. So Hill's simple four-cylinder engine was quietly buried, and David Brown decided that henceforth the Lagonda-engined car would be described as purely Aston Martin. He had other plans for Lagonda. . . .

At about that time, Monaco Engineering (with whom Wyer had prepared pre-war Astons, among other cars) lost one of its principals, Peter Monkhouse, in a tragic crash. Wyer went to Feltham as team manager in 1950, with responsibility for preparing DB2s for Le Mans and the Tourist Trophy. This was the beginning of Aston Martin's most glorious years in competition. Under Wyer's direction, works cars entered practically every serious race for sports and GT cars. Of this period, the first three works cars, or team cars as they liked to call them, were the DB2s, VMF 63, 64 and 65. These cars, prepared with the military precision which characterized everything that Wyer did, were a good deal lighter than their predecessors—one of which, the Lagonda-engined UMC 66, was retained as a spare. In the event, this proved to be a wise precaution. One of the team drivers, Jack Fairman, was involved in a crash on the way down to Le Mans in VMF 65, injuring himself and his wife and damaging the car. The spare driver John Gordon and UMC 66 were hurriedly pressed into service, but the car suffered from lack of preparation and retired early with Eric Thompson driving. The other two cars ran well, however, and George Abecassis and Macklin in VMF 64 tied with a Monopole-Panhard for first place on performance index, finishing in fifth place overall. Immediately behind, in sixth place, was Reg Parnell and Brackenbury in VMF 63. The winner was a thinly disguised 4.5-litre grand prix Talbot driven by Louis Rosier and his son, Claude, with another Talbot and two bigger British cars ahead of the Astons. But both the Allard of Sydney Allard and Tom Cole, and the Healey of Tony Rolt and Duncan Hamilton, had large American engines which meant that Aston Martin scooped the patriotic publicity.

Plate 1 A fine example of the DB2, pictured at the Aston Martin Owners' Club concours at Fort Belvedere in 1969. This car was re-registered in Great Britain in 1968 after having been raced in Belgium in its earlier life.

Plate 2 Only ten Aston Martin DB3 competition cars were built, between 1951 and 1953. Of these, number seven, was extra special: It was fitted with a fixed-head coupé body to reduce driver fatigue in long-distance events, in which it enjoyed some success, chiefly in the hands of Tom Meyer. During 1955 it was driven by David Brown's daughter Angela before eventually being acquired by Rob Walker, at whose garage it was pictured before being sold to Shaun Magee for restoration.

Plate 3 The DB2/4 Mark II fixed-head coupé is one of the rarest first-generation Aston Martins produced after the war. The car pictured here during a St John Horsfall meeting at Silverstone has proved to be a formidable competitor in club racing.

Plate 4 One of the most famous of Aston Martins, 63 EMU, started life as a Le Mans fixed-head coupé before being rebuilt with a late-style works open body to win the Goodwood Nine-Hour race. It is pictured here more than twenty years later, still racing in historic events.

Plate 5 Three production DB3Ss were built with coachwork based on the Le Mans fixed head. This car, one of the prettiest Aston Martins made, is pictured at the home of its owner, Nigel Dawes.

Plate 6 Aston Martins command just as much respect abroad as they do in their home country. This immaculate 1958 DB Mark III was bought by the Aston Martin Owners' Club Swedish representative, Tommy Blank, in 1975 and was extensively refurbished during the following three years.

Plate 7 Nostalgia Trail; Stirling Moss laps Silverstone again in a DBR1 twenty years after he drove it to so many victories.

Plate 8 One of Aston Martin's keenest supporters is Geoffrey Marsh, who runs DBR4/1, pictured here fitted with the engine from his Le Mans-winning DBR1.

Plate 9 The beautiful DB4 saloon introduced the second generation of post-war Aston Martins. It is pictured here in fourth series form.

Plate 10 One of Aston Martin's and Lagonda's chief assets has always been the craftsmen who build the cars by hand. Here a coachbuilder works on one of the early Newport cars in the time-honoured tradition which remains unchanged.

Plate 11 Spectacular shot of a spectacular car, the Aston Martin DB4 GT Zagato, pictured here as part of the Owners' Club's award-winning display at the Town and Country motoring festival in 1978.

Plates 12 and 13 Historic racing involves rather more than roaring round a track: often total rebuilds in the paddock are the order of the day.

Plate 14 One of the cars that John Bolster loved best: *Autosport*'s road test DB4 GT pictured near the factory in 1961.

Plate 15 The DB4 Vantage was quicker than the standard saloon but still docile enough to potter down to the pub, Aston Martin's demonstrator (the first one made), proved here.

Over:
Plate 16 The fastest Aston Martin on the track today: Robin Hamilton's turbocharged V8 storms past the pits at Silverstone.

Plate 17 One of the most-prized Aston Martins has always-been the convertible, pictured here in DB5 form. With the hood up it makes a snug, sophisticated grand tourer, with the hood down it's enough to turn anybody's head.

Plate 18 And as for the interior of an Aston Martin, it is second to none.

Plate 19 The Aston Martin DB5 has always had a firm following among enthusiasts who appreciated the reliability of its 4-litre engine and the relaxed manner in which it could be driven, and who didn't worry too much about small rear seats.

Plate 20 The DB6 was the first of the four-seater Aston Martins made after the war and was more stable than the DB4 and DB5 at high speed because of its revised roofline and rear spoiler.

Plate 21 Soon after the introduction of the DBS, Aston Martins had a V8-engined version with alloy wheels on the road. Their development car, pictured here in 1968, eventually went into production in substantially unaltered form in 1970.

Plate 22 The car that captured William Willson's heart: his personal Lagonda, one of seven built towards the end of Company Developments' reign at Newport Pagnell.

Plate 24 The series one DB4 owned by Ian Moss and Pete Foster is the ideal clubman's car. It cost little to build, it has won numerous awards, and it makes an exciting road car!

Left:

Plate 23 The latest Lagonda is impressive from any angle, emphasizing how well William Towns has adapted the current trend towards wedge shapes.

Plate 25 The car for all seasons, the Aston Martin Vantage, pictured here on test with *Motor* magazine.

Plate 26 Great car, great driver, Mike Salmon in the historic Project 212 Aston Martin.

Other events were less auspicious but, nevertheless, served to publicize the DB2's virtues as a long-distance car. Macklin finished second in class (to Sanesi's Alfa Romeo) in the Inter-Europa Cup at Monza in a 1949 works development car, UMC 272, before it 'fell into a ravine' in the Targa Florio. Meanwhile UMC 66 was making a record attempt at Montlhery that had to be abandoned owing to fog after five hours at 103.98 mph.

Then came the Silverstone Production Car Race with Jaguar, Healey, Frazer-Nash, Allard and so on for opposition. Macklin wasn't well, so his place was taken by French grand prix star Raymond Sommer with Parnell and Thompson backing him up. Sommer drove like a man inspired in VMF 64 till Whitehead's Jaguar XK 120, in third place, blew up, covering the track and Sommer's windscreen in oil; towards the end, Hamilton's works Healey squeezed past to put Sommer back into fourth place with Parnell in VMF 63 and Thompson in VMF 65 close behind.

The same three cars appeared at Dundrod for the Tourist Trophy with Astons proclaiming that this sort of race was better suited to them than a one-hour 'sprint' round Silverstone. As it worked out, the Jaguars (admittedly with bigger, 3.4-litre engines) were more successful, with young Stirling Moss winning in a borrowed car; but Parnell in VMF 63 was fourth, Abecassis in VMF 65 fifth, and Macklin eighth in VMF 64. This meant that Aston Martins had won the first three places in the under 3-litre class, the subject of further good publicity. They also took the team prize at the Shelsley Walsh hill climb soon after.

Later, in November, Macklin and Moss had a great time in VMF 65 in the *Daily Express* 1000-mile rally. What with driving down to events, a practice Aston Martin were to continue for years, even with long-distance events and rallies, team cars had a hard life.

Other Aston Martin drivers were doing well in 1950: Count J. R. de Wurstemberger (the Aston Martin Owners' Club Swiss representative) contested the Alpine Rally in his DB1, and despite being eliminated with electrical trouble on the third day, still won the award for the best-looking car. DB1s really were charming cars.

Two more team cars were built for 1951 while Aston Martin's new designer, Eberan von Eberhorst, continued to work on the DB3 he had started in the winter. The new cars were the DB2s registered XMC 76 and 77, which together with the veteran VMF 64 rebuilt in similar trim, were about 300 lb lighter than standard, with 3.27 : 1 rear axles. Team drivers were Macklin in VMF 64 again, with Thompson, Abecassis and Brian Shawe Taylor in XMC 77, and Parnell and David Hampshire in XMC 76. They were somewhat overshadowed by Jaguar's magnificent win by the Peters Walker and Whitehead, in their new C type (which was in many ways like the DB3 to come). Nevertheless, Aston Martin took 1-2-3-5-6 in class with Macklin and Thompson third overall in the faithful VMF 64, Abecassis and Shawe Taylor fifth and Parnell and Hampshire seventh. Nigel Mann and pre-war Aston exponent Mortimer Morris-Goodall were tenth in a private DB2 with Clark and Scott's similar car thirteenth.

In fact, VMF 64 had yet another good year, with Tommy Wisdom and Tony Hume winning the unlimited closed car class in the Mille Miglia by taking eleventh

Two of the most successful DB2s raced in the early 1950s were PPJ 2 and XMC 77. PPJ 2, driven by Nigel Mann and Mortimer Morris-Goodall is seen here leading XMC 77 (in the hands of George Abecassis and Brian Shawe-Taylor) at Le Mans in 1951. PPJ 2 finished tenth, the first private Aston Martin after the three team cars, of which XMC 77 finished fifth overall.

Geoff Duke sets the pace in his DB3 in the British Empire Trophy race on the Isle of Man in 1952 before he had ignition trouble and Pat Griffith won in a Lester-MG.

Reg Parnell storms to victory in the Goodwood Nine-Hour race in 1953. The car he shared with Eric Thompson is DB3S/2, later sold to Peter Collins and registered UDV 609.

place overall. Second overall in this 1000-mile Italian road race, behind Villoresi's 4.1-litre Ferrari, was Bracco's amazing 2-litre Lancia Aurelia (ninth in the Mille Miglia's sports 2-litre class was Ernest Stapleton in the 1946 Belgian GP winner!) Aston were looking to their laurels. Wisdom took his wife with him to win an Alpine Cup and four special stages in the Alpine Rally in VMF 64 later that year to emphasize its versatility.

In other Continental events, Charles Pozzi's DB2 finished second in the Nice international road race's 3-litre class behind Mme Simon's Ferrari, and Mann/Morris-Goodall finished fourth behind a trio of Ferraris in the 3000-mile Tour de France road race-cum-rally.

The Tourist Trophy in September was the last big event for the team cars in 1951 with the Le Mans DB2s, XMC 76 and 77 entered for Shawe Taylor and Abecassis with Thompson in VMF 65, now owned by whisky magnate Rob Walker. There was a fourth team car for Macklin, the first of the new DB3s.

'Perhaps it was the after-effects of a strike that had taken place at Feltham for a month, or perhaps it was a design fault, but Macklin was robbed of second place in the race by a trailing exhaust pipe', said Dudley Coram in *Aston Martin: The Story of a Sports Car*. Abecassis also retired, with clutch failure, leaving Shawe Taylor and Thompson trailing Bobby Baird's class-winning Ferrari as Jaguar scooped the race overall and team prize.

However, the DB2 had showed considerable promise and the AMOC did manage to launch the Snetterton motor racing circuit soon after to give more opportunities to club drivers (whose exploits in Aston Martins were already becoming too numerous to mention) to develop, besides the big names.

One of the 'new boys' was haulage contractor's son Peter Collins from Kidderminster, who landed himself a drive in a team DB3 for 1952, along with Parnell/Thompson, Dennis Poore/Pat Griffith, and Macklin. Those were the pairings for Le Mans that year, with Collins sharing Macklin's car. They nearly took fourth place until their rear axle seized with only an hour to go—an Achilles heel that was to prove troublesome with the inboard-braked DB3. The same trouble stopped Parnell and Thompson early in the race and the Poore/Griffith car also had to retire due to water pump failure. The only Aston to finish, in fact, was Peter Clark's faithful MKC 306, driven into seventh place with Griffiths's Monkey Stable mate Mike Keen. It was a fine effort by the private entrant of a car which had already finished at Le Mans the previous year, taken fifth place in the Wakefield Trophy race of 1951 and tenth place in the TT, and was now running in supercharged form.

If it was any consolation, the Jaguar works cars had an equally ignominious defeat, all retiring with cooling problems to let Mercedes Benz win the race with their sensational 300SLs, although the DB2 did manage to split two works Lancia Aurelias.

In fact, private owners did much to bolster the works efforts in all types of events in 1952, starting with the Monte Carlo Rally won in fearful conditions by Sydney Allard in one of his own saloons. Aston Martin didn't enter, but Dubliner Cecil Vard abandoned his successful Mark V Jaguar to try his hand with a 2½-litre

Lagonda, ploughing through to 113th place! At least he was showing the flag for Feltham: pre-war Lagondas made in Staines had supplied the marque's only post-war representation, and that in minor club events. Still, perhaps it was only to be expected; the Aston Martin DB2 was regarded as a production racing saloon at the time!

The DB2 was still capable of putting up a good show in top class international events, however. Incredibly, for such a hard-worked car, VMF 64 (which had also doubled as David Brown's personal transport) was still in the works line-up for the Mille Miglia, with Wisdom at the wheel, backed by Parnell in XMC 76 and

The Mann and Lewis DB2 chases the Hazlehurst and Thompson central-seater Kieft-Bristol and the Rolt and Hamilton Jaguar C type during the 1953 Goodwood Nine-Hour. The DB2 finished sixteenth overall and eighth in its class.

Parnell gives the Lagonda V12 its first public outing at the Silverstone sports car race in May 1954. He finished fifth, 1 minute 4 seconds behind winner Froilan Gonzalez in the car David Brown wanted to beat, the Le Mans-winning 4.9-litre Ferrari. Parnell lapped only four seconds slower than the Argentinian ace, however, and the Feltham camp were quite encouraged by the Lagonda's performance.

Abecassis in XMC 77. Private Aston entrants consisted of Mann and AMOC president Morris-Goodall in a DB2, and Mr and Mrs Stapleton in the ex-Horsfall Speed Model!

The pace over the rough Italian roads proved to be too much for the pre-war car's front suspension, although it did not affect the softer-sprung VMF 64. The vastly experienced Wisdom won his class again with Parnell second, his unlucky passenger having to hold damaged bodywork together in atrocious conditions. Overall winner was Giovanni Bracco's 3-litre Ferrari with Luigi Fagioli driving at amazing speed in his Lancia Aurelia to finish well ahead on the road. But VMF 64 wasn't finished yet. Wisdom went on with it to take fifth place in class in the Alpine Rally before it went into honourable retirement from serious competition.

In most other races, in which the DB2 by now stood little chance of an award, the works was represented by the new DB3. By 1952 international sports car races had become really serious for all manufacturers as Formula One fell into decline. Several grands prix that year were run for sports cars, which were becoming so highly developed that they cost as much as grand prix cars. One of the areas in which they needed highly specialized development, for instance, was in the rear suspension and transmission, as they had to be capable of carrying heavier loads of fuel for much longer distances than all-out racing cars.

Overheating differentials apart, the DB3 was quite well equipped, but did not enjoy too much success until late in the year, for a variety of reasons. New team driver Geoff Duke, the ace motor-cyclist, was out-handicapped to be beaten by two XK 120s at Goodwood on Easter Monday. He was then beaten by a loose

The most successful Aston Martin at Le Mans in 1954 was the supercharged DB3S of Parnell and Salvadori, pictured here leading Briggs Cunningham's Cunningham and the Moss and Walker D type Jaguar. It was an unhappy event for the Feltham firm however, with all their cars vanquished.

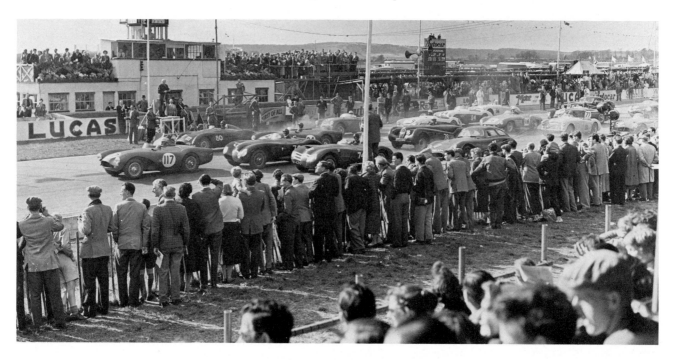

Mike Sparken and Duncan Hamilton jumped the start at Goodwood in April 1955 and were penalized one minute with the result that Salvadori won in YMY 307. It was his first race in this DB3S as a private entry. He is seen here leading the pack in pursuit of Sparken and Hamilton at the start with the second row made up of two C type Jaguars and a Cooper-Jaguar with team mate Collins in his private DB3S.

electrical connection and Griffiths's Lester-MG after a storming drive in which he nearly won the British Empire Trophy before a wildly excited crowd on his 'home' Isle of Man circuit. However, the team did manage a 1-2-3 class win (Parnell, Abecassis, Macklin) and team prize at the *Daily Express* Silverstone meeting, beaten on the road only by Moss's Jaguar C type in the larger class.

Bad luck struck again in the Monaco Grand Prix. Parnell was eliminated by trouble with his new 3-litre engine and an almighty crash; Macklin was put out by overheating while in seventh place, which was then inherited by Collins (who broke a con-rod in his 3-litre *after* he crossed the line!). The team's fortunes looked brighter, however, when Parnell won the under 3-litre class at the West Essex Car Club's 100-mile race, finishing third overall behind Moss and Hamilton in C types.

Their luck couldn't have improved at a better time. Petrol restrictions were being lifted in Britain, racing enthusiasts were just beginning to enjoy themselves again and were counting the days to their own mini-Le Mans: racing by headlights at Goodwood in the first Nine-Hour event to be held there.

'For most of the race a Jaguar victory seemed certain, then fate dealt one of those blows that are inseparable from motor racing,' said *Autosport*. Tony Rolt's C type took an early lead only to be passed by Parnell, exploiting the Aston's roadholding to the full on a slippery circuit. Then, as the surface dried, Moss's C type overtook Abecassis for third place behind Rolt, who promptly passed Parnell, followed by Peter Whitehead's C type, which relegated Parnell with the only 3-litre Aston to fourth place, Collins moving up to fifth. Whitehead was then eliminated by a crash and Roy Salvadori moved up to fourth in Baird's Ferrari, behind Thompson in Parnell's Aston, which had begun to smoke ominously from the back axle. As the car was being refuelled, petrol spilled on the hot axle casing

Salvadori wins again in YMY 307 at Ibsley in 1955 from Blond's Jaguar.

Parnell won his heat in the British Empire Trophy race in 1955 but could finish only third in the final when the 2.5-litre engine in his DB3S started misfiring badly. The car was the former David Brown road machine, re-registered 9046 H.

Line-up for the British Grand Prix meeting's sports car race at Aintree in 1955. Number one is driven by Collins, who finished second with the lap record; number five is driven by Parnell (third); number nine is a D type Jaguar driven by Mike Hawthorn; number seven was the Spa production car race-winning DB3S driven into fourth place by Peter Walker after being converted to twelve-plug, disc-braked works specification, and number three, partly obscured on the extreme right, is Salvadori's winning DB3S, 63 EMU.

and the whole lot went up in flames. Fred Lownes and chief mechanic Jack Sopp, were badly injured together with Wyer as he sprang to their aid. John Bolster, commentating for the BBC, escaped with singed hair, while Parnell, who was waiting to take over the car, jumped clear and then took over Wyer's role in the pits as his chief went to hospital with the mechanics.

The drama wasn't over. Soon after Poore in the Abecassis Aston lost all except top gear, and Collins and Griffiths soldiered on in fifth place behind Moss, Hamilton (in the Rolt car), Salvadori and Tom Cole in another Ferrari. As the Ferraris stopped for fuel, Collins moved up to third place. But Salvadori was soon looking the more menacing behind, and took the Aston. Two shattering blows then hit the leading Jaguars: Hamilton's car lost a wheel and Moss's machine broke a radius arm. This left the Ferrari in the lead till it refused to restart after a fuel stop and lost four laps! But all was not well with the Aston: it had a blown gasket as everybody could hear . . . but Collins hung on to the end. Cole and Graham Whitehead were second. Salvadori was third, after being docked a further lap for a push start. It was midnight on a perfect August night and the Astons had made it at last.

This success fired David Brown into ordering work to start immediately on the DB3's successor, the smaller, lighter DB3S. Sports car racing reached a peak for 1953 with works teams from Alfa Romeo, Ferrari, Maserati, Lancia, OSCA, Talbot, Gordini, Panhard, Renault, DB, Porsche, Borgward, Cunningham, Austin-Healey, Jaguar, Bristol, Frazer-Nash, even Kieft—besides Aston Martin. Sports car racing really did help sell cars!

As the Feltham team laboured on the DB3S, the DB3 continued to race with notable success in the Sebring Twelve-Hour which opened the 1953 season. Collins led for the first three hours before being eliminated by a crash which was caused

The 1956 RAC Rally-winning crew, from the left: Tony Ambrose, Lyndon Sims and R. Jones, with their DB2 and trophies. The car is the veteran NGO 651 which went on to win its class in the Tulip Rally that year for Lyndon Sims. Ambrose was co-driver again and went on to become one of the top men in this branch of the sport, and one of the first to use pace notes, which have transformed modern rallying.

when marshals failed to warn a slower car that he was overtaking. America's top road racers, Phil Walters and John Fitch, won in a Cunningham from Parnell and Abecassis, who were handicapped by having only one headlight after a first-lap fracas.

Although the DB3's days as a top-flight works racer were numbered, the team took three of the 3-litre cars to the Mille Miglia, for Parnell, Collins and Abecassis, with Wisdom aiming at the unlimited touring car class in his DB2, XMC 77. This all entailed three weeks away from Feltham, with the prototype DB3S for testing at Monza and a 2.5-litre supercharged DB3 and the other ex-team DB2, XMC 76, for training.

To add to the burden of producing three more DB3Ss to race at Le Mans the following month, the works were building DB3s for customers (Graham Whitehead being the most successful with a car registered TPB 641), and were continuing to help clubmen (such as Tony Everard) racing DB2s.

In the Mille Miglia, Parnell put up a magnificent drive, taking fifth place after wiring up the throttle at fully open when the linkage broke, driving from then on by switching the ignition on and off. Collins took sixteenth place and Abecassis retired with steering trouble—but this was no disgrace, with more than 400 entries and Marzotto winning in a 4.1-litre Ferrari from Fangio in a 3.6-litre Alfa Romeo.

The DB3S that followed was one of the prettiest sports/racing cars ever built, if one of the most frustrating. As Denis Jenkinson said in *Car Classics*:

'With the inspiration of Claude Hill gone, chassis development was handled by a German designer, Professor Eberan von Eberhorst, a gentleman connected with the grossly tail-happy Auto Union of pre-war years. At Feltham,

NGO 651 ploughs on to twenty-second place overall and second in class in the 1958 RAC Rally in the hands of Sims and Walton.

Eberhorst went out of his way to make Astons understeer, giving them great stability and balance on corners at the expense of a lot of tyre drag. Though more stable than the D type Jaguar, the DB3S by comparison could almost be seen losing speed through fast bends, as drag overcame available power.

'Though Aston drivers saw success in many events, a Le Mans victory continued to elude them. Always down on sheer horsepower compared to rivals, the Aston Martin approach was to set a pace and stick to it, hoping that the faster and more powerful machines would break down in their struggle amongst themselves—the twenty-fourth hour was the most important at Le Mans. Unfortunately, this policy never paid off. Whenever the faster cars had trouble, the Aston Martins seemed to have trouble; if the Astons were trouble-free at least one of their faster rivals would prove equally reliable—too often this was Jaguar. Second, third, fourth places were won continually, but Aston Martin were never first. Sometimes there looked to be a chance of victory, when young tigers like Stirling Moss or Peter Collins were going flat out in a win-or-bust effort, but John Wyer ruled the team with rigid autonomy, and refused to countenance such tactics, insisting on maintaining the calculated set speed. Moss often got very upset by this refusal to let him have-a-go at the opposition.'

Le Mans 1954 was a good example of Aston Martin's other problem: trying to do too much. The three new DB3Ss were entered for Parnell and Collins, Abecassis and Salvadori, Thompson and Poore. All were eliminated, Parnell by a crash, Abecassis by clutch failure and Thompson by water pump trouble as Jaguar went on to a magnificent win with Wyer commenting wryly in *AM*, the AMOC quarterly:

'The things which happened to us were exactly what might be expected with very new and untested motor cars, and could all have been eliminated had there been adequate time for test and development. On the other hand, it is certainly true to say that if we had not attempted to build the new cars in time for Le Mans, we should have won nothing else for the rest of the season.'

Within days of the Le Mans débâcle, the Aston Martin team were heading for the Isle of Man (as the Jaguar team went to win at Rheims), where Parnell was to drive the prototype DB3S in the British Empire Trophy race. He won at 73.96 mph, more than 3 mph faster than Duke's previous sports car record. There were still some races in which roadholding was at a premium.

Then it was on to Silverstone and the British Grand Prix's supporting sports car race which, in the absence of the works Jaguars and with a fleet of DB3s entered, driven by Graham Whitehead, Dickson and Clark, they won convincingly. All looked well for the Goodwood Nine-Hour, but once again it was not without drama. Salvadori retired with engine trouble early on, Collins left the road twice when tyres (which were consumed at a prodigious rate on this short circuit) blew up, and Parnell lost his clutch. The disc-braked works Jaguars held a convincing lead until the last hour, when constant cornering caused their oil pressure to falter and their engines to blow, leaving Parnell and Thompson to win, without an operative clutch, from Collins and Griffiths. Aston Martin roadholding had stood them in good stead again on this twisty circuit.

Good roadholding also helped win them the TT, with victory going this time to Collins and Griffiths from Parnell and Thompson, the works Jaguar opposition succumbing either to gearbox or running-out-of-road problems (although it must be admitted that Poore's DB3S also whacked one of the banks lining this tortuous Dundrod circuit). This, in effect, ended Aston Martin's most successful season to date with the DB3S unquestionably the best racing sports car on twisty medium-paced circuits, the Jaguar ahead on ultra-fast circuits such as Le Mans, and Ferrari fighting it out everywhere with an extraordinary variety of models.

Salvadori helped Mike Sparken to fourth place in the Casablanca Twelve Hours on 20 December 1953 with his Vignale-bodied DB3, and the Whitehead brothers finished fifth in Graham's DB3. Pit manager was Wyer, who could probably have done with either a holiday or just staying at Feltham to supervise preparation of new team cars.

At this time the works were concentrating on their new project, the Lagonda V12 which it was hoped would be fast enough to vanquish cars such as the 4.9-litre Ferrari at Le Mans. Meanwhile the DB3s passed down the line for 1954, Everard buying the Whitehead car, and Sir Jeremy Boles buying NUV 925, which had been driven in 1953 by Downing. Tom Meyer continued to race his DB3 (a fixed-head, registered NXY 23), in major events and Dickson, horror of horrors, fitted a C type Jaguar engine to his for 1954! At least it was certain that he wasn't taking up the works' time. The Parnell Mille Miglia DB3 went to AMOC stalwart Mann to race with Brackenbury and Sparken continued to race his in French-held territories. The supercharged DB3, TMT 124, which had been fitted with a hardtop for Le Mans in 1952, was returned to standard bodily form for Eric Forrest Greene to race in Buenos Aires, unfortunately with fatal results. Meanwhile the factory retained their team DB3Ss, and the DB2s XMC 76 and 77, to race while they concentrated on Lagonda development.

Wyer was well satisfied with the DB3S chassis design and, until the advent of the DBR1, this remained unchanged; modifications were confined to seeking more power or improving the aerodynamics.

The dual development of the Lagonda was based on Ferrari tactics. These were to try all sorts of combinations in the hope that one would prove to be outstanding. Unfortunately Feltham didn't have Ferrari's resources, and this is where they foundered. They started off with all the right ideas, namely, that the DB3S could do with more power and better streamlining, but after that everything fell apart. The Lagonda, the chassis of which was based on the DB3S, couldn't be made to handle properly because of the weight of the engine (virtually a doubled-up DB3S) and experiments with wishbone and coil front suspension to give more wheel movement were started too late; and the crankshaft location wasn't strong enough for all the torque of the two DB3S engines, even when their capacity was reduced to a combined 4.4 litres. If it had been reduced any further there wouldn't have been much point in having a V12 anyway, as an increased frontal area and extra drag from the bigger wheels, needed to cope with the extra power and weight tended to slow the beast too much.

When it was obvious that the Lagonda presented serious problems, two new DB3S team cars were built for Le Mans with fixed-head coupé bodies that the Vickers plane makers calculated would reduce drag by twenty-five percent. As an alternative, the long-suffering prototype, YMY 307, was fitted with a Wade shaft-driven supercharger operating through a single Weber carburetter in a further attempt to make the DB3S faster in a straight line or through a long curve.

To add to all this work, the three 1953 Le Mans DB3Ss were prepared for the Buenos Aires 1000-kilometre race with the supercharged DB3 prototype for a training car (which had been its purpose at the 1953 Mille Miglia) and eventual sale later to subsidize the trip. The idea then was that these three team DB3Ss should go on to Sebring and then be used for the Mille Miglia before being re-placed by the new cars for Le Mans—which remained David Brown's chief objective. He was also running around in an experimental DB3S with fibreglass body, like that of the new Chevrolet Corvette which had been introduced in the United States following the success of using fibreglass in power boat racing.

Air freighting racing cars to Buenos Aires was out of the question in the winter of 1953, so the DB3Ss were hurriedly modified in the light of the season's experiences. These changes were chiefly confined to moving the brakes outboard and redesigning the engine mountings, and the cars were dispatched six weeks before the race in January. This left Wyer time to go to Casablanca to keep alive the French connection before returning to England to supervise design and race preparation, before then flying to the Argentine.

It was with high hopes, however, that the team drivers, Parnell and Salvadori, and Collins and Griffiths, joined the Argentinians, Roberto Mieres and Carlos Tomasi, to drive the DB3Ss with Forrest Greene in the blown DB3. Tragedy struck Greene a third of the way through the race, but Parnell raced on in second place behind Farina's Ferrari until his distributor drive sheared. Collins and Griffith annexed third place.

This left only a fortnight to prepare the cars for Sebring before shipping them to North America, a task that proved difficult for the small team far from Feltham. Meanwhile Wyer flew back to find that von Eberhorst had left; this meant that he had to take over engineering as well, because it was mostly racing in any case. There was also the 3-litre DB2/4 to launch. In addition, there were far more demanding projects than those already mentioned, including the development of the 12-plug head for the DB3S and disc brakes.

All too soon he had to return to Sebring to find the team there struggling desperately, with even the drivers helping change engines—quite revolutionary in those days! All the cars ran reasonably well in practice but in the race none lasted more than three hours—mainly through lack of the detailed preparation that Wyer had made his watchword.

It was a poor start to the season, but the Feltham men were not inclined to

Les Leston and Philip Salamanca competed in the Monte Carlo Rally in 1956 in the Prince of Palitania's left-hand drive DB2/4 Aston Martin registered OXE 469. Starting from Glasgow, they ploughed through ice and snow in Britain to reach Monte Carlo and take fourth place in the speed test on the sea front before being eliminated by engine trouble on the last stage.

give in. 'With hindsight, we should have forgotten all about the Mille Miglia and concentrated on Le Mans', Wyer said later. They had only eight days to prepare the best of the Sebring cars, UDV 609, Parnell's Buenos Aires car, and UXC 999 (Collins's car in that event), between docking and leaving for Italy. In the event, they crashed, with Wyer saying that they could have won with better preparation.

Nevertheless, they still fielded four cars at Silverstone a fortnight later, two new Le Mans coupés, the old prototype DB3S (now with Lockheed discs on the front), and at last the Lagonda. Salvadori was best of the Aston Martin drivers, in seventh place with one of the new coupés, 62 EMU. Parnell was fifth in the Lagonda, behind the car it was meant to compete with, Ferrari's 4.9-litre driven by the 'Pampus Bull', Froilan Gonzalez.

All this was too much for Wyer, who was sent home to rest by David Brown. He returned in time for Le Mans, but the results only added to his agony: none of the Feltham cars finished, heavy rain contributing to the toll. First the Lagonda was eliminated after smashing its back in during a spin; then Jimmy Stewart crashed the coupé he was sharing with Graham Whitehead, breaking his arm badly; the open DB3S of Belgian Paul Frere and Texan Carroll Shelby retired soon after with a stub axle damaged in another accident; and Siam's Prince Bira, sharing Collins's coupé, crashed heavily. To everybody's surprise the supercharged DB3S of Parnell and Salvadori lasted 222 laps before it was forced to retire with a blown gasket while in sixth place. And to make it all worse, Rolt and Hamilton covered Jaguars in glory by coming within an ace of beating Gonzalez and

Throughout the 1950s, the Monte Carlo Rally was of equal importance to Le Mans in terms of publicity. British enthusiasts were treated to special BBC Light Programme radio reports by their 'Mr Motoring', Raymond Baxter, who competed in a variety of cars. He drove an Aston Martin with Jackie Reece in 1958—a DB2/4 Mark II that was the prototype DB Mark III—equipped with disc brakes all round. The car is pictured here after reaching Monte Carlo in some of the worst conditions ever encountered en route from Glasgow before being eliminated by a flat battery caused by a slipping fan belt during the final 1000-kilometre test.

Stirling Moss makes his traditionally good start at Le Mans in 1956 in the DB3S he shared with Collins (number eight) for eventual second place. Close behind are the D type Jaguars of Hawthorn and Bueb (number one) who finished sixth, Flockhart and Sanderson who won (number four) and Fairman and Wharton (number three) with Walshaw and Bolton's Jaguar XK 140 (number six), and the DB3S (number nine) of Salvadori and Wharton.

Trintignant in the all-conquering 4.9-litre Ferrari.

'So Astons went home, John Wyer in a state of nervous collapse and the rest of the equipe wondering why they had chosen motor racing as a career', said Christopher Nixon in *Autosport*.

Only by a tremendous effort did the team manage to appear at Silverstone a few weeks later, with Collins winning in the prototype DB3S, without a super-charger. Salvadori was second in David Brown's personal DB3S, fitted with a conventional body, and Shelby was third in the car he had shared at Le Mans with Frere. They won the manufacturers' team award, which did wonders for their spirits. Further consolation was provided by Parnell rumbling in fourth with the Lagonda, which had a new rear end to its bodywork. This was really amazing—the first four places in an important race from a motley collection of the only running machinery they had left.

The TT was the next big race and proved to be a setback for Wyer and Brown. Against strong opposition from Lancia, Maserati, Ferrari and Jaguar, two DB3Ss retired and the other, driven by Poore and Graham Whitehead, scraped home thirteenth. Soon after, the DB3S went into production, with the first three going to the Australian Kangaroo Stable to race in Europe. These cars had the six-plug head and drum brakes; and the three oldest team cars were also sold. Another team car was built, making four for the factory to race in 1955. These were all fitted with Girling disc brakes and twelve-plug heads, and on some bodies wheelarch flares were fitted to clear the wide offset of the Borrani wire wheels. An assortment of air scoops were fitted to their noses.

One good aspect of 1954 should not be overlooked. Aston Martins had continued to do well in international rallies, with Wisdom competing in the Alpine and the Liège-Rome-Liège in XMC 76 or 77, and private owners Burton and Burke winning an Alpine Cup and their class in the Alpine Rally of 1954 in their DB2.

This led the works to prepare three DB2/4s for top-line crews in the 1955 Monte Carlo Rally. This most famous rally of them all was reaching the height of its popularity at the time, with people (including small boys such as myself) lining the traditionally snow-covered routes everywhere. Good luck signs festooned buildings all along the roads to Monaco and, on paper, Aston Martin stood a good chance of winning if the weather held. So they prepared three DB2/4s for the GT and modified class although the modifications extended little further than fitting extra windscreen wipers front and rear.

Three crews were assembled: the 1953 Monte Carlo Rally winner, Dutchman Maurice Gatsonides, partnered by Marcel Becquart of France; Parnell and photographer Louis Klemantaski; and Belgian Johnny Claes, with Peter Collins. Illness forced Claes to give his place to Graham Whitehead, however.

In the event, touring cars had an eight per cent handicap advantage over the GTs, which proved to be too much for the Astons on the vital Gap-Monaco and Mountain Circuit stages which had been made tortuous by sudden frost, massed ice and snow. An error cost Parnell a lot of time on one special stage and punctures delayed Collins badly on the Mountain Circuit, but Gatsonides forged on for seventh place overall, close behind Lier and Ziegler's Lancia Aurelia and not far adrift from the winning Norwegian crew of Malling and Fadum in a Sunbeam. The Astons took first, third and fourth places in the over 2-litre class. The first place, and the RAC Comfort and Road Safety trophy went to Gatsonides. The third and fourth places went to two private DB2/4 crews, Mariage and Boris and da Silva Ramos and Lucas.

This was the start of a good year for Aston Martin, chiefly because they had learned from their mistakes and concentrated on fewer races. They also did more development work on the DB3S, strengthening the crankshafts and connecting rods, and spent less time on the Lagonda, although they did race it at Le Mans with a new chassis. It was an easier season, too, because several races that they might have entered were cancelled following the Le Mans disaster in which eighty-two people were killed.

They gave the first two races of the World Sports Car Championship, Buenos Aires and Sebring, a miss, although private owners were in action in early season events. Graham Whitehead took his ex-team DB3S (UXC 999) to the Agadir sports car race, only to retire with final drive problems in a race won by Sparken, now Ferrari-mounted. Whitehead was running an ultra-high ratio for this very fast race, and without this equipment it was not worth running in the Dakar Grand Prix a fortnight later, so the next appearance of an Aston Martin was in the British Empire Trophy. Parnell won his heat in a 2.5-litre DB3S, the ex-David Brown car, now re-registered 9046H. There was a handicap or class limit advantage in running a 2.5-litre engine in some events and it was the contemporary Formula One capacity—a fact not lost on David Brown. Salvadori retired in the bigger car class with the throttle broken on his ex-team car, the prototype DB3S. In the final, Parnell, who had beaten Archie Scott-Brown's Lister-Bristol in his heat, was plagued by a chronic misfire and could finish only third behind Scott-Brown and Kenneth McAlpine's Connaught.

Aston Martin's luck returned for the *Daily Express* meeting at Silverstone when Parnell and Salvadori took the first two places in the sports car race with 62 and 63 EMU after Hawthorn's Jaguar blew a radiator hose when leading with four laps to go. Across the Channel at Spa, Frere outran the Ferraris with the new team car, 39 RH, which was temporarily fitted with six-plug head and drum brakes, to win the 175-mile production sports car race at the impressive speed of 107.91 mph.

By then Tony Gaze had got his Australian national team, the Kangaroo Stable organized. He had tried to get D type Jaguars, but the Coventry firm couldn't quote any firm delivery date and his friends at HWM (run by George Abecassis) were equally uncertain about their Jaguar-powered cars. So Gaze, who had already had a DB3 (chassis number nine) written off in an 'awe-inspiring' crash in the 1953 Oporto Grand Prix, contacted Wyer, who supplied production DB3Ss fitted with Weber carburetters giving 210 bhp. Their first race was the Hyeres Twelve-Hour in the South of France, with Gaze sharing his car with David McKay, Les Cosh paired with Dick Cobden and Tom Sulman sharing with a bright young recruit called Jack Brabham. The Whitehead Brothers had also entered a production DB3S (GH 30) which was faster in practice than the Kangaroo cars because of

their better knowledge of axle ratios. Mann and Morris-Goodall made up the Aston contingent in Mann's old DB3, UPL 4. In the race, on the final stint, McKay was misled by his amateur pit crew into thinking he was just over a lap behind the leading Ferrari and slowed to finish second on the same lap when he could have beaten Canonica and Maunaron in their ailing Italian car. Cosh and Cobden were third, Sulman and Brabham were fourth, and the DB3 repeated its sixth place of the previous year when Brackenbury was the co-driver. It was a typical weekend in which enthusiastic owners campaigned their Aston Martins many miles from Feltham while the works concentrated on the major events.

With such a start, the Australians looked like being on to a big success. 'Already the team were being approached by small unobtrusive men in quiet suitings who were acting for race organizers throughout Europe. These men offered starting money to us Aussies which seemed like fortunes', said David McKay in his book, *Behind the Wheel*. They had races lined up at Oporto, Rome, Lisbon, the Pescara Twelve Hour and the 1000 kilometres at the Nurburgring, before the Le Mans tragedy (two weeks after Hyeres) ruined their season, causing numerous sports car races to be cancelled.

The works were really saving themselves for Le Mans that year with a relatively low key entry in the Mille Miglia: Frere and Wisdom in two of the Monte Carlo Rally DB2/4s (54 and 56 DMF) and Collins in a DB3S (9064 H). All retired with clutch or engine trouble and Feltham concentrated on the French classic: David Brown was determined to win it after six years of trying. Three DB3Ss were entered, 62 and 63 EMU for Collins and Frere and Salvadori and Peter Walker,

Peter Whitehead in 63 EMU leads his brother Graham in DB3S/10, the wishbone and coil car, in the British Empire Trophy race at Oulton Park in 1957. Of these private entries, Graham Whitehead finished fourth in his class behind overall winner Archie Scott-Brown in a Lister-Jaguar and Salvadori's second-placed works Aston Martin.

Scott-Brown's Lister-Jaguar proved almost unbeatable in British sports car races in 1957, except at Silverstone in September where Salvadori beat him convincingly in the DBR2. Salvadori is seen here in DBR2/2 (number seventy-four) about to lap Stuart Lewis-Evans (eventually sixth) in DBR1/1 with Brooks on the extreme right in DBR1/2. Scott-Brown is in the centre of the picture on the inside of the track in the striped car next to Bueb's D type Jaguar. Aston Martins won the team prize.

Determined driving by Brooks and Lewis-Evans in the 1958 Nurburgring 1000 kilometre race came to nought when their Aston Martin, DBR1/2, was forced off the road by a small saloon when holding fourth place only fifty kilometres from the end. The paint on the driver's door has been scarred by an exhaust blow-back during a spin at the Karussel.

The Aston Martin entry for Sebring in 1958 consisted of DBR1/2 for Moss and Brooks (number twenty-four), DBR1/1 for Salvadori and Carroll Shelby (number twenty-five) and a DB Mark III (number twenty-six) entered by Elisha Walker for George Constantine in the GT class. The DBR1s were among the favourites for the race on this circuit, which was so punishing for their brakes, because they had discs as opposed to the rival Ferraris' drums. In the event Moss and Brooks led for half the distance and set the fastest lap; Salvadori and Shelby led at one point before being eliminated with gearbox trouble; Moss and Brooks had to retire with rear axle maladies and Collins won with Phil Hill in a Ferrari. The DB Mark III, running with a DB3S engine, retired early—a disappointing day for Aston Martin.

and the Spa-winning 'production' car, 39 RH, uprated to twelve-plug, disc-braked, limited slip, specification, for Brooks and Risely-Pritchard. A Lagonda was also entered for Parnell and Poore. This car had a new spaceframe chassis which reflected some of Wyer's philosophy: to develop a car gradually rather than to build a completely new one to solve inherent problems. Von Eberhorst had always wanted to change everything at once.

Collins and Frere proved to be the fastest of the quartet, effectively killing any future the Lagonda might have had at Feltham before it retired in the seventh hour with fuel leaking from an improperly closed filler. An hour later Brooks and Risely-Pritchard were out with a flat battery, and soon after Salvadori and Walker were stopped by engine trouble. It looked as though Aston Martin's jinx would never end, but Collins and Frere kept moving up the field as other cars were either withdrawn, following the crash in which Levegh's Mercedes ploughed into the crowd after a collision with Macklin's Austin-Healey, or when they broke down. Eventually there was only Mike Hawthorn and Ivor Bueb ahead in the D type Jaguar, and in the four hours that remained Collins couldn't catch him. In any case, Wyer would not have allowed a hell-for-leather chase. His tactics were to lap at a constant, pre-determined pace, and wait for the others to break down. As it happened the D type didn't, but David Brown was not too unhappy: the DB3S won its class and took third place on index of performance.

The immediate impact of the Le Mans tragedy was the wholesale cancellation of Continental races and rallies, although the British and Portuguese carried on. This gave the Kangaroo Stable considerable problems. 'There were several English races we could get a start in, but they wouldn't be to our advantage', said McKay. 'Firstly they were short races and the little Lotuses and Coopers would make mincemeat of us and secondly we weren't the drawcard in England that we were on the Continent; consequently £25 a start would be about the most we could expect!'

However, they raced in whichever British or Portuguese races they could, saying goodbye to much of the £3000 starting money they had had lined up for Continental events. They were unable to repeat the promise of the Hyeres event, however, and Sulman and McKay exported their cars to Australia at the end of the season. Cosh sold the third car to America, where it achieved considerable success in West coast events until 1960.

Meanwhile the works concentrated on British events with conspicuous success. The four works Astons of Salvadori, Collins, Parnell and Walker easily disposed of Hawthorn's D type to mop up the Aintree sports car race. This was some kind of revenge after Le Mans and before going on to win the Goodwood Nine-Hour for the third successive time. This win emphasized that this was their circuit every bit as much as Le Mans belonged to Jaguar and Ferrari. In practice at Goodwood, only the Ferrari of the Marquis de Portago and Hawthorn was faster than the works Astons, and the rest of the field, which included works Jaguars, HWMs, a Cooper-Jaguar, and Cuff-Miller and Hinde in Graham Whitehead's old DB3, TPB 641.

The Aston Martin team were nervous when Parnell retired after only three laps with hub trouble, but Collins and Poore quickly established themselves in first and second places in a race in which repeated tyre changes played a vital role. Eventually Collins and Brooks dropped back to third place with electrical trouble behind Sanderson and Titterington's D type, but there was no holding Poore and Walker: they won as convincingly as the Jaguars had at Le Mans.

With Jaguar having won two World Sports Car Championship events and Mercedes and Ferrari one each, and the Nurburgring having been abandoned in the aftermath of Le Mans, the TT at Dundrod assumed vital importance. It turned out to be an epic struggle between Moss's Mercedes and Hawthorn's Jaguar, resolved in Moss's favour when the Jaguar seized near the end. This allowed Mercedes to win 1-2-3, with Walker and Poore as the best-placed British car immediately behind with 63 EMU. Moss, who had won the Mille Miglia and went on to win the Targa Florio had now established himself as the unofficial world champion sports car driver.

During the winter months some of the British contingent headed for the rich pickings of the Australian and New Zealand racing season, which was reaching its height then. Tony Gaze acted as a contact man, frequently persuading the top Europeans to sell their cars after the races! All manner of machines were allowed in these races, two of which were the national Grands Prix, the Kangaroo Stable even entering their Astons in the Australian GP. However, in the event they both retired, but they shipped their cars over to New Zealand for the grand prix supporting events in which they stood a better chance. David Brown built up a single-seater DB3S for Parnell with a 3-litre supercharged engine, which unfortunately blew up when in practice for the New Zealand Grand Prix. A 2.5-litre engine was installed for the Lady Wigram Trophy a fortnight later and Parnell managed fourth place behind Peter Whitehead's winning 3-litre Ferrari. Gaze in a similar car made fifth place, and Leslie Marr's all-enveloping D type Jaguar-engined Grand Prix Connaught finished sixth. McKay and Sulman took third and fourth places in the sports car races. A week later Parnell improved to second

Moss is pictured here leading a gaggle of cars at Sebring in 1958: number fifty-three is a Stanguellini driven by Carl Haas, number fifty-eight an Elva driven by Bill Bradley, number forty-one a Porsche driven by Harry Schell, number forty-seven on OSCA driven by Hal Stetson and number fifty-one an Alfa Romeo driven by Louis Comito.

place at Dunedin behind Gaze's Ferrari, and third place soon after at Invercargill. The project convinced David Brown that there was a future for a single-seater Aston Martin, but work had to be shelved as the team's sports cars were being redesigned.

As development went on, combining the best aspects of the Lagonda with the DB3S to make the DBR1, a second-hand DB2 won the RAC Rally!

Former Riley exponent Lyndon Sims bought an ex-Tony Everard Vermin Stable car, NGO 651 (Everard had progressed through a DB3 and DB3S to the Cooper-Aston) and, with a youngster called Tony Ambrose, had no difficulty in beating the well-established Jaguar rally stars, Ian and Pat Appleyard, to win Britain's premier event in this field. This wonderful old car (which I remember seeing overturned at least once at Snetterton in 1953) carried on rallying for years, winning its class in the Tulip in 1956 and finishing 22nd in the RAC in 1958!

Back at the works, they were concentrating on improving the aerodynamics of the DB3S as they developed the DBR1. Changes to the four existing team cars included dry sumping, allowing a lower nose line, and modified tails to reduce drag and improve stability at Le Mans, besides the fitting of a full-width screen to meet new regulations. Two more team DB3Ss were also built; they were chassis numbers nine and ten.

Following their policy of previous years, three of the oldest team cars were sent to Sebring, with the later machines, and the DBR1 was scheduled for Le Mans. The DB3Ss were among the front-runners for the American event despite the entry of works teams from Jaguar, Ferrari, Maserati and Porsche. This was partly due to the signing of Moss for three races and partly due to really well-developed disc brakes for this tortuous circuit. Sebring rules decreed that any spare parts other than tyres used on the cars had to be carried on board, so Wyer stowed extra brake pads in the cars, besides bulbs and the like.

Moss and Collins were up to second place after three hours before their engine seized; Parnell and Brooks lasted for ten hours and held third place before similar

Moss is pictured here winning the British Empire Trophy at Oulton Park in 1958 in his DBR2 3.9-litre from Brooks's DBR2 and Scott-Brown's Lister-Jaguar. Moss made fastest lap but the writing was on the wall for the Aston Martins and Jaguars in top British sports car events as Graham Hill shared the fastest lap in a 2-litre Lotus-Climax Fifteen.

The Whiteheads storm to second place
at Le Mans in 1958.

trouble befell them in 62 EMU. But Salvadori and Shelby in 63 EMU hung on to
finish fourth behind Fangio and Castellotti's 3.4-litre Testa Rossa Ferrari, and win
their class.

Moss mopped up an event at Goodwood on Easter Monday in the oldest team
car, 9046 H, at stage two of his three-race contract. Soon after, Parnell won the
under 2700 cc heat of the British Empire Trophy race at Oulton Park in 9046 H
with a 2.5-litre engine, but was handicapped down to eleventh place in the final,
won by Moss in a 1.5-litre Cooper-Climax! However, Salvadori had no trouble
winning at Aintree the next weekend in 9046 H which was then back to 3-litre
form. All this was a build-up to the great Jaguar versus Aston match in the *Daily
Express* Silverstone meeting. There, Salvadori made a brilliant start in his Aintree-
winning car, only for Titterington to spin his D type behind him, taking out
Parnell and Collins and another Jaguar. Moss managed to avoid trouble and kept
station behind Salvadori to make it an Aston 1-2 and complete his first contract
with David Brown.

The DB3S in its final form was proving to be highly competitive everywhere,
with Parnell taking second place at Spa in 9046 H, and Salvadori repeating his
Aintree win in the same car at the Liverpool circuit in June; in its earlier form
it was still a force to be reckoned with. Graham Whitehead took third place in the
Grand Prix des Frontières at Chimay in YMY 307, bought for the season from
Salvadori. Berwyn Baxter won club races with the first of the production series,
which had been raced the previous year by Ken Wharton.

So prospects looked good for Aston Martin when they sent two cars to the
Nurburgring for the 1000 kilometres, despite the might of the Ferrari, Maserati
and Jaguar works teams. Moss was back with Maserati again; Collins and Brooks
had the old faithful, 9046 H, and Salvadori and Walker had 39 RH. Despite their
wonderful roadholding, the DB3Ss fell behind the higher-powered Ferraris and

Maseratis, with Hawthorn's Jaguar falling back, too, because it was so difficult to handle on this twisty classic of a course. Not for the first time a duel between Moss and Fangio, in Maserati and Ferrari developed, with Moss winning to confirm his unofficial world sports car title.

Of the Astons, Collins and Brooks brought 9046 H home fifth while the other car broke its de Dion tube on the last lap. Obviously, with more power, they could look forward to this event with more confidence.

No works Maseratis were entered for Le Mans, so Moss was free to share one of the new DB3Ss with Collins; Walker and Salvadori drove the other with Parnell and Brooks in the new DBR1, which in some aspects of appearance and mechanical configuration, bore a strong resemblance to the Mercedes 300SLR. The DBR1 had a 2.5-litre engine for this race, to fit in with the prototype regulations, whereas the DB3Ss really took the series car class rules to their limit with their special wheels, body and engine modifications.

The race, in foul weather, became a duel between the Moss/Collins car and the Jaguar D type of Ron Flockhart and Ninian Sanderson, with the Jaguar narrowly defeating the Aston after Collins lost second gear with five hours to go. Once more, Aston had won their class but not the race; however, the future looked better. The DBR1 ran raucously and well for 246 laps before a universal joint gave way—a most encouraging début. The other DB3S crashed after being delayed for fifty minutes with starter trouble.

To wind up the season, four works cars were sent to Oulton Park for the International Trophy. Moss drove the second-placed Le Mans car, with 39 RH for Brooks, 63 EMU for Parnell and 62 EMU for Salvadori. They took the first four places in that order, before Brooks and Salvadori did a 1-2 at Goodwood with 63 EMU and the Le Mans finisher.

Throughout the winter, development continued on the DBR1, particularly on

Moss set the Sicilians on fire with a fantastic drive in DBR1/3 in the Targa Florio as part of Aston Martin's attempt to win the world championship in 1958. He buckled a wheel when he slid off the road on the first lap then limped into the pits to have the crankshaft damper removed in twenty-five minutes while in tenth place. 'He returned to the race like a bullet', said *Motor Sport*'s Continental Correspondent, Denis Jenkinson, hitting 145 mph along one brief straight on this tortuous mountain circuit and taking corners in a series of seemingly wild and uncontrolled slides. In one lap he broke the circuit record, one minute quicker than the winning Ferrari driven by Luigi Musso. Then he broke the lap record again before his transaxle gave up at 225 miles, leaving poor Tony Brooks in the pits vainly awaiting his turn at the wheel. But Moss was at his best when the odds were against him and everybody appreciated his magnificent effort.

Moss sets a new GT lap record to win at the British Racing Drivers' Club meeting at Silverstone in 1959 in the prototype DB4GT, chassis number DP199/1.

The body of Moss's Targa DBR1 was destroyed by the fire in the pits during the 1959 Tourist Trophy race, so it was rebuilt in 1960 to meet new regulations at Le Mans. These specified a large windscreen and luggage boot, and the car was registered FSH 360 and raced in this form by the Border Reivers for Jim Clark and Salvadori. They are pictured here finishing third in the 1960 Le Mans race.

its 3-litre engine, and a new DBR2, with 3.7-litre engine, was built for even more speed. The four oldest team DB3Ss were sold off, the Whitehead brothers having the EMU cars, 62 for Graham and 63 for Peter. One of the remaining DB3Ss, the car Walker crashed at Le Mans, was fitted with wishbone and coil front suspension to test its suitability for the forthcoming production DB4 and the planned DBR4 grand prix car. A second DBR1 was built which, with the DBR2, gave the team five cars, one too many for their needs that season. The DB3S with standard suspension was shipped to Australia for McKay to use as a promotional exercise, which was to include competing in the top sports car races 'down under' and attacking the national Class D record for the flying kilometre. After much searching, McKay found a stretch of outback suitable for this venture and had a road constructed! In a claustrophobic plastic bubble top and with trouble from wheelspin, he took the record at 143.1 mph.

Meanwhile the works entered the Le Mans DBR1 with 2.5-litre engine for the British Empire Trophy race at Oulton Park with their DB3S for Noel Cunningham-Reid, assembling a pile of spare parts up into another DB3S just in case! They had the Whitehead brothers to back them up though, and it was interesting to note that Cunningham-Reid's DB3S was fitted with experimental fuel injection based on diesel engine equipment. Archie Scott-Brown ran away with the event in his Lister-Jaguar, becoming almost invincible in British club racing at the time, with Salvadori and Cunningham-Reid in hot pursuit. It stayed that way to the finish, with Graham Whitehead beating his brother into sixth place.

Scott-Brown and Salvadori met again at Goodwood on Easter Monday, the Lister-Jaguar scoring a runaway victory from the 2.5-litre DBR1, with Brooks third in the DB3S. But better things were brewing, and the team had the 3-litre engines and the second DBR1 chassis ready for the 180-mile Spa sports car race in May. The wet conditions on this high-speed circuit proved to be just right for the DBR1s with Brooks and Salvadori finishing first and second; an ideal warm-up for the Nurburgring in a fortnight's time.

This is where according to Denis Jenkinson the car really proved itself:

'The DBR1 of Tony Brooks and Noel Cunningham-Reid literally trounced all opposition and was among the front-runners from the word go. It was not one of Wyer's "tortoise and hare" victories [Parnell had taken over as team manager by then] with Aston running a schedule and letting rivals do the in-fighting. This time the Aston Martins were in the thick of the battle, and they came out covered with glory. It was undoubtedly their finest victory, about which no one could argue, and it showed the DBR1 to be the equal of anything at the time.'

Salvadori and Les Leston were sixth in the other DBR1 and the Whitehead brothers ninth, in the last race for a DB3S as a works car (the 1957 spare going to America to be raced by Rod Carveth on the West coast and for one season in Australia and New Zealand). Dalton, followed by Sgonina, took over the other one for a long career chiefly in club events.

The DBR1s, however, had beaten the might of Maserati and Ferrari, and were looking forward to Le Mans. The same two DBR1s with the same drivers were entered with the Whitehead brothers in the DBR2. The DBR1s were eliminated however, with gearbox trouble, and the DBR2 was handicapped by a fuel system that cost it 50 bhp before it, too, retired with gearbox trouble. 'It was one of our silliest mistakes', said Wyer.

Meanwhile the Jaguars, who had retired from racing as a works team the previous season, had the satisfaction of seeing the Ecurie Ecosse D type of Flockhart and Bueb win with other Jaguars in three of the next five places, most of the Italian cars having retired following a private grand prix. It really did seem as though Astons were fated never to win at Le Mans. Only one finished in 1957, a production DB3S driven by Frenchmen Kerguen and Colas into eleventh place, although they did win their class.

Consolation, if there could be such a thing for an eight-times loser, came in the Belgian Grand Prix when Brooks led from start to finish with his DBR1 equipped with the four-bearing wide-angled head engine. Once more, Ferrari were vanquished, and Salvadori took fourth place in the other DBR1, with the Whiteheads in sixth and seventh places with their DB3Ss. This gave the team the coveted marque prize and all they had to do was pick up the pieces of the DBR1 crashed in practice by Cunningham-Reid.

Salvadori, in a new DBR2 beat Scott-Brown in a thrilling duel at Silverstone in September, the only time the Lister driver was beaten that season in his 3.8-litre car. Cunningham-Reid was third in the repaired DBR2 with Brooks hard on his tail in a DBR1. Brian Naylor took fifth place in this high-speed race with an incredible 2-litre Lotus-Maserati from the second DBR1, driven by Stuart Lewis-Evans. Le Mans apart, it had been a great season for the team cars.

Sadly, the DBR2, along with the 3.8-litre D type Jaguar, was rendered ineligible for the 1959 World Sports Car Championship when a 3-litre engine limit was introduced. But, for the first time, Aston Martin had an ideal car for this prestigious title: the DBR1. Therefore they decided to concentrate on that— particularly as Le Mans was now included in the championship. This meant shelving the grand prix cars, one of which they actually had running that winter. Their task in sports car racing was made easier in that Jaguar built a 3-litre XK engine but could not make it sufficiently reliable, and Maseratis gave up for a while through general disorganization and lack of finance. But there were still the menacing Ferraris, and Porsche were always waiting in the background should one of the giants fall. The DBR2s were therefore fitted with 3.9-litre engines for non-championship events that would not stretch the team too much, while the DBR1s were prepared for the world championship. This meant building a third DBR1; such had become the expense of sports car racing that these cars were not built in DB3S quantities. Jaguar couldn't afford the expense either, and the Ecurie Ecosse certainly couldn't afford to take their ex-works D types to Buenos Aires for the first round in January 1958.

Astons gave it a miss, too, because they weren't quite ready and they still remembered the débâcle of 1954. This meant that Ferrari had a relatively clear run for that event, with Collins's car winning from another, with Moss's Porsche snapping up third place when the remaining works Ferrari failed. Naturally, Aston Martin treated the next round at Sebring very seriously, and so did Jaguar, although they appeared in the guise of Lister-Jaguars for Briggs Cunningham.

Astons took two DBR1s to Sebring, one for Moss and Brooks and one for Salvadori and Shelby, with a Weber-carburetted DB Mark III for George Constantine. This car in fact belonged to Elisha Walker. It retired with differential trouble in the race, but went on to win the Avon International Trophy in 1957 and to take second place in the SCCA Category C.

Moss stormed into the lead, setting a lap record in the process, with Salvadori moving up into second place before he had to retire with a broken frame, much to Aston Martin's surprise. Then the gearbox failed on Moss's car and Astons began to rue having given Buenos Aires a miss: at least they would probably have had more time to work on the gearbox problem.

In 1957, the Mille Miglia was not run following an inevitable crash involving spectators, but the Targa Florio was still held in Sicily. While the works concentrated on their gearbox problem Moss took the new DBR1 and lapped fantastically fast till he was eliminated—by his gearbox. With this threat removed, Ferrari's only opposition came from the incredible Porsche of Behra and Scarlatti, which eventually finished second behind Musso and Gendebian. That left Ferrari with an almost invincible lead in the world championship with twenty-four points to fourteen for Porsche and none for Aston Martin. One more victory and they would be sports car champions again. But the next round was at the Nurburgring. . . .

In the meantime, the DBR2s were entered at Spa, against the Lister-Jaguars and D types, for Frere and Shelby; who stayed over in Europe for a season or so because 'there was nothing much left to achieve in sports car racing in the States'. Masten Gregory won in his Ecurie Ecosse Lister, against Frere and Shelby, with Bueb fourth in a Jaguar; but Scott-Brown lost his life when his Lister skidded off the track and caught fire.

British spirits rose again when Moss's Aston Martin outran Hawthorn's Ferrari to score another win at 'the 'Ring'. Brooks should have been second, to score more points in the world championship, but was forced off the track by a slower car near the end, and Salvadori went out with gearbox trouble. But Ferrari were not champions yet.

Then came one of the wettest Le Mans ever. Astons were fastest in practice, which was dry, with the Jaguars close behind and the Ferraris lazing around. But burned pistons sidelined the Ecurie Ecosse within half an hour and Moss led till his engine blew. Heavy rains fell at 6 pm. Phil Hill and Gendebian sailed into the lead in their Ferrari speedboat with Brooks ploughing along fourth and Lewis-Evans losing the third DBR1 under the Dunlop Bridge. Bent cars littered the course, and the Aston Martin of Brooks and Trintignant retired with gearbox trouble. Meanwhile the Whitehead brothers were moving up in 62 EMU, which was a private entry. When Duncan Hamilton crashed into a ditch and nearly drowned himself, they inherited the Jaguar's second place, but Hill and Gendebian in the

Semi-works Aston Martins were entered by the Essex Racing Stable in major events in the early 1960s. Here one of their DB4 GT Zagatos driven by Tony Maggs takes third place in the 1962 Oulton Park Trophy.

Aston Martin DB4 GT Zagatos proved quite competitive in GT racing in the early 1960s: here Mike Salmon wins the EMU Trophy at the Aston Martin Owners' Club's 1962 Silverstone meeting.

Jim Clark tried all he knew to stay with the Ferraris in the 1962 Tourist Trophy race at Goodwood, but he overdid it when the leading 250GTO (number six) driven by John Surtees was about to lap him. Clark lost his ill-handling Ogier DB4GT Zagato and took Surtees with him at Madgwick, leaving Innes Ireland to win in another Ferrari 250GTO.

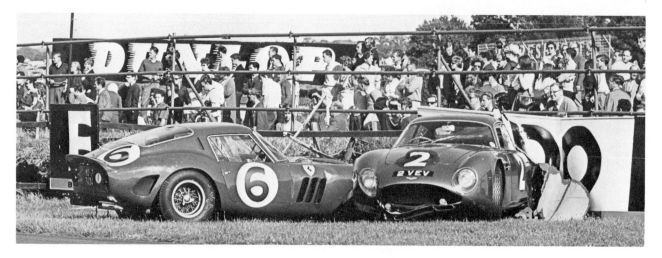

Zagato bodies on DB4GTs varied in design from car to car. One had a front similar to the standard DB4GT and the car pictured here, driven by Kerguen and Franc at Le Mans in 1963 had different rear wings. Kerguen and Franc's car retired after six hours with rear axle trouble. The following car is Elde and Dumay's fourth-placed Ferrari 250GTO.

Salmon continued to campaign Project 212 after it was sold to Viscount Downe and fitted with a 4.2-litre engine in 1964. He is pictured here leading Peter Sutcliffe's lightweight Jaguar E type in third place before retiring with final drive problems in the rain-soaked *Autosport* Three-Hour race at Snetterton in 1964. Ten years later Salmon won the British Classic Car championship for Viscount Downe in the same car.

Ferrari lasted out to win. David Brown was so grateful he promised to build Graham Whitehead a DBR1. But his gratitude was tinged with sadness for Enzo Ferrari had won the championship.

The Commandatore could see little point in entering the TT at Goodwood after that, but Aston Martin fielded a full team of DBR1s for Salvadori and Brabham, Moss and Brooks, and Shelby and Lewis-Evans. They had it all their own way with Jaguars and a flying Porsche RSK putting up the only opposition to their 1-2-3 result—Moss, Salvadori, Shelby—which had been a demonstration of speed and reliability. It was left to *Autosport* to remark that it was a pity they couldn't have done it a bit earlier.

Constantine had been doing so well in the States that David Brown sent over a DBR2 with a 4.2-litre engine for USAC racing, where it showed itself to have the legs of assorted Ferraris, Maseratis and Porsches, and where it went on to win the US sports car drivers' championship in 1959. Salvadori also drove a DBR1 at Riverside on its way to Sebring to share with Shelby. The other DBR2 was fitted with a 4.2-litre engine for Oker to drive in USAC racing with similar success. The DBR3 made an appearance at Silverstone in the BRDC meeting in 1958 to test the DBR4's grand prix engine, but it seized after Moss had set a class lap record and the car was converted into a fourth DBR1 for the 1959 season.

John Wyer summed up 1958 as 'the year we should have won the world championship and didn't. The car fulfilled its promise by making fastest lap in every race in which it competed, but won only two important events. It was a classic example of conflicting aims and policies and failure to concentrate on the main issue.'

The next season was to be different. Aston Martin were tired of world championship racing and decided that they would concentrate on Le Mans and getting the DBR4 (which had run as much as a year earlier) ready for grands prix. In fact, things looked gloomy for the British. No new Jaguar team was forthcoming despite rumours about the new E type; all the rest of the Jaguar-powered devices were either outdated or lacked a reliable engine. Ferrari, on the other hand, had at last recognized the value of disc brakes and there seemed to be no end to the speed Porsche could extract from their little cars. When Ferrari practised for Le Mans, the cars just walked away from the Astons along the straights although Wyer and Parnell knew they were over-revving.

The Buenos Aires races were cancelled because not enough people could afford to go to them and Sebring became the first world championship event. Astons did not want to attend but sent one DBR1 at the last moment when the organizers twisted their arms. Salvadori fought valiantly but the car succumbed to all manner of minor problems and Wyer wished they hadn't bothered, especially when Ferraris scooped eight points for the championship and Porsche four. The Stuttgart cars eventually nailed Ferrari in the Targa Florio, leaving them on twelve points to Ferrari's eight, Astons having declined to enter. However, David Brown couldn't refuse the Nurburgring organizers and sent along his oldest DBR1 for Moss—who was convinced he could win with an Aston Martin—and Fairman. Old as this DBR1 was, it had a four-bearing engine, and it was faster than the more durable seven-bearing cars. Happily Moss and Fairman won and suddenly enthusiasm for the world sports car championship returned to Feltham as everybody prepared for Le Mans. That is, everyone except Salvadori. He just concentrated on playing cards. He had been driving there for years and still had to finish a race.

However, it was to be a do-or-die effort for Astons with their three youngest DBR1s for Salvadori and Shelby, Moss and Fairman, Trintignant and Frere, with Whitehead and Naylor in the private DBR1 and the DB4GT prototype for Frenchmen Patthey and Calderai. The Frenchmen were soon out with engine trouble, followed by Moss and Fairman. Moss had frightened the Ferraris by provoking their fastest car, that of Behra and Dan Gurney, to go far too fast for its own good. As Moss and Fairman retired in the four-bearing car and the Whitehead DBR1 crashed, Salvadori and Shelby and Trintignant and Frere were cruising round on a schedule set by Wyer in their slightly slower seven-bearing cars. This time the plan worked, despite one heart-stopping moment when a piece of metal in Salvadori's back tyre caused such severe vibration that they thought their race was over. A wheelchange cured all that, and the Ferraris followed by the Porsches fell by the wayside. The two DBR1s swept in, also taking second and third places in the performance index. Salvadori had finished a Le Mans at last, and David Brown had achieved his ambition after ten years' trying.

Suddenly it became apparent that the world sports car championship was there for the taking, almost by accident. After Le Mans, Ferrari had eighteen points (a 250GT had finished third), Aston Martin sixteen and Porsche only fifteen. Only then did the Feltham team start to treat the last event, the TT, seriously, shelving the grand prix car yet again. As the Ferrari driver concentrated on learning this difficult circuit, the Aston Martin team concentrated on saving seconds at the numerous pit stops. They even had an Indianapolis-style air-jacking system which cut the time it took to change all four wheels and refuel to a fantastic 33 seconds. This time the pairings in the three DBR1s were Moss and Salvadori, Shelby and Fairman, Frere and Trintignant, it being reasoned that the first combination was definitely the fastest. Whitehead had his repaired DBR1 there for support. The Ferrari team were tremendously fast but suffered from poor roadholding compared to the Astons and Porsches. The Jaguar-powered cars were outclassed on this circuit.

Moss and Shelby shot straight into the lead, with Whitehead well up until he was overwhelmed by Ferraris and electrical trouble. Although the Ferrari drivers, particularly Brooks, Phil Hill, Gurney and Gendebian, drove like men inspired, the Astons stayed ahead with Jo Bonnier looking threatening in the lighter Porsche, which did not have such an appetite for tyres. Then another refuelling disaster struck. Spilled petrol was ignited by hot exhaust pipes. Salvadori leapt 'like a frog' from his blazing DBR1 and rolled himself in grass around the pits to put out his flaming overalls; fortunately he did not incur serious injury. But the car was out and at the next pit stop Moss took over from Fairman in the second car, by now chasing Bonnier. Whitehead retired so that the works could use his pit. Moss soon took the Porsche, leaving a titanic struggle behind him

Another famous DB4GT, one of the Project 214 cars, also made a comeback in British historic racing. Nick Cussons is pictured here behind the wheel in 1973.

Current club racing at its best: British Airlines pilot Pete Foster corners his DB4 series one to take second place in the modified David Brown Aston Martins class at the Aston Martin Owners' Club Curborough sprint in September 1978. This event is so popular that it is usually oversubscribed, with as many as twenty reserves listed in the programme.

between Taffy von Trips (in the Bonnier Porsche) and Brooks with world championship points at stake. The Aston had only to finish first to win the championship, no matter where the Ferrari finished. Ferrari was third, giving Porsche second place in the title fight. David Brown had won this coveted title, almost by accident!

Christopher Nixon summed up this historic season in *Autosport*:

'It is quite easy to see how and why Aston Martin won the championship. To begin with, there was nothing really new about the DBR1. It was a proven design, the Feltham team's organization was second to none and nothing was left to chance. Reg Parnell had gathered a team of drivers, not a bunch of individualists, and this paid hand over fist.

'On the other hand, there was a lot of grumbling in the Ferrari team, and it was never a really happy one. The drivers were seldom satisfied with their cars, which, in comparison with the Astons and Porsches, were sadly lacking in roadholding, although more powerful.

'Porsche, in this writer's opinion, could have snatched the championship from Ferrari and Aston Martin, but they suffered a complete débâcle at Le Mans, which set them back a bit. The real tragedy, from the German point of view, was surely that Porsche used bolt-on wheels. Had they had knock-ons at Goodwood they must have won the race. . . .

'The drive of the year was undoubtedly that of Stirling Moss at the 'Ring. He drove splendidly at Le Mans and Goodwood, too, of course, and there is no doubt that without "The Master", Astons would never have won the championship . . . and the most pleasing result of the year was surely Roy Salvadori's Le Mans victory. He is one of the most experienced and versatile drivers around and it is surprising to realize that this was his first really big win.'

David Brown chose this moment to get out of sports car racing and concentrate on the grand prix cars which had been racing spasmodically throughout 1959. This project had looked good when Salvadori managed second place and a lap record in the International Trophy at Silverstone behind world champion-to-be Brabham's Cooper-Climax in May. Shelby had over-revved when the pit told him to try to take Flockhart's BRM for third place on the last lap, and blew his engine. After that, engine trouble eliminated both DBR4s in the grands prix they contested, with the exception of the British Grand Prix where Salvadori took sixth place; the Portuguese, where he had another sixth and Shelby eighth; and the Italian where Shelby took tenth.

'A revolution was taking place in Grand Prix racing [said Jenkinson] started by Cooper and Lotus with the aid of Coventry-Climax, the engine firm, and encouraged by changes in the grand prix rules. All was aimed towards a much watered-down type of event that encouraged small, simple, cars, taking much of the endurance characteristics out of the races.

'The single-seater DBR4 Aston had been bred especially for the old school, long, tough, and rugged grand prix race, and developed through knowledge gleaned from sports car racing. So the whole concept of the GP car was wrong; in the "small car circus" which comprised GP racing by 1959, the car was simply outclassed. The team struggled against all the odds . . . but it was hopeless and the DBR4 never made its mark. This was really a pity. Had it appeared, say, two years earlier, it might well have stopped the degenerate slide down the slope greased by "special builders" like John Cooper and Colin Chapman.

'In passing it is worth recording that Lance Reventlow's all-American Scarab formula one car suffered from the same quirk of fate that affected the DBR4. Had these two cars gone GP racing even a year earlier they might well have changed the whole course of grand prix history, by preventing the doldrum of 1961–5 with its little 1.5-litre formula one cars.'

But, then, David Brown might not have won Le Mans, and he would almost certainly not have won the world sports car championship had he gone overboard on formula one. . . .

The DBR5, which was an updated DBR4, was raced in 1960 alongside two of the four DBR4s. It finished only once (in eleventh place), in the British Grand Prix, driven by Trintignant, before the entire project was dropped and a couple of DBR4s with a spare chassis were sold to Australians Lex Davison and Bib Stilwell. They enjoyed equally small success, although other Aston Martin's were still proving successful in Australia. McKay resurrected his ex-works DB3S to win the Australian TT in 1959 and Sulman was still mopping up local events in his Kangaroo car!

Private owners took over from the works in racing the sports cars in 1960 while Feltham tried to get the DBR4 and 5 right, although it was the last year of the 2.5-litre Formula One. The Border Reivers were the most successful with the car which nearly burned out at Goodwood, and which had been rebuilt to new regulations with high 'luggage boot' and windscreen. The up-and-coming Jim Clark was their star driver: he took third place at Le Mans in 1960 with Salvadori, and Ferrari occupying the rest of the first seven places! The Border Reivers also led the Nurburgring 1000 kilometres before retiring in fourth place and Clark managed a third place at Oulton Park in an early season warm-up. Major Ian Baillie took the Le Mans-winning DBR1 back to the Sarthe circuit with Fairman for ninth overall in 1960: he also competed at the 'Ring with the Hon. Eddie Greenall. Whitehead persevered with his DBR1, retiring at the 'Ring and lending it to Fairman for fourth place at Rouen.

Meanwhile the DB4GT was being campaigned in lesser events: Moss had won the International Trophy GT race in 1959 with the prototype before it went to Le Mans. The introduction of the Zagato enabled private owners to compete on reasonably equal terms with the Ferraris and Jaguar E types in GT racing. These included, notably, John Ogier's Essex Racing Stable, who also had the original DBR1 and borrowed the fourth DBR1 in 1961. Ogier's lightweight DB4GTs and Zagatos did well in GT racing and the DBRs were campaigned as

Fractionally faster at Curborough was another good representative of current Aston Martin club competition, Dave Ellis in his V8. It is pictured here at the St John Horsfall meeting at Silverstone in 1978, characteristically trailing smoke from its final drive. This very fast car has a habit of consuming one differential unit per race meeting!

Roy Salvadori makes an encouraging debut with DBR4/1 in the International Trophy race at Silverstone in 1959. He finished second with the lap record behind world champion-to-be Jack Brabham in a Cooper-Climax. Sadly, Aston Martin were never able to improve on that performance in Formula One.

often as possible, the original returning twice to the 'Ring—making five times in all—and finishing fourth in 1962 with Bruce McLaren and Tony Maggs at the wheel!

With the demise of the 2.5-litre Formula One and for Moss the dream of the world championship, David Brown authorized work on some special DB4GTs for Le Mans, providing their development was of logical use for road cars. These were the Projects 212, 214 and 215 cars. There was also a DB4GT (the second prototype) which was prepared for the Monte Carlo Rally. This event was still of considerable importance for publicity and it was felt that Sims ought to be given a chance with a more modern car than the DB2! But this DB4GT was not really suited to the event because smaller cars had highly favourable handicaps. However, its crew took it to third in class and not surprisingly won the special stage around the Monaco GP circuit.

Project 212 in the hands of Graham Hill (who had won the world championship that year) and the American Richie Ginther, held second place early on at Le Mans in 1962 before falling back and retiring with engine and ignition trouble. Zagatos driven by Kerguen and 'Franc' and Baillie and Mike Salmon retired with blown engines midway through the race which was won, inevitably, by a Ferrari far removed from anything that could be driven on the road. The Project 214 cars were campaigned extensively in GT racing in 1963 with Salvadori winning the Inter-Europa Cup at Monza and Jo Schlesser winning the Coupes de Salon at Montlhery. Engine trouble struck them down at Le Mans, however, and Kimberley and Schlesser were forced to retire when in third place. McLaren and Innes Ireland retired after being as high as sixth. Project 215 for Phil Hill and Lucian Bianchi lasted three hours before its transmission gave up. Ferraris took the first six places . . . and the DBR1s were consigned to club racing. Viscount Downe, who now owned the original DBR1, using it for club racing, bought Project 212 to use on the road, and for occasional races with Salmon at the wheel. Salmon and Salvadori, when the latter's Ford GT40 commitments allowed, raced Project 214 with little success, although it did last seventeen hours at Le Mans before running out of oil. Brian Hetreed and Mike Kerrison raced the other Project 214 car before Hetreed was killed in it at the Nurburgring.

Unlike a lot of famous racing cars, many of the Astons continued to be used in club racing, remaining popular because they were so rewarding to drive. Even a Lagonda Rapide saloon competed between 1962 and 1964 against hordes of Minis and Anglias. It won at Snetterton and recorded 29.50 seconds to win the over 2-litre class for four-seater saloons in the Brighton Speed Trials in 1964!

As historic racing caught on in the late 1960s, Aston Martins were well placed, having been maintained to high standards. The DBR4s were bought back from Australia for Neil Corner to win almost every race he entered between 1968 and 1974, annexing lap records all over Britain, Peter Brewster enjoyed similar success in the ex-Stilwell car between 1966 and 1970. David Ham and Corner raced the Le Mans-winning DBR1 and Charles Sgonina the ex-Border Reivers cars, with Clive Aston notably successful among DB3S owners with 9046 H, re-registered PAP 625. Van Tilburg enjoyed some success in the ex-Whitehead DBR1 after it had been raced in Angola and Rhodesia by Whitehead and Fairman. In addition to this other Astons were also racing; they were being raced in far higher proportions than most marques.

The factory had only one more serious attempt at Le Mans with the two abortive V8-engined Lolas which were both out within a couple of hours as the Ford GT40 went on to complete a double over Ferrari in 1967. Corner's exploits apart, Aston Martin enthusiasts had to wait for Salmon to bring Project 212 out of retirement and to win the first Classic Car Championship in 1973 for their next major national title. By this time thoroughbred racing was catching on, with cars such as the DB4s (shared by Ian Moss and Pete Foster, and run by Dave Preece) enjoying success. Today there are two classes of Aston Martin in this branch of racing: the ultra lightweight machines such as Preece's and Dave Reade's (prepared by Moss), and the heavier, more standard cars of which the Moss and Foster machine, 358 DLW, is a good example. Earlier cars are well represented by enthusiasts like Shaun Magee with his DB3S-engined DB2. Equally successful is the modified V8 driven by Dave Ellis. In a class of its own is the V8 prepared for Le Mans by Robin Hamilton. This magnificent, much modified, machine finished seventeenth at Le Mans in 1977 (with Hamilton, Preece and the veteran Salmon driving) to confound many people's predictions. Hamilton turbocharged the car in 1978, but couldn't fit in enough testing before the event, so now Aston Martin enthusiasts everywhere are waiting with bated breath for their next excursion to the French classic and also for the fulfilment of the reports that the works will be racing a V8 in production sports car events in 1979.

X

Strengths and Weaknesses

THE STRENGTHS of any Aston Martin or Lagonda made since the war are well known: they are beautiful-looking machines which are synonymous with quality and which are positively seductive. Their handling has always been in a class of its own, with the exception of the early Lagonda, which could be rather tail-happy when driven in a spirited fashion. But then, that was a car designed for a dowager rather than a demon driver. With the exception of the Feltham cars and the DBS six-cylinder, particularly the automatic, their straight-line performance has been of the highest quality. So why have these rewarding Aston Martins and Lagondas acquired a troublesome reputation with so many people? It is because they are thoroughbreds which need every bit as much care as a racehorse, and because they are made of many diverse materials, which inevitably lead to corrosion. It is thus a question either of accepting underbody corrosion, in most parts of the world, or dried-out woodwork and leather where there are desert-like climes in which you never see a spot of rust.

None of these factors need be a major problem, providing that the car is in first-class condition to start with, and that it is maintained properly after that. However, there was a period, between about 1960 and 1975, when many unfortunate Aston Martins and Lagondas received hardly any of the care they deserved. Before 1960 most garages were more attuned to keeping cars running than scrapping them, were better versed in the art of proper maintenance than just bolting on replacement units, and were staffed by men who, in the majority, had had a good training in the forces. This was ideal for the person running an Aston Martin or Lagonda. Britain then introduced the Ministry of Transport test for cars of more than ten years old (this limit is now down to three years old), and the average garage changed almost overnight. Many cars that had been kept running by sheer ingenuity and dedicated maintenance were scrapped because it was uneconomic to keep them running when they had to face this stiff test every year. At the same time, county councils in Britain became wildly enthusiastic about the qualities of rock salt. We had a wonderful summer in 1959 followed by some awful winters, and the councils started laying more and more salt on their roads to combat ice and snow. They really went overboard on its use, frequently salting roads for as much as 250 days a year, as I discovered to my horror in a survey for *CAR* magazine in

1978. As the salt diggers worked overtime, trying to meet the ever-increasing demand, cars started to crumble. There is no worse enemy for any car than rock salt, and the saline solution thrown up from wet roads. These factors accelerated the change in the garage industry: the combination of salt and the MoT test was enough to turn many into 'scrap 'em and sell you another' car merchants, rather than 'we can keep it on the road for you' service establishments. Fairly soon the average garage mechanic became little more than a fitter of replacement parts. The comprehensive servicing schedules of old also became prohibitively expensive; labour rates soared as Britain's economy took a hammering in the early 1960s. Aston Martins and Lagondas suffered badly from a number of these factors: they have always needed the comprehensive servicing and maintenance that demand the skills practised by the garages of old. And they are as susceptible to salt as any other car. Their special weaknesses in corroding centre on the use of alloy for body panels with a steel frame, and all-alloy engines since 1959; the blocks and heads often suffer particularly from internal corrosion when the cars are laid up for a long time 'to protect the investment'.

Another factor that influenced the decline of so many Aston Martins and Lagondas between 1960 and 1975 was the fact that they commanded incredibly low second-hand prices. This was due to Jaguars, as they offer comparable, if not superior, straight-line performance for a far lower starting price, and their body-work is just as beautiful to look at. This meant that Astons and Lagondas suffered dreadfully from lack of maintenance, often receiving only the attention associated with cars in the cheaper price brackets. It applied particularly to oil changes, which, as any Aston owner should know, cannot be extended beyond the 2500-mile limits if good oil pressure is to be preserved. Other cars, with lower-pressure systems, have been able to get away with extended intervals between oil changes as modern technology has improved the lubricant. (Just remember that expensive as oil might be, a set of bearings costs a lot more.)

The enthusiasts who buy and own these cars today are still frequently 'picking up the tab' from that age of neglect. Their problems are heightened by the fact that since Aston Martin were saved in 1975, the cars have commanded rapidly rising retail prices, and the cost of spares has inevitably risen at the same time. There is a good side to this, however. At least the owners of these later cars, and the ones made since 1972 that look like them, have usually forsaken the back-street garages for specialist establishments to protect their investments. And Aston Martins have always been made in such small quantities that the customer has had to do much of the minor development work and sometimes the major work as well. Happily, the company are now in a situation where everything (Lagonda's electrics accepted) has been in production for so long that the development bugs have been ironed out, and where the new cars are now selling at a realistic price so that there is enough money for the proper development work.

The brakes were one of the worst weaknesses. In common with so many high-performance cars made between 1950 and 1957, Aston Martins and Lagondas suffered from brake fade. This was because not enough air circulated around the drums enclosed in the cars' new all-enveloping bodywork. Strangely, it was not

Rare view of a Claude Hill pushrod engine as fitted to the DB1.

The massive cruciform chassis of an early post-war Lagonda saloon.

so bad on the racetracks, where the drums were subject to a constant cooling blast of air. It must be remembered, however, that Aston Martins weren't as bad as many production cars, because their adherence to wire wheels, even when they were unfashionable between 1950 and 1953, and the use of Alfin drums later, helped to disperse heat. The problem was at its worst in the heavy, disc-wheeled Lagondas, and was never properly cured until the advent of disc brakes. Even then, the early disc brakes, particularly those on the DB4, could suffer from an alarming rate of pad consumption till matters were improved on the series three DB4. It didn't really matter how you used the brakes, they were expensive to maintain. This was because the Dunlop system on the early disc-braked cars had a bad habit of seizing brake pistons. The pistons were less liable to seize if the brakes were used hard, but then the pads wore out very quickly. The general problem of pad wear affects all disc-braked Aston Martins and Lagondas; they are heavy cars capable of high speeds, so heavy use of the brakes means that the life of a set of pads can be as low as six or seven thousand miles. They may well last about 15,000 miles with more moderate use, but then there is a risk of seizing pistons on Dunlop-braked cars. This can often be felt when the car pulls to one side or the other, as the pads wear unevenly. The same factors influence tyre and clutch wear: drive the car hard and they won't last long, there's so much weight to cope with.

Cross-ply tyres, to which the pre-DBS cars are so well suited, frequently last less than 10,000 miles; radial-ply tyres last, perhaps, 15,000–20,000 miles in the same circumstances, although the ride suffers. Clutches have a life of 10,000 to, maybe, 25,000 miles, this being influenced by how much the car is used in heavy traffic. But at least you do not have to take the engine out to change the clutch, which is the case on the majority of Jaguars! Never economize on changing the

The rolling chassis of a 2.6-litre Aston Martin.

The front suspension of one of the 2-litre prototype Aston Martin DB2s.

flywheel; if there is any sign of scoring you must fit a new one or the new clutch is likely to last no more than a few hundred miles. It is not advisable to have a scored flywheel skimmed; it frequently leaves 'hot spots' which are no better than scoring.

Be prepared to have the engine overhauled after about 70,000 miles' use; this can be as little as 2000 miles with highly tuned racing units! Standard engines, Vantage or not, frequently last for more than 100,000 miles with little attention, but it depends on how they have been used and looked after. Any untoward noises should be checked immediately, particularly in the alloy-blocked engines, because these noises can lead to thrown connecting rods, which are, inevitably a very expensive repair. The place to look for previous repairs to the Feltham cars' engines is around the number five cylinder because that is the weakest part of the block. The early 2.6-litre engines are less prone to trouble than the later 3 litres and this is because the crankshafts and connecting rods are less highly stressed. Generally, the lower the power output of these units the longer they are likely to last. But whichever engine you have, whether it is the six or eight-cylinder, make sure the operating readings are right. Unlike Jaguar engines, for instance, they will not tolerate low pressures because they were designed to operate at much higher pressures. The relevant minimum oil pressures at normal running temperature at 4000 rpm are: 2-litre, 90–100 psi; 2.6- and 3-litre, 60 psi; 3.7-litre series one and two DB4, 75 psi; series three DB4 and following six-cylinder cars (which have bigger sumps), 95 psi; V8, 80 psi. Water temperatures before the V8 Vantage should hover around 75 degrees; 85 degrees if it is the 'blanked-off' grille model.

Gearboxes are generally reliable, if somewhat noisy. Severe noise with the David Brown gearbox heralds trouble, although the synchromesh never lasts long anyway; ZF gearboxes are generally noisier but last much longer in this condition.

Side by side in the service department at Feltham, a DB2/4 and a Lagonda 2½-litre saloon.

The massive chassis and body super-structure of the Aston Martin DB4.

The final drive and brake assembly used on the V8 Aston Martins and Lagondas.

Overdrives, where fitted, hardly ever give trouble and then it is usually traceable to the electrics. Early automatic gearboxes can be troublesome but they are not a mystery to the specialist; they are similar to those fitted to cars, such as Jaguars, of the same period. The later Chrysler gearboxes are superb. Differentials are quite reliable, although those fitted to cars with independent rear suspension frequently suffer from leaking oil seals. This condition is caused by the intense heat generated by the inboard brakes and is not a problem for immediate concern in normal use, unless the oil is contaminating the brake discs, providing that the level is kept topped up, but not overfilled. When the oil seal starts to leak it seems to become better lubricated and doesn't deteriorate so quickly from then on! Any other oil leaks (which are typical of alloy-engined cars) should receive immediate attention, although I should hasten to add that Aston Martin engines are particularly good from this point of view. No doubt it is because they are hand-built. Brake and clutch hydraulics can suffer from lack of use. The hydraulic fluid absorbs moisture very easily, which leads to corrosion of the operating pistons, to the detriment of the cylinder seals. Everyday use and changing the fluid every 15,000 miles or annually can alleviate this; otherwise it is worth having the system drained and the seals lubricated if the car is to be laid up for any length of time.

Suspension systems are basically very strong; the earlier cars' reliance on coil springs has stood them in better stead than leaf-sprung rivals in later years, and torsion bars are rarely troublesome. Also, the entire suspension system is so well engineered—far better than those on modern Ferrari and Lamborghinis for instance—that with decent servicing and with the possible exception of ground clearance, it is unlikely to give trouble.

Lack of ground clearance has always been an Aston Martin problem: everything worked well when the cars were in top-rate mechanical condition and running on British roads, which used to be better maintained than in many parts of the world. As soon as an Aston hits the ripply roads of France, however, it is liable to bang its back end on the surface. This is a problem that has survived even to the V8, because of the compromise needed with a soft suspension that is low enough for good roadholding, and the necessity to hang a large exhaust system under the car. If the exhaust system was indented into the underside it would roast the inhabitants. Engine heat was a big enough problem on the early Newport cars, and it was only alleviated by comprehensive insulation. The ground clearance problem has not been completely eradicated on the V8 because it is so much more powerful and so much more can be loaded into the back. The only cure is proper—and expensive—maintenance. In this respect, the rear dampers seem to suffer at roughly the same rate as tyres when the car is driven hard or when heavily laden.

Proper maintenance is also essential for the wire wheels, particularly those with chromium-plated spokes. The actual chroming process weakens the spokes, although the wheels of any heavy, powerful car, capable of high cornering speeds, are bound to suffer. Alloy wheels are trouble-free in this respect, although they can suffer far more from corrosion. The only cure is to keep them very clean, inside and out, and to not let their protective coating deteriorate.

Exactly the same problems afflict Aston Martin and Lagonda bodywork, with

The bare chassis of the Aston Martin V8 convertible, with strengthening around the doorline to make up for the rigidity lost by the absence of a metal roof.

the potential for far more danger in the frames of early cars than many people realize. The basic problem is that water gets into the chassis and jacking points all along the outer edges of the car. Because water thrown up by the wheels often contains salt, it is even more corrosive. It seeps in through the felt liners around the inner wing splash panels and runs along the door sills inside the body. Obviously it has to get out somewhere and this fine salt solution eats it way out through the jacking points, attacking the chassis sides on the way. As the jacking points are weaker than the chassis sides, so they go first.

The situation becomes potentially perilous because of the fact that the brake and clutch pedals on cars from the DB4 onwards, are mounted on one of the front jacking points. The effects of a jacking point collapsing underfoot have only to be imagined. The other danger areas where rust attacks are at the rear suspension radius rods' mountings points and the shock absorber mountings. The bottoms of the doors corrode as well (because of blocked drainage holes) and bumpers are prone to rust through. All these items are expensive to repair or replace, particularly on the DB4, 5 and 6, although the DBS cars are little different in construction and will, no doubt, suffer from these conditions in years to come. A peculiarity of the Feltham cars is that corrosion is starting to show in their chassis tubes, and is obviously striking at the very hearts of these cars. Their alloy front suspension pillars can also suffer from corrosion as, in fact, can any of the alloy used in all Aston Martins and Lagondas. Just because their body panels are made from aluminium, it does not mean that they are proof against the dreaded salt— far from it.

The only cure for cars suffering from these conditions is replacement of the parts affected and of those in the immediate area. This can be a dreadfully expensive business, especially when added to the realization that it is becoming necessary to spend as much money or time on the maintenance of a car's bodywork as it is on the mechanical side. Fortunately one of the strong points of any Aston Martin or Lagonda is the very high quality of their interiors: with decent treatment and maintenance they will easily outlast those of practically any car other than, perhaps, a Rolls-Royce or Bentley. But like the rest of the car, the inside responds only to loving care.

How Aston Martins and Lagondas are made

Aston Martins and Lagondas are not like other cars. They are still built almost entirely by hand. A guided tour of the factory at Newport Pagnell can be a fascinating exercise as these pictures show:

The basic steel floor pan, welded up from numerous small parts.

Parts of the body structure are welded to the floor pan in a jig.

When it is removed from the jig the car begins to take on a recognizable shape.

At this stage the chassis is nearing completion. This is an Aston Martin.

And this is the much bigger Lagonda built alongside it.

Aluminium body panels are formed on a wheel.

Then they are beaten into actual panels.

The various panels are then welded together into a bodyshell with the help of the jigs in the foreground.

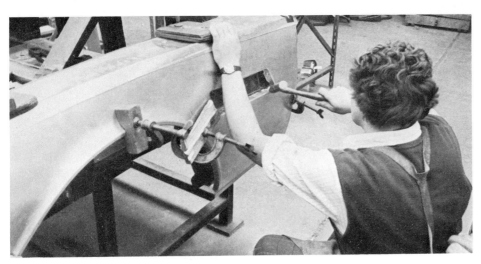

This picture of a front wing being made shows clearly how it is essentially a hand operation.

Completed front sections with the
tools of the body builders' trade in the
foreground.

It's quite simple welding aluminium,
it just needs about twenty years' experience.

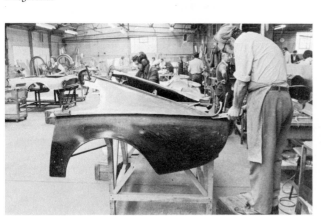

More panels being made on a jig.
Many operatives wear ear muffs to
protect them from the constant noise
of panel beating.

Completed body panels awaiting
assembly.

Hard at work on a front section.

A nearly completed tail section for a new Aston Martin convertible.

Fixed heads and convertibles are built side by side.

Cylinder head assembly in the engine
shop follows machining.

Engine castings are delivered ready to
be machined in Newport Pagnell's
own shop.

Block assembly is carried out at the
same time.

Engine specifications vary considerably. These pistons are for a North
American low-compression engine.

An overall view of the engine shop
with a number of units nearing completion.

Engines and transmissions waiting to go into the rolling chassis.

In another part of the factory the de Dion tube is being assembled for the rear suspension.

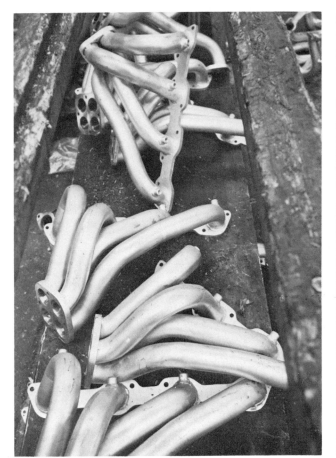

Exhaust manifolds are fitted after the engine is installed.

And front suspension components are being assembled near by.

Once the steering rack is in place, the engine can be dropped in.

The rear suspension sub-assembly awaiting its car.

Preparing for the engine to go into the car after the suspension and steering have been fitted.

Engine fitting takes place in a separate bay.

Instruments, wiring and so on are fitted after the engine. At this stage the car uses slave wheels.

The cars are then removed to the trim shop.

Fitting up a Lagonda in the trim
shop—rather like measuring up for a
Savile Row suit.

Large quantities of sound-deadening
materials are used.

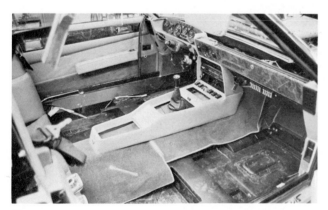

Then the trim is fitted part by part.

Cutting seat material from complete
hides.

The seat trimmer at work with completed seats in the background.

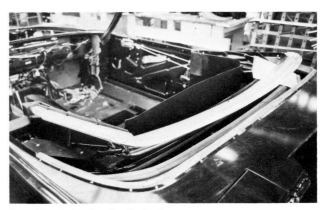

Assembly of the drop-head's hood irons.

Testing takes place before the convertible is trimmed.

The paint shop occupies another part of the factory. Cars are painted twice, for the second time after the major trim components are in place.

Then the external and internal accessories are fitted.

More work on a convertible.

The engine compartment during fitting up.

The V8 convertible before its final trim is fitted.

Completing the hood trimming.

Fitting and adjusting the lights is one of the final jobs before road testing and fitting new wheels and tyres.

XI

What to Look For

It has often been said by salesmen that connoisseurs can see more clearly than they can think; an adage that certainly applies to people who think that they can buy a good Aston Martin or Lagonda on the cheap. The trouble is that so many people are seduced by the beauty of an Aston or Lagonda, by their graceful, yet aggressive bodywork and by their engines which are seemingly sculptured from a block of shining alloy. All this is just part of the pleasure of owning an Aston; the problems can be more complex.

The engine can only be rebuilt by an expert. Bearing clearances on the alloy engine are so fine that they are bound to be tight when running in and it frequently overheats as a result. This is a problem that has afflicted Aston Martins and Lagondas for years. If the engine is not overheating and keeps a constant oil pressure, it is unlikely that there will be much wrong with it, so long as it is fitted with a thermostat to keep up the temperature. But if it does overheat, the possible causes are many. First check the water hoses as there are so many of them, and they all need replacing every other year.

In the case of the early DB4s fitted with electric fans, the cooling system can be the cause of the trouble. These fans are mounted in front of the radiator and simply do not force enough air through the matrix. Unskilled labour and rank amateurs have even connected them up the wrong way, with the disastrous result that the engine quickly overheats the moment they are switched on! But even running the right way, Aston Martins could not mount them in the proper place, which is behind the radiator—because there wasn't enough room. So they switched to a viscous coupling fan, which effectively cured the problem.

Overheating can also be caused by a blockage or obstruction in the radiator core. That is another point to check, plus the basic tune of the engine itself. Timing chains don't last for ever, rarely more than 60,000 miles in fact. But at least you can hear that they need attention, even if you can't see them. Carburetters need careful attention of course and, although Webers are the Rolls-Royce of such instruments, they are more difficult to set up than the more-forgiving SUs.

Fuel injection is a different matter. In theory it is great, in practice it can be awful. The pumps, in particular, need very careful maintenance and cost a fortune to rebuild let alone replace. If it wasn't for the bigger bulge on the bonnet of a V8 it would be well worth converting a fuel injection car to Webers. In fact, it's probably worth it anyway to ensure good performance, and dependable starting. Hot starting has always been a problem with Webers, however, and can be difficult unless you have the knack. The trouble is that so much engine is crammed under the bonnet of any Aston or Lagonda that high temperatures can cause vapour lock with these carburetters; modifications to the fuel return system of later V8s have since alleviated this problem. With earlier cars it is a question of knowing just when to 'catch' the engine.

Be careful to avoid flooding your triple 45DCOEs if these beautiful instruments are fitted, a flashback can set fire to the vapour! If they are flooded, mop up the surplus and start all over again.

Automatic gearboxes in earlier cars have been known to overheat, too; this is usually caused by inadequate cooling arrangements, particularly on the early V8s. The only real cure is to update the system to include a separate oil radiator. This problem often occurs with Astons made early in a model's production run; many of the subsequent changes were made purely as the result of development work by the customers, although I must hasten to add that the factory has always been extremely honourable. If a fault could be attributed to them they have never hidden behind the small print of a warranty, and they have frequently provided replacement vehicles as well as parts.

The best-known instance of this was with the early 3.7-litre DB4 engine. The model's introduction coincided with the opening of the M1 motorway in Britain. As a result, owners started travelling 25 mph faster than they had done before and they kept it up for mile after mile. Unfortunately their oil pressure didn't, with the consequent loss of connecting rods. As Leonard Setright reported in the late-lamented *Automobile Connoisseur*:

'The lubrication troubles came as a shock to the factory, too. They had concentrated on designing a stiff engine with a stiff crankcase and a stiff crankshaft, but it had not dawned on them at the time that when the engine got hot the clearances in the bearings could grow to three times the designed figure. Even between seventy degrees and 100 Centigrade oil temperature, the clearances grow nearly twice, and the engine's oil requirements increase correspondingly until there comes a time when the pump cannot deliver sufficient oil because the clearances are too big. Pretty soon they fitted an oil cooler to the cars, though the early DB4s missed out on it, and this usually kept the oil temperature below the 100 degrees C mark. Then the factory revised the initial bearing clearances so that there was not too much oil between the crankshaft and the main bearings when the engine was hot. But they had to be careful, because the engine has to be capable of starting in winter, and if the clearances are tightened too much the high coefficient of linear expansion of aluminium would see to it that at some degree of frost everything binds up solid. Eventually they compromised at a gripping temperature of minus 25 degrees C.

'Why did they not put a bigger oil pump on the engine? Simply because

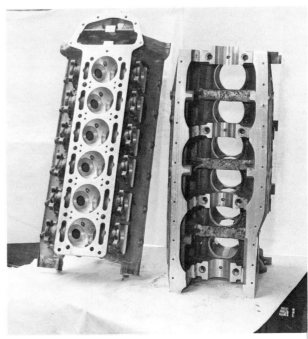

the output of the pump was already about 20 gal/min at full engine revs, at which rate it swallowed the entire sump contents and spat them out again in a mere eight seconds. So there was the danger that the oil would go up faster than it would come down, so to speak, and the pump would start sucking air whereupon the same trouble would recur. And there was nowhere to put a larger sump. They were stymied. Aston Martin, under their chief engineer, Tadek Marek, worked very hard; but the problem was never completely overcome until the engine was redesigned as a 4-litre for the DB5 some time later.'

One of the most exacting jobs on an Aston Martin or Lagonda is bearing assembly. The picture shows clearly the 'cheeses' on the crankshaft of one of the first generation of post-war Aston Martins.

The crankcase and a cylinder head from a first generation Aston Martin, in this case a DB3S.

There's a moral there, obviously. Watch your oil temperature as well as pressure and update the engine if at all possible. Ideal opportunities present themselves from around de-coke time, at about 60,000 miles. In the same way as it pays to keep a close eye on the instruments, the oil and the water themselves can tell you tales about your Aston Martin or Lagonda engine, that are easy to see. They should never mix, of course. Cylinder liners are as easily broken as piston rings on assembly and should always stand an exact amount proud of the cylinder block. Too close, and water gets into the cylinder; too far, and the head gasket leaks. What with these fine tolerances and precision needed with the bearings, plus the steaming that is needed to fit liners, engine rebuilds are definitely best left to the experts.

Useful pointers to the state of an unknown engine include a compression check and the condition of the six liner bleed holes on the carburetter side of the engine block. If they are weeping, it shows that the coolant has penetrated the normally empty gap between the upper and lower liner sealing rings. A tin of Bar's Leaks (called Bars at Newport, they don't like the sound of leaks, although they recommend the use of this ginger-based goo for its corrosion-inhibiting properties) can often solve the problem, and should be used in an Aston engine anyway.

It also pays to make sure that an Aston gearbox is really hot before passing an opinion on a David Brown gearbox. Sometimes it can be impossible to locate a gear in a worn box when the oil is hot because the synchromesh cones can tip in their saddles, and block the selection.

You can see, hear and feel suspension troubles. No Aston Martin or Lagonda feels right if the suspension or steering is worn; it becomes sloppy or inclined to wander. Feltham cars clank if the front suspension is worn and they react badly to only moderate amounts of wear. Deterioration in the rubber gaiters and rack mountings on Newport cars requires immediate attention as the dirt that gets past worn rubber causes rapid, and expensive, wear. In the case of the rack-mounting rubbers it can lead to wander.

Shock absorbers can be tested by depressing the car vigorously while it is standing still and seeing how it rebounds. Be careful to spread the load on the front wings if you apply the pressure at that point: the alloy panelling is delicate and you may dent it. The same restrictions apply to the elbows of mechanics, amateur and professional! If replacing the rack rubbers does not keep a Newport car on course, the rack probably needs re-shimming, although radial-ply tyres are

Top left:

Meticulous care is needed while working on the cylinder head of an Aston Martin or Lagonda. The car in the picture is an Aston Martin DB Mark III.

Top right:

A production DB3S receives attention from one of Aston Martin's top 'backroom boys', Ted Cutting, at Feltham in the 1950s.

Right:

An early DB4 pictured with its rather problematical engine.

better than cross-plies for directional stability.

Brake rubbers need constant surveillance, too, and servos do not last for ever. Often they can absorb brake fluid and eventually convey it to the engine, causing a mystery loss of power and smoke that is not reflected by anything amiss with the oil temperature or pressure. If brake fluid does get out to the engine this way, replace any carburetter balance pipes besides the appropriate braking components, as they do not take well to this mixture. Brake lines should be inspected regularly as they deteriorate with constant exposure to road dirt and sometimes rub through in contact with other parts of the car.

Really the only way to preserve an Aston Martin or Lagonda when it is in good condition is to keep it immaculately clean underneath and inside as well as outside, and then you can see any corrosion developing. To check spokes on wire wheels run a pen round them. Listen for a regular 'ping'; if it 'pongs' you've got a loose spoke!

The best bargain any potential owner can make is to call in a specialist. The Aston Martin Owners' Club or Lagonda Club can advise on names and addresses, and arrange to inspect the car before a price is agreed. This price should always reflect the potential cost of repairs or rebuilding against the potential value of the vehicle when completed. The actual inspection might cost the equivalent of two or three tanks full of petrol, but is worth every penny, cent, yen, mark, franc, lire or whatever. With a car far from Newport it might even pay to fly somebody out to it, such is the possible cost of putting some troubles right.

Aston Martin and Lagonda enthusiasts are well served for specialist attention. The stores in the picture are at Aston Services in Dorset.

Triple Weber carburetters like those pictured here, boost the power of Aston Martin and Lagonda engines, but they are more difficult to set up than SU carburetters and less economical for road use.

XII

Getting the Best Out of Your Car

MAINTAINING your Aston Martin or Lagonda is relatively simple if you stick to the schedules laid down by the manufacturers and keep it immaculately clean. There are a lot of things that are beyond the average amateur, however, and this means that the car will need specialist attention. This applies particularly to preparation for competitive events, whether racing or concours. It is still possible to pick up a DB2, DB4 or V8 in poor condition, and it is worth exploring the sort of work that would be needed to bring it up to the most competitive condition for racing or concours, and how it can be improved for road use. The DB4 makes the most economical racing car although the V8 can also be quite competitive.

Once in first-class condition, any standard Aston Martin is suitable for racing and extensive modifications are scowled upon by the Aston Martin Owners' Club. However, a first generation car can be made to lap a lot faster by bringing it as close as possible to production DB3S mechanical standards with, perhaps, Mark III disc brakes and telescopic shock absorbers. The DB4 can be turned into a really rapid car by the extensive use of GT and DB5 components, special cams and telescopic shock absorbers. The V8 can be made considerably faster by lightening its weight—there are many things you can remove!—and uprating the engine to Vantage specification. Limited slip differentials are a boon if the car is not already fitted with one.

In general terms, the earlier a model is in the first, second or third generations, the faster for racing it is because it is usually lighter. One of the quickest first-generation cars is the DB2 raced by Shaun Magee, the Hampshire garage proprietor who, along the Forshaws in Bournemouth, specializes in these cars. His DB2—which is, incidentally, smart enough to win a concours—has a six-plug 3-litre engine which puts out around 200 bhp with modifications similar to those used on the production DB3S cars.

Second-generation cars come into two categories: the ultra-light DB4s such as those of Dave Preece and David Reade, and the heavier, more standard, but no less powerful DB4s such as that used by Ian Moss and Pete Foster. There are also the DB4GTs and Zagatos of drivers such as Simon Phillips and John and Rachel Goate. The DB4GTs and Zagatos were as far advanced as was possible for racing even in standard form, except for the fact that they are not allowed to use the later ZF five-speed gearbox except when competing in modified classes. This rule applies to the DB4s as well. The lightweight DB4s are similar to the Moss and Foster car (registered 358 DLW), except that they carry only fittings essential for racing and the floor pans are lightened. Cars such as 358 DLW still make some concession to the needs of road users. Its engine is basically a DB4, with a DB5 head, DB4GT pistons, cams with a profile based on that of the Project 214 Le Mans car, revised oil cooling and triple 45 DCOE Webers with a special long exhaust system. DB5 brakes are used with Koni telescopic rear shock absorbers and twin servos in the boot to improve the weight distribution. Fifteen-inch competition wire wheels with six-inch rims are fitted with American stock car tyres for some events and Dunlop L-section racing tyres for others in which the regulations demand them. A 3.54 limited-slip rear axle is very carefully located so that it cannot move under vigorous use. One of the 'demon tweaks' Moss uses in assembly is to make sure the drive from the David Brown gearbox is absolutely in line for better traction. He would like to use a ZF gearbox but regulations won't allow it in his class. The DB5 can be prepared in much the same way, but it has the disadvantage of extra weight to cancel out its additional 300 cc and five-speed gearbox.

The racing V8s are basically the same in chassis preparation with all unnecessary weight and power-sapping appliances, such as air conditioning, removed and the engine uprated to 485 bhp against the 300 of the hottest DB4s.

None of these modifications, other than the racing tyres, linings and exhaust, render these cars unsuitable for road use and some of them actually improve the road cars. Obviously oil coolers in conjunction with a temperature gauge are an advantage for any Aston engine, particularly the 3.7-litre. And now that lever arm shock absorbers are becoming scarce, Koni or Spax adjustable telescopics are ideal substitutes. Spax shock absorbers are far more easily adjustable on the car, incidentally. Some modifications, such as wider wheels on all except the DBS six-cylinder, are positively undesirable, however. In the case of the wheels, the cars are so finely balanced that they actually detract from the roadholding.

The current cult in the concours world is for absolute standardization and oil coolers aside, it is here that Aston Martin owners are at their most fortunate. In 'bog-standard' form their cars are still ideal for everyday use, concours or club racing.

Preparation for concours involves the basic decision of how far it is necessary to dismantle the car. For potential winners it is necessary to strip virtually everything down to the last nut and bolt. Second- and third-generation cars are more difficult, of course, because it is an enormous, and expensive job to dismantle much of the body. First-generation cars are easier because the entire front comes off easily and it is not such a difficult job to expose the rest of the chassis. Ironically, racing cars are the easiest in this respect, although they are far more expensive to start with and present special problems of spare parts.

To restore a car it is necessary first to carry out a detailed examination, noting everything that needs attention or replacement. Secondly, find out how long it will take to get the work done and how much it will cost. Thirdly, providing you can afford the time and money involved, work out a Wyer-style battleplan and assemble a vast number of boxes, and a lot of old blankets to protect the parts and to prevent losses.

When dismantling the car it is essential that the owner, or the same trusted operative, is present throughout the whole procedure to make notes on any potential problems. As parts are removed they should be labelled if there is likely to be any difficulty in recognizing them months, or maybe years, later when they are returned to the car, and filed in separate boxes. Use a logical sequence here: put the windscreen wiper in with its drive, blades and so on. Don't just put it in a corner with back axle parts because there's more room in their box. Keep the car on its wheels as long as possible unless you have a big workshop, so that it is possible to move it around.

Many parts, such as chromework, must be sent away to specialists for restoration—the Aston Martin Owners' Club can help with names and addresses. When they have been returned, wrap them in the blankets and store them somewhere safe and dry until they are needed when the car is rebuilt. Many other parts can be restored or checked in the home workshop or garage. Clean them meticulously, then if they are found to be in excellent condition, wrap them up in blankets, too, and store them for later. Otherwise, have them restored or replace them. Keep notes of the specialists you have dispatched parts to so that you can chase them at appropriate times. A desk diary devoted entirely to the car's restoration is best for this purpose. But don't just confine the notes to the specialists' names, addresses, telephone numbers, delivery dates and possible delays: include further notes of wedding anniversaries and the St John Horsfall meeting so that you do not lose contact with everyday life.

When the mechanical cleaning is done and the specialists are well under way you can start on the bodywork and chassis. Sandblasting on steel parts is ideal as it quickly shows up imperfections such as rust holes, while dramatically cutting the cleaning time. But don't let the stuff near your precious alloy panels except in the most skilled hands as it can blast them to pieces or dent them very quickly. There's no substitute really for removing all the old paint by hand—and there's a lot of it on any old Aston! But be patient or you'll be in deep trouble and have to take out a second mortgage to get everything put right.

The interior should be relatively easy to remove as it is all hand made. Interior panels in good condition or just restored are suitable cases for the blanket treatment while the rest of the work is under way because the dirt raised from body and chassis stripping and the spraying to follow can be horrifying.

Once everything is in good condition, it is not too difficult to put the car back together again. The first thing to do is to get the fully prepared body/chassis unit back onto its wheels. Then fit all the awkward parts such as pipes and wiring that will be difficult to reach when major components are in place. Next, it is best to fit the heavy parts such as the engine and gearbox, before connecting everything up and making sure that it works. The trim comes last.

The labour content of a proper restoration can be enormous. But it is the only way to win a concours, and you stand a chance of success with an Aston Martin or Lagonda because there are hardly any parts that are unobtainable on the production cars. Racing cars present different problems, as recounted by Geoffrey Marsh, owner of the Le Mans-winning DBR1 in the award-winning *AM* magazine:

'Why would the car not start? No, it was not the petrol, or rather the lack of it; with the battery fully charged the engine seemed to turn over. Yes, all the electrics were correct. There seemed to be nothing for it but to investigate further. This showed that the distributors were not turning but the crankshaft was! There seemed nothing for it but to remove the head, and there, lying next to the gear train, was a gearwheel that appeared to have fallen out of mesh. For the record, only 2.5- and later 3-litre engines in the RB6 series had gear-driven camshafts and many people will, therefore, not realize that each gear-wheel runs on nineteen needle roller bearings which, in turn, run on a fixed shaft. You can imagine the potential damage caused by nineteen needle roller bearings dropping down through a complicated gear train! Further examination revealed that number two and four pistons were very slightly marked but the number two inlet valve was extremely badly bent. Numbers four and six inlet valves were slightly marked and it would not be safe to re-use these. The related exhaust valves were also marked and it became apparent that this was not the end of the damage when pistons collide with a number of open valves.

'The lubrication of all the gear wheels and idler gears is through a very low pressure supply to the gallery on the camshafts but when a shaft holding a gear wheel drops out, the oil is then allowed to go through a very large hole, thus allowing very little oil to reach the camshafts. On further dismantling, the exhaust camshafts had become very blue as a result and the temper had been drawn such that it was now soft. The bearings had "picked up" in places and those valves that had been hit very hard had smashed cam followers. The exhaust camshaft had been running hot for some time, due to lack of lubricant and the cam follower, where it had been in contact with the valve, had accelerated the wear very badly. The cam followers that had smashed became very hot on jamming in the head, leaving mechanical carnage everywhere. It is very expensive to repair an aluminium cylinder head, for which there is no replacement, and an engine for which there are virtually no spares. It must be remembered that perhaps only seven 3-litre engines were built in all, so it was not exactly a production run! It is good for the mental state that the dismantling process took place slowly to allow a chance to absorb each disaster with a time interval in between. It was certainly apparent that it would now be worthwhile doing a total rebuild on the car.

'It is perhaps because I enjoy the historian/archivist part of the job of rebuilding that I keep a notebook to record the work on each of my cars. I learn from referring to this particular book, that dismantling is quite a quick process, and entries read: October 21, body removed, October 24, engine removed from chassis, October 26, complete inventory of spares taken to reveal that none of the parts that we wanted are available from these spares. Then the time-consuming research must start. . . .'

There is an inspiring story behind the immaculate Aston Martin DB5 pictured here. It was in poor condition when it was bought by Detective Constable Robert Morris of the West Midlands Police stolen car squad in 1972, but after two years' painstaking work in the drive outside his home in Great Barr, Birmingham, it won the Portman Trophy at the Aston Martin Owners' Club Fort Belvedere concours in 1974. 'Initially it returned about 15 mpg and leaked more oil than it used', said Robert Morris. 'I soon found that the bodywork had been cheaply "blown in" in places, particularly around the rear wings and valance. I began patiently cutting away all the rotted metal, but was pleasantly surprised that the damage was not so bad as I had feared at first. The whole body was meticulously prepared, while various fitments, including the front bumper, were sent for re-plating at Sercks in Birmingham.

'At this stage the car was resprayed in white, then I decided that it did not do justice to the beautiful lines of the body, so over the next few months the car was resprayed silver grey. However, I was still not satisfied with the effect and decided to go the whole hog and prepare the car with concours in mind.

'Four months were spent preparing the body and it was finally sprayed with twenty-five coats of Aston fiesta red, each being meticulously rubbed down. I might add that all preparation and painting took place in the open air!

'The chassis was steam cleaned, treated for rust, and painted from end to end with protective black paint.

That was in 1975, and

'after much research we found a supplier who was willing to cut gears in limited quantities to our requirements if we were able to supply the "blanks". We learned that we should make the gears out of EN26 and my local precision engineering shop undertook to make these blanks. The diary records that it took some four months to complete the process of making these gears as after blanks are made the teeth must be cut and this was very excellently carried out by Spencer Gears of London. After gear cutting they must be case hardened and only then the internal diameter ground so that the needle rollers can make a precision fit.

'Fortunately the DB4GT valves appeared to be all right as replacements for the inlet valves but nothing made seemed to substitute for the original sodium-filled exhaust valves. After researching the problem with Farnborough Engineering, a turbocharged Ford diesel valve, it was found, could be adapted if machined. All those involved with restoration work will understand that unless one has no job then work and one's family make large demands on one's time and so it was fortunate that at the end of 1975, during the works close-down for nearly two weeks, I had time for further investigation, research, cleaning, checking and so on.

'Having known John Clarke for some time I found that the restoration work he carried out is of extremely high standard. I found that he was now in business on his own at PAO Preparations, and so it was agreed that our fitter, Jim Stokes, should go to work with John on the chassis. Stripping is always easy but must be done methodically. Every part dismantled must be checked, crack-detected and identified so that some months (or sometimes years) later it can be assembled in its former position. When the chassis was completely stripped there were a number of tubes found cracked or completely broken. After welding, the chassis was therefore zinc sprayed and stove enamelled. We were fortunately able to mix some paint to the original Aston Martin colour which is light cream tinged with green. The chassis was returned

Bushes were renewed in the front and rear suspension, the rack and pinion was rebuilt and four reconditioned shock absorbers were fitted. The old exhaust system was discarded and replaced with a new one from Burgess. Four new discs, most of the brake piping and a very awkward master cylinder were replaced. Reconditioned brake servos were fitted and a set of factory reconditioned chrome wire wheels and new Dunlop RS5 tyres completed work on the chassis.

'A new clutch and a decoke came next. I completed both jobs on my own, but found the gearbox particularly heavy to handle. A new water pump was fitted with a rebuilt distributor. The three SU carburetters were rebuilt using new spindles, butterflies, bushes, jets and needles. Synchronization was not easy, but once completed, the car tends to stay in tune well.

'Fortunately the interior was in excellent condition and only two new carpets were needed. The car, now completed, was a joy to own. It took a considerable time to learn to drive well, but gives endless driver satisfaction. The handling is superb, enhanced by the five-speed gearbox. Petrol consumption is around 20 mpg and oil consumption negligible. The car is not terribly expensive to run, and in any case repays all expenditure by providing somewhat unusual transport in these days of strangulated tin-box driving. No other car could satisfy my requirements to such an extreme— except perhaps a DB4GT!'

The Aston Martin DBR front suspension, engine and radiator can be seen clearly in this picture.

Bottom end of the DBR engine, with the sump off.

to John Clarke in January 1976. It was further decided (from photographs kindly supplied by *Motor Sport*) that we would repaint the chassis as near as possible in the original colours, with the Watt linkage and Panhard rods black. The original casing of the transaxle looked very shabby and corroded, so with "restorer's licence" we repainted this to a similar appearance but with a durable finish that would not further corrode. The original bulkhead was very scruffy, so we agreed to make a new one in our own body shop and it was about this time, after much discussion, that we agreed to undertake to produce a replica body for Lord Downe's DBR1.

'By February all the parts in good order had been cadmium plated, the brakes had been rebuilt, new brake pipes had been made up and the sub assembly was beginning to take shape. It is only when you start to make some progress that you begin to understand the tremendous delays that can take place on a restoration job. We were now beginning to have troubles which were very difficult to remedy. No doubt we could put parts back in a worn condition, but when undertaking restoration of a really worthwhile car such as this it is far better to tackle difficult jobs now and hope that you will not have any major work to repeat for ten to fifteen years.

'It was fortunate that at that time a few spares came to light from Richard Forshaw of Aston Service, Dorset. Richard has been very helpful over the years with Aston problems, and when his firm bought all the old pre-1960 stock from Aston Martin, there were many parts he was unable to identify. We spent an evening going through these parts and with certain items that had been stripped from the car, we would be able to identify part numbers which related to the original build specification, which I had been lucky enough to obtain from Roger Collings, owner of DBR1/3.

'It is interesting to study the records where part numbers are available as it shows how much of the DBR1 evolved from the DB3S. The trailing arms of the front suspension caused us a great problem. They had to be built up by a hard chroming process, new bearings found and the chrome ground down to the correct size. It proved almost impossible to find someone with

The DBR chassis exposed for total restoration.

The DBR's transaxle.

a big enough machine to swing the trailing arms and grind the bearing surfaces. However, we eventually found a specialist aircraft sub-contractor who completed the job, but this is where restoration becomes so costly!

'At the time of writing we are at the stage of finding that Vandervell must make up new main bearings, as there are none available, although the big ends are those of a Perkins diesel engine.

'The clutch assembly is almost identical to a D type Jaguar multi-plate unit but corrosion of magnesium electron components on the outside of the engine is leading to other problems and we may well have to resort to either casting replacements in aluminium, or repairing water ducts to the cooling pump with Polythene inserts, kept in place with Araldite.'

A year went by, before Marsh could complete his tale in *AM*.

'"Never forget, it is easier to take it apart than put it together again." This is a message to any would-be restorer. Repeat these words fifty times before undoing the first nut and bolt [he began].

'During 1976, with our greater activity in the motor trade, we at Marsh Plant decided to become more involved in historic motor racing. We entered our ex-Le Mans Daytona Ferrari in the 1976 St John Horsfall meeting and then bought the Lola T70 111b in November. The historic motor racing season usually starts with the Jaguar Drivers' Club meeting in early March, so after Christmas preparation must start in earnest.

'The decision was made to leave the completed DBR1 chassis at my home and take the Lola to our one-car preparation shop. All the DBR1 parts had been carefully labelled, boxed where necessary, and laid out in racking in this shop. We did make various attempts to complete the engine during the year, without much success. The crankshaft was crack-detected and found to be in good condition; connecting rods all right, and pistons capable of re-use, but we do have five new ones, all with their original RAC homologation marking. The liners are "wet" and rely on two "O" rings to keep the coolant

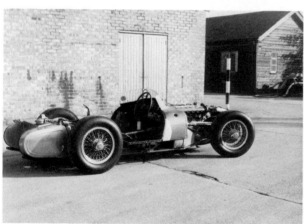

The rear suspension and cockpit area of the DBR.

The space frame and dry sump equipment of the DBR.

The DBR's rolling chassis.

A unique occasion: two consecutive-numbered DBRs—number one and number two—side by side, being re-built at Marsh Plant Hire. Number one, with the body·on, is Lord Doune's car, and number two, awaiting its body, is Geoffrey Marsh's Le Mans winner.

out of the sump, but here a horror was revealed.

'Research showed that at some time in the past someone had tried a little "improvement" in the method of sealing the liners in relation to the aluminium block. Machining had taken place, the mistake realized, and then welding repairs carried out. We still are not sure that the block has not distorted from the heat of the welding repair. Thank goodness that Astons seemed to learn from the weakness of the DB3S cylinder block, which relies on the liners locating in the crankcase and the cylinder head holding the top of them in place. The DBR1 liners are properly located in the top of the cylinder block, allowing for correct measurement of their required projection from a rigid cylinder block. It must be remembered that this aluminium block does not have a barrel type of crankshaft and bearing assembly: it has proper bearing caps bolted to the block. Astons could not seem to make up their minds about how many main bearings this engine should have. . . .

'Now for the bodywork, which was the next major job. It was Mike Salmon's suggestion that I contacted Lord Downe to propose we build him a replica body using our DBR1/2 as the "master". His car had not had a body for twelve years and after all, these Astons are part of our mechanical heritage. The only trouble is that DBR1/1 was the prototype and not quite the same as the other four cars. . . .

'There are many small aluminium panels on the car and one wonders why the whole project was so complicated. . . . When restoring an aluminium body it is essential to remove all the paint. The body of DBR1/2 has revealed much of her history and to that end we have kept as much of the original as possible. Each separate panel has DBR1/2 stamped on it from original manufacture. Modifications, such as jack pick-up points for the 1959 Le Mans, rear wheel spats, and so on are uncovered. The matching modifications to partly fair-in the front wheels, later returned to normal, are noticed. The bulkhead section just in front of the driver's door shows the position of the inlet valve for the pneumatic jacking system used to great effect in the 1959 Tourist Trophy race.'

Fascinating, rewarding and years of hard work, that's what goes into restoring an Aston Martin or Lagonda. As this book was being written, Marsh had yet to complete the restoration of his DBR1. But he had bought a DBR4 as a stablemate, using the DBR1's engine to make it a runner! Some Aston Martin enthusiasts will never admit defeat.

XIII

The Men Behind Aston Martin and Lagonda

THE STORY OF the post-war Aston Martins and Lagondas is almost entirely the story of one man, David Brown, an old-school Yorkshire tycoon whose ideas and influence survive in the cars even today now that the current directors Peter Sprague, George Minden and Alan Curtis have picked up the pieces. Motoring correspondents who should know better are still calling the Aston Martin V8 the DBS V8! Quite understandably this annoys today's management who have at last turned this aristocrat of English car makers into a viable enterprise.

To all those who snipe at the ten years it took Aston Martin to win Le Mans and point to their sometimes shambolic financial affairs, it should be made clear that without David Brown neither Aston Martin nor Lagonda would have survived the war to have built more than a few prototypes. If he had not rescued them the world would have been robbed of some great sports cars and a few extraordinary saloons. To all those who point out that he was only a part-time boss—Aston Martin and Lagonda were never more than two per cent of his turn-over—let it be emphasized that he was the only person sufficiently detached from the diverse camps of Aston Martin and Lagonda to realize that they could be welded together to make a commercial success. That they were only rarely a commercial success under David Brown is a tribute to his patience and pocket.

Sadly, two of the key Aston Martin men, designer Claude Hill and development engineer Jock Horsfall, left soon after David Brown took over, and W. O. Bentley, who was technical director and designer for Lagondas, and who had been responsible for David Brown's last car in 1940, never did join him after the war. This didn't end their influence, however, as Hill and Horsfall left behind them their chassis, which was used in shortened form in the DB2. Bentley left behind his engine which was used in the Lagonda built by Brown, and the DB2, and he went on to design a still-born prototype for Armstrong Siddeley, which was very much like the Lagonda. The other priceless assets that David Brown inherited were a dedicated band of craftsmen at the old Aston Martin works in Feltham and Lagonda's body designer, Frank Feeley. A number of the Lagonda design staff went with Bentley to set up an independent office in Byfleet while others stayed on at the Lagonda factory in Staines, which was not part of the deal with David Brown.

David Brown celebrates his greatest moment with the men who were to make his Aston Martins champions of the world: from the left Reg Parnell, John Wyer, Roy Salvadori (in the DBR1), mechanics Eric Hinde and Jack Sopp, Carroll Shelby (toasting fellow driver Salvadori), Brown and pacemaker Moss whose brilliant driving broke the Ferraris in opposition.

To understand David Brown, and his purchase of the Aston Martin and Lagonda companies, it is necessary to understand his background. In 1921, when he was seventeen years old, he started work as an apprentice in the gear manufacturing works founded by his grandfather in 1860. At that time he wanted to be a racing motor cyclist, but his father refused to allow him to ride for the works Douglas team. He had to weigh the advantages of a relatively secure path to the top in the gear-making industry as the boss's son against the temptations of a sporting life. He loved to participate in all manner of sports when he could afford it, but he realized that it was essential to secure his future first. So he stayed in the family firm and became foreman in the worm-gear shop in 1926—a position he could not have achieved without a lot of hard work. His only involvement in motor sport at the time appears to have been building a 'special' car from bits and pieces in his spare time. He made some good contacts in the car world, however, including Amherst Villiers, who made the superchargers for the Le Mans-winning Bentleys designed by W. O. Bentley. At this point, David Brown also showed considerable business ability, pulling off a good deal to drive a Vauxhall Villiers in Northern speed events after his firm had agreed to make the gears for Villiers's superchargers. By 1927, David Brown had been made assistant works manager; by 1928 he had become manager of the Keighley Gear Company; by 1929 he was on the board of David Brown and Sons Ltd; and in 1932 he became managing director. He worked hard and played hard, racing horses and cars with moderate success. He also had firm ideas on the design of his companies' products.

When they diversified into farm tractors he made Plasticine models for the prototypes himself, so that their styling suited his taste. It had to be admitted that the
results, Ferguson and David Brown tractors, were much better looking than most
of their contemporaries!

Meanwhile Aston Martin and Lagonda were producing good-looking cars, but
just as the Second World War provided work which left the David Brown group
in a strong position in 1945, so it left Aston Martin and Lagonda high and dry.
Aston Martin were in rented premises at Feltham with some good craftsmen and
Claude Hill's Atom saloon; Lagondas were rather better placed for property with
a big factory at Staines, but they had not only scrapped the tooling for the
magnificent V12 which David Brown had loved so much but they had even
destroyed most of the drawings.

At that point, in 1946, David Brown had money to invest and was complaining about the waiting lists for new quality cars. It was then that he saw an ad-
vertisement in *The Times*, inviting offers for the purchase of a sports car company.
Remembering the fun he had had with the Vauxhall Villiers, he inquired and
found to his amazement that the firm was Aston Martin—'a very famous name'.

He tried the Atom saloon and found that he loved its roadholding but hated
its styling. He also considered that it would take more power than that produced
by its pre-war Aston Martin two-litre engine. He knew that Claude Hill was
designing a new engine and thought he could put this in its place, remove the
Atom's top, and make a real sports car. So he bought Aston Martin lock, stock
and barrel for £20,000, only a little more than double the price he would have
had to pay for a Rolls-Royce or Bentley car in those days.

At that time Aston Martin weren't the only firm scratching around for money
to make their cars. With a keen eye to trends in the motor industry, Bentley had
designed a new economy car to replace his V12; which was much the same idea
as Hill's in fact. But Bentley, with a history of high-powered Le Mans wins behind
him, wanted it to go fast too. So he gave it a twin-overhead-camshaft engine and
again there were similarities between his thinking and that of Hill. The Aston
Martin man was designing a four-cylinder engine that could be made into a 3-litre
six; Bentley's idea was for a six-cylinder that could be reduced to a four for a
cheaper car, and stretched to an eight for a luxury liner.

As it turned out, Bentley's six was powerful whereas Hill's four favoured
economy: Bentley's chassis was rather ponderous whereas Hill's was light and
very advanced.

Meanwhile, Rootes, Jaguar and Armstrong Siddeley had shown an interest in
the entire Lagonda operation—factory and cars—for around £250,000. That was
too much for erstwhile Lagonda owner David Brown, but fate was on his side.
The 'Export or Bust' trade minister, Stafford Cripps, came out with a gloomy
economic forecast and the big three forgot about Lagonda. Two other, much
smaller, offers were made, then David Brown stepped in and topped the lot with
an offer of £52,500. The factory, however, was not included in this price; that
went to Lagonda owner Alan Good, who turned it into the world-famous Petters
diesel engine works. Within weeks, Brown had moved everything else three miles

down the road to his new works at Feltham. He wouldn't have to wait long for his ideal cars now, they'd be exclusive, and he could cover the cost of the money he'd put up by selling them to like-minded enthusiasts . . . he could even go racing! He had the basis of a good sports car and a fine saloon already, plus two of the most famous names in British motoring history.

At the beginning, all went well. Hill and Horsfall worked themselves into the ground turning the Atom into a sports car and working on the Lagonda project. Everybody was pleased with the Aston Martin's performance at Spa, so it seemed worth waiting for Hill's new six-cylinder engine.

Meanwhile Brown got down to work with Feeley. Feeley, who had joined his father at Lagonda on leaving school in 1926, was especially gifted at designing flamboyant bodies that left managing directors thinking 'That's just what I would have drawn myself'. David Brown couldn't have had a better man to work with as they produced the DB1. Naturally it followed Lagonda lines; it was more a post-war development of the nostalgic pre-war styling Lagonda used on their $2\frac{1}{2}$-litre. And as the Lagonda had a recognizable radiator grille linking it to the glories of the past, so did the DB1. It still looked like an Aston.

But something lighter and more lithe was needed for Le Mans, which was already occupying much of David Brown's attention. He fancied a car that looked like a Ferrari. That Feeley's definitive DB2 body looked even better than an Italian thoroughbred, yet was still unmistakeably Aston Martin, was a tribute to his genius and that of David Brown.

Hill was as much part of Aston Martin as Feeley was of Lagonda. He had been with them for the same length of time, living with their successes and their financial disasters, leaving twice when they couldn't pay his wages, only to return a few months later (Feeley left Lagonda once in similar circumstances, only to be recalled by the receiver!). Styling apart, the DB1 and the DB2 chassis were among the pinnacles of Hill's achievement. He was a designer who never switched off, living for his work, convinced that his final product was right. And it was, most of the time. It wasn't his fault that the pushrod engine had been conceived under a different management; and who is to say that Aston Martin might not have had a better chance of survival with a cheaper product? Not many firms had a boss with as deep a pocket and such staying power as David Brown. Anyway, Hill had seen the worst of financial disasters caused by expensive products before the war and his mind was made up. His car should have his engine.

But David Brown was equally strong-willed: he had an excellent six-cylinder engine already and it was going into the DB2. He didn't need another even if it was the life and soul of his great designer. So Hill quit, ironically to go to Harry Ferguson, the tractor man David Brown had worked with so closely before the war.

As Horsfall and Johnson were winning at Spa, there were two men in the pits who were to have a profound influence on Aston Martin racing successes to come: John Wyer and Jack Sopp. Wyer was an engineer with a great gift for organization on a military scale which made him the ideal man to run a racing team, particularly as the object of racing at that time was not only for publicity,

Jock Horsfall devoted many miles to road testing the prototype DB1 chassis and engine with Claude Hill in the passenger seat. They are pictured here in the car with its temporary 'body-work'.

but to develop road cars to come. His firm, Monaco Engineering, was doing this very job for one of the pre-war Aston Martins as Jack Sopp, with Fred Lowne, was working on Jock Horsfall's car. It was hardly surprising that they wound up working together when one of the partners in Wyer's firm died in a racing crash just before David Brown decided to start racing seriously.

As part of this policy, he hired a real racing man, Professor Eberan von Eberhorst, as his new designer in November 1950. This Austrian had been discovered by Leslie Johnson and journalist Laurence Pomeroy working with Dr Ferry Porsche at the Cisitalia factory in Italy. Von Eberhorst, who had done much of the chassis work on the fearsome pre-war Auto Union racing car in collaboration with Porsche's father, was helping design the rear-engined flat-12 Cisitalia formula one car.

When this project collapsed through lack of finance, the Professor came to England at Johnson's behest and took charge of the technical side of the ERA racing car firm. Pomeroy, like many other motor industry personalities, was of the opinion that there was a market for a small sports car. Von Eberhorst produced the Jupiter chassis which was subsequently built by Jowett at Clayton, only a few miles from David Brown's main works at Huddersfield. It was while he was working there that David Brown approached him to work for Aston Martin Lagonda.

Von Eberhorst's first brief was to design a Le Mans-winning car. He was a theoretician with an ivory-tower approach, so he tried to sweep aside all existing designs and create something entirely new. He didn't succeed because his ideas were beyond the production ability of Aston Martin and Lagonda. But much of his work appeared in their cars in the 1950s. The first example was the DB3 chassis. It bore a close resemblance to the Auto Union, Jowett Jupiter and E type ERA with which he had been associated; the front suspension of the DB3 was similar to that of the later Porsche laboratory designed Auto Unions and the rear suspension followed the same principles. The Lagonda V12 engine was largely his work

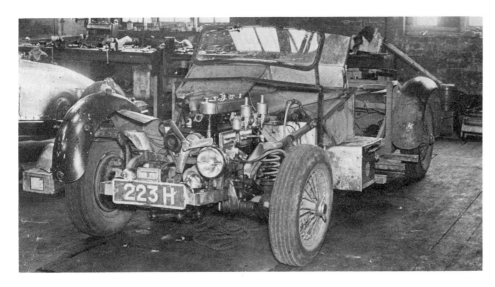

The prototype in Jock Horsfall's workshop in Suffolk with part of the bodywork and the radiator removed to show clearly the engine installation.

and so was the Lagonda saloon's Tickford body. He even started experimenting with fibreglass in the two years he was at Feltham, with the body on David Brown's personal DB3S as an example. But he clashed with Wyer, whose approach was more that of a practical racing man: it was his belief that you should improve the car a little bit at a time, not change the whole thing overnight and spend the next two years trying to make it all work. So it took only the offer of a seat on the board as Director of Development at Auto Union in 1953 for von Eberhorst to return to Germany, leaving behind him a great racing chassis, a V12 engine that consumed crankshafts and the fibreglass DB3S body. He worked well with the new plastic body medium—pioneered in California by speed boat enthusiasts—producing the ultra-rapid DKW saloons. In many respects, he was years ahead of his time, saying of fibreglass: 'It is essential to design in this material and not to try to use it as a steel substitute.' Who knows which path Aston Martin and Lagonda might have taken had he stayed on at Feltham? Only Colin Chapman at Lotus was to follow his lead with fibreglass construction in his successful Elite four years later.

Meanwhile Feltham decided that it was better off with tried and tested practices, like making bodies out of aluminium, so David Brown bought the Tickford works at Newport Pagnell to ease the pressure on Feltham.

Feeley's last task for David Brown was to design the strikingly beautiful DB3S—the DB3 was just a sawn-off DB2 with a bigger opening at the front to help cooling, a real racing man's car. The DB3S was an altogether better affair showing a much more scientific approach with its low drag nose and wheel arch extraction which combined with Italian styling was obviously influenced by the lovely little Maserati A6GCS driven by Roy Salvadori.

Meanwhile, on the production side, a draughtsman called Harold Beach had been hired in 1950; in twenty years he had worked on coachwork for such great cars as Bugattis, Alfa Romeos and Delages—and he knew just as much about the rest of a car. Under Jock Stirling and Frank Ayto (from Lagonda) he worked on the DB2's successor, till von Eberhorst scrapped the lot! One of his chief ideas was for wishbones and coils to replace the trailing link front suspension; but von Eberhorst, following the example of Auto Union and Porsche decided that the links must remain. Some of Feeley's work found its way into the DB2/4, however: the back seats were just like some he had designed for Lagondas before the war.

Soon after, Beach started work on a new replacement for the DB2 design, with wishbones at the front, de Dion at the back and a perimeter frame. Even then, in 1954, it was called the DB4. This car, fitted with a 2.9-litre engine and four-seater body, carried a Lagonda badge and came in for some intensive testing from the works most influential driver: David Brown! He was still getting his bespoke motor cars, and with Yorkshire canniness, saving himself money at the same time!

David Brown liked to be deeply involved in everything he did: he never went to a motor race except the Monaco Grand Prix unless he was a driver or an entrant. He liked hunting, when he was Joint Master of the South Oxfordshire; he liked a day at the races, when one of his horses was competing; he spent a lot of time at water-skiing, essentially a participant sport, and numbered shooting among his other hobbies.

That's what he liked about his cars: he could drive them all himself. He lost a lot of interest when racing cars developed to such an extent that you couldn't drive them on the road. He kept up his life style by flying himself everywhere possible in his de Havilland Dove, the rest of his travelling being carried out in prototype or pre-production Aston Martins or Lagondas, plus his yacht in the Mediterranean.

'He succeeds in doing all these things without the slightest trace of high pressure simply because he orders his life this way. He knows exactly what he is going to do all the time. He never shows any sign of haste or excitement—when his world champion Aston Martins were winning at Le Mans (one of his most cherished ambitions) he calmly went to his hotel for six hours' sleep instead of staying up all night. He will devote just so much time to whatever he is doing, whether it is discussing the state of one of his factories or water skiing, and no more—for his whole life would be unmanageable otherwise', said *The Motor* in one of the rare profiles on David Brown.

Essentially Aston Martin and Lagonda started as a hobby for him and rapidly became far more serious. From the moment they dropped the Lagonda engine into the Aston chassis the potential was so great that the operation had to be made to pay for itself. After all they were producing cars in enormous quantities compared to Aston Martin and Lagonda before the war! In fact the operation did pay for itself sometimes; there were years when Aston Martin made a few thousand pounds. The racing programme was run in a similar way. On the face of it, it consumed money, but in reality it wasn't such a drain; a works Aston Martin team drew considerable starting money and component suppliers helped subsidize it. It was also deeply involved in development, and David Brown would often drive the Le Mans cars home after the race to see how they had stood up to the ordeal (he did it with the winner and loved every mile!).

He was full of enthusiasm, providing the programme did not cost a ridiculous amount of money. At first Wyer tried to go along with all the suggestions and keep check on von Eberhorst at the same time; but the task was too much and he learned from his mistakes, with Beach playing a bigger role after von Eberhorst left. But not before Wyer had seen to it that the Lagonda engine was abandoned, Aston Martins were on the way to winning Le Mans, and that the grand prix car project had been shelved, so that it did not get in the way.

As Beach worked on the DB4, Wyer brought in Tadek Marek from BMC to design a more powerful engine to take over from the ill-fated Lagonda project. Marek was a Polish engineer who had found himself in Britain in 1941 following a colourful career in which he had won the Polish Grand Prix in 1937 and competed in the Monte Carlo Rally before escaping to Britain via Casablanca. He helped design the Morris six-cylinder engine that powered BMC's Austin Westminster and did a lot of design work on the Centurion tank before joining Aston Martin to finish development on their three-litre engine and start the all-alloy 3.7-litre engine. He was a good designer but relied heavily on development staff to make his engines work properly. The DB4 engine gave a lot of trouble until it was finally developed into its DB5 form with modifications to the bottom end to keep up the oil pressure and to stop its gaskets blowing. The same sort of troubles were experienced with his V8 engine but they were eliminated before it went into production. Marek didn't like to be rushed, which was one reason he was against his six-cylinder engine going into the DBR2. But Wyer and David Brown believed firmly in using the race track as a testing ground. That's why the V8 was tried out in the Lola racing cars in 1967; an outstandingly successful venture when it is realized what problems might have manifested themselves in production cars. Nevertheless, it is to Marek's credit that nobody has yet designed another V8 from scratch; the one he built is so light and so powerful.

Reg Parnell, on the left, shares a joke with John Wyer over a late model Aston Martin DB2.

Beach's design work had to undergo the same sort of rigorous testing. After his ideas on suspension had been vindicated on one of the DB3Ss, he was dispatched by Wyer, by then general manager, to Touring, Milan, in 1957 to have a new body designed around his perimeter frame. Imagine Beach's surprise when they turned down his idea flat and promptly inveigled him into designing a platform chassis with them to go with their proposed Italian-style body! 'I really accepted this idea of regarding the body and chassis as one rather than as separate entities because of the tremendous weight-saving and improved stiffness', said Beach in *The Power Behind Aston Martin* (Oxford Illustrated Press).

Meanwhile Wyer had been relieved of some of the responsibility of running the whole show under David Brown by Reg Parnell taking over racing responsibilities. Many people wondered why Parnell raced so long for Aston Martin, retiring from driving only when he was forty-nine years old. It was quite simply because he was at his peak as a sports car driver during those years; he was as good as anybody in the team till Brown landed Moss. Moss was unquestionably the best driver that Aston Martin ever had. One of his best races was in the Nurburgring 1000 kilometres which won the world championship for Aston Martin every bit as much as Le Mans.

This race was one of the greatest of his career. The opposition seemed overwhelming: a phalanx of works Ferraris and Porsches against the lone Aston Martin. In the first lap Moss, at the peak of his powers, pulled out an eighteen-second lead, extending it to five and a half minutes by the time he refuelled and handed over to his steady co-driver, Jack Fairman. Then it rained and the lead was whittled away before Fairman spun off at Brunchen. He was a never-say-die character renowned for his ability to keep a car going in the most adverse conditions, an ideal partner for Moss. He heaved their Aston out of the ditch single-handedly and headed for the pits. Two Ferraris and a Porsche had passed him, but Moss caught them within six laps. When he handed the car back to Fairman at three-quarters distance they had a lead of forty-three seconds, but within two laps Phil Hill's Ferrari was back in the lead. Fairman was called in and Moss started his chase all over again. Four laps later he was back in the lead, holding on to finish forty-one seconds ahead. This was the sort of form that made Moss unofficial world sports car champion and the best driver never to have won a world championship. Collins and Brooks were in the same class, and so, on occasions, were Salvadori and Shelby. Wyer and Parnell selected their drivers purely on ability and for reliability; no amount of money or sentiment could buy a man's way into a full-blown works car. If drivers were not quite good enough for the team cars of the day they could always buy an ex-works machine or perhaps a production DB3 or DB3S. Only Graham Whitehead got a DBR1 for sentimental reasons and he was a good driver anyway! It was the same with the technicians and mechanics. Jack Sopp became a legendary engine builder leading a team that prepared racing cars as individual as any of the road-going Astons. They rebuilt the same cars over and again with engines in all sorts of states of tune (for performance or reliability or mid-way between) and chassis to match (big Lagonda discs for some circuits, smaller Aston brakes for others), culminating in winning

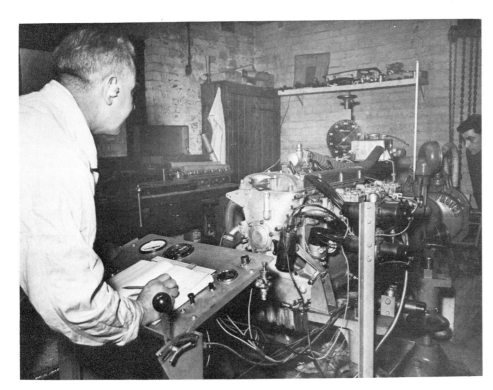

Jack Sopp, on the left, hard at work on the dynamometer with an Aston Martin competition engine. The cotton wool in his ears was essential!

the world championship on a handful of engines! Every works car was tailor-made for the driver(s) and circuit; no wonder the team was a happy one.

With the winning of the world championship, David Brown got his chance to insist on grand prix cars. Too late. Wyer had stuck out for making haste slowly and the cars were based on their existing long-distance sports racers. Grand prix races, however, had become the province of short-distance mid-engined machines and this was the way David Brown wanted to go. There was neither the time nor the money to beat the world in the existing Formula One that was due to end in 1961, so David Brown didn't complain. He accepted it all philosophically although he wasn't too pleased with the half-hearted attempts at Le Mans that followed with the Project cars. It just wasn't like the old days.

Aston Martin and Lagonda had a great deal of work at the time developing the DB4 and Lagonda Rapide as well as moving the works to Newport Pagnell. They laboured long and hard to make the David Brown gearbox work with a de Dion back axle and had to give up in the end and fit Borg Warner automatic boxes to all but one Rapide, and ZF boxes to Aston Martins. When David Brown's companies were in the position of suppliers to Aston Martin and Lagonda they could be just as tough as anybody else. He gave as much as he could to Aston Martin and Lagonda and then called a halt.

Much as David Brown liked the earlier DBs, he loved the DB5 best, twisting the works' arms for an estate version so that he could go shooting in an Aston Martin. It caused a lot of disruption and so did the James Bond cars although the film-makers paid for all the modifications. The publicity they got from it,

The men at Aston Martins were adept at making rather more than full-scale cars. This is a 'DB2 drop-head coupé' pedal car pictured beside the real thing in 1950. Sixteen years later they made a similar car based on the James Bond DB5 for Prince Andrew of the British royal family.

Frank Feeley, on the right, at home in a corner of the body shop where scale models of future projects were made. The models in the background are of a production DB3S and a DB2/4 fixed-head coupé.

however, was as good as winning Le Mans or the Monte Carlo Rally (which had eluded Brown). It was his personality that sold the car in this case. The James Bond author, Ian Fleming, could think of no other car as being so thoroughly sporting and English after meeting David Brown at a house party.

Sales soared, then slumped, as economic crisis hit Britain in the early 1960s. By 1967 there were reputed to be 200 unsold DB6s stored around Newport Pagnell and in dealers' showrooms. Brown, who by now had far less time to spend on Aston Martin and Lagonda as his other businesses had mushroomed, repeated a ploy of the mid-1950s which had wiped up a surplus of Lagondas. He slashed the price by £1000 and the DB6s were gone in no time. But Aston Martin needed a new model and heroic efforts by Beach and a new Engineering Chief, Dudley Gershon, brought out the DBS in record time. They did it in such a hurry that the chassis was made too wide and they didn't have time to take much weight off—which is why the current cars are so big and heavy. However, Marek's last engine, the V8, provided plenty of power to make up for this and the weight and size worked out to be something of a bonus. At least Beach could feel some satisfaction from the DBS in that it used the rear suspension he had wanted to see on a production Aston Martin for ten years.

Gershon was a significant figure at Newport Pagnell in the late 1960s in that he absolutely refused to lower engineering standards. One of his pet hates was compliance in the suspension. If customers asked: 'Why can't you make my DBS ride like a Rolls?' they were told that Aston Martin's engineering would not sacrifice safety for comfort and if they wanted a Rolls ride they would have to buy a Rolls and put up with its handling.

He was a great admirer of Ferrari engineering, but he was openly scornful of European manufacturers who used American engines. 'Mere assemblers of bits', he called them and American cars were beyond contempt as far as he was concerned. Gershon was a purist who would have nothing to do with pushrods or single overhead camshafts when twin overhead cams were more efficient. So when

Tommy Wisdom pictured with XMC 77 (still bearing its Liege-Rome-Liege Rally sticker in one side window) on the way to practice for the 1955 Mille Miglia in which he was to drive a DB2/4.

he redesigned Marek's V8 it was twin overhead cams or nothing. Unfortunately these principles extended to fuel injection and they just couldn't make it work properly, although it was far better in theory. Mind you, Gershon had to compromise sometimes, like when the jigmakers made a mess of the DBS platform. However, he absolutely refused to allow anybody to remove the front crossmember to just see if a big American V8 would go in. Apart from his horror of agricultural engineering it would have made the chassis sloppy and ruined his precious roadholding. The car would have wound up just like a Cadillac—'Out of control on bends at speeds 40 mph below the Aston's.' All along he was backed up by managing director Steve Heggie, who also made some memorable quotes, in *CAR* magazine:

> 'I have come to the conclusion that 70 mph for a great many of our owners is quite fast enough, but similarly the reason the car feels like an Aston Martin at that speed is because of the endeavour for maximum performance. You get into one of our cars with your eyes shut, if you like, and you ask yourself what car is it. You know it's an Aston Martin, and the evidence of this endeavour for top performance out of a road vehicle is there whatever one may be doing. . . .'

Aston Martins have always been as distinctive in appearance as they have been in feeling. The DBS styling, although still based on Italian ideas, was the work of William Towns. His designs have always been cleverly arranged for a variety of wheelbases: his DBS looking just as good in its later Aston Martin Lagonda form. He was (and still is) a great universal designer and went freelance in the late 1960s. Another great freelance, Trevor Fiore, was hired to design a successor to the DBS by Heggie's successor, Malcolm Montgomery. Montgomery was a realist who wanted a lower, slimmer and lighter car than the DBS to achieve the volume sales which would make Aston Martin and Lagonda in its old form viable into the

1980s. His ideas were based on a variety of trends: balanced weight distribution like that on the DBR1 with engine at one end and transaxle at the other; passenger area was spacious but more intimate than the DBS (rather like an Austin 1800!); road and wind noise had to be reduced (to Jaguar XJ6 levels); a convertible body option had to be available (the Volante had always sold well); space had to be created for air conditioning (to combat Cadillacs); engine access had to be improved (to keep down servicing costs); tank capacity had to offer at least a 300-mile range (you were always having to stop to fill up your DBS); the body had to be of a type that would greatly reduce repair costs (Aston Martin insurance premiums could be intimidating for potential customers, especially if they went into the volume production field); and it would have to conform to all known impending US regulations. To his eternal credit, so far unsung except by *CAR* magazine, Fiore designed an Aston Martin to meet these seemingly impossible demands, made in May 1971 during the year of their first great post-war financial crisis. Montgomery's inspired ideas—to pitch new Aston Martins (and stretched Lagonda versions) progressively lower in the market to achieve greater volume sales—were radically different from those which turned out in practice. He even had a new model in mind, a mid-engined coupé with Aston Martin body and BRM engine. Agreement in principle with BRM had been reached when David Brown really began to run short of money. As Aston Martin struggled to produce a new world-beater the losses were mounting, at a time when other parts of his empire were going through a liquidity crisis. A third of the labour force at Newport Pagnell were sacked—people there at the time said there were too many people doing too little anyway—but the losses mounted to £1.2 million at a time when the turnover was only £3.2 million.

Company Developments took over with a pledge to keep the firm going and they very nearly succeeded. Their chairman, William Willson, did everything in his power to preserve Aston Martin and his company did their best to improve the existing cars. First of all, they brought in an engineering consultancy to replace Gershon and then decided they were better off as they were. Gershon had gone but fortunately they still had Beach. He set about cleaning up the V8 exhaust emissions to get it into the States. They tried turbocharging, then settled for the current Webers. The next project was getting the Lagonda ready for production. Willson fancied the car and wasn't interested in Fiore's futuristic projects. He didn't even ask to see them although he had bought an option on the design as part of Aston's assets! Instead, he concentrated on selling the existing product. Andrew Furnival and Chris Philips portrayed him in *Industrial Management* as a go-getting businessman who tempered any aggressive instincts with not inconsiderable charm. They said:

> 'He's also Aston Martin's self-appointed public relations officer, taking great pains to put across his ideas of how any company should be run. Willson's style ranges from entertaining potential clients over champagne at the Earls Court Motor Show (where he says he "thoroughly enjoyed" himself) to wandering round the Newport Pagnell factory in his shirt sleeves.

'He said at the time of the takeover: "I know there will be a lot of raised eyebrows at the idea of a banking man becoming managing director of one of the most respected car names in Britain."

'But he doesn't think the idea at all odd. "Let's make no bones about it: if you have the resources as we have, you can buy the technical expertise needed to run a company such as Aston Martin and link it with your own management skills."'

At first, all went well. Company Developments ploughed £600,000 into Aston Martin and component suppliers stopped screaming for their money. The loss was reduced to a few thousand and there was even the possibility of breaking even by the end of 1974 and going into profit in 1975. The only trouble was that there was an energy crisis just when they were launching the luxurious new Lagonda. There was still hope of selling enough—about a dozen a week with the work-force as it was—if they could get into America. But half a million pounds was needed to crash enough cars into concrete blocks and so on to meet the ever-changing American regulations. Ironically, the Aston Martin and Lagonda V8s had such a clean engine by now that they had no problem passing emission tests and thanks to Gershon and Beach they were incredibly good at missing concrete blocks even if they had fallen into the road in front of them. They were also so solid that the concrete block would have been in more danger than the occupants of the car should there have been a collision.

Willson made these points to the Department of Trade and Industry and emphasized what a fine set up they had for selling the cars in America if they could only borrow the money to get them through these awful tests. However, he came up against Tony Benn who wasn't exactly into luxurious Lagondas, although he had been of considerable help to motor cycle manufacturers struggling with the same sort of problems.

As ever, other people became involved and Willson became the victim of a most undignified row between the Conservative and Labour candidates for Buckingham, whose potential constituency included Newport Pagnell. As Judith Jackson, motoring correspondent of *The Sunday Times* wrote in *CAR* magazine:

'The resultant publicity turned a liquidity problem—which had been accentuated for Aston Martin as well as for the rest of industry by the three-day week earlier in 1974—into a liquidity crisis. There is nothing like the thought that a company may be in financial trouble for sending all its creditors, including the milkman, to hammer on the front door.

'Enter the incredible loyalty factor. The workers agreed to forego a five per cent pay increase and agreed to a year's wage freeze. The Aston Martin Owners' Club formed a support group to back the company and offers of help arrived daily. One owner even sent a cheque for £1000 to use in any way the company thought fit. One of the imponderables is why Aston Martin commands such incredible loyalty. One of the founders of the support group,

Dudley Coram, says that it's because the Aston Martin V8 is the finest GT car in the world—and its British.'

Dudley Coram, the advertising man and king of Aston Martin enthusiasts, had revived the owners' club after the war to build it into one of the strongest marque clubs in the world. Now, with other members just as keen, he was fighting to preserve the firm as well. They won a six-month moratorium from the creditors and members Peter Sprague from New York and George Minden from Canada bought the company for a million pounds. One of the people who had been interested was Alan Curtis, and a few weeks later Sprague persuaded him to join in the attempt to make Aston Martin and Lagonda viable again, together with retired steelman Denis Flather—Aston Martin owners all. Curtis was busy with his property interests so he didn't have much time to spend at Newport Pagnell until early in 1976 when Sprague and Minden were dreaming up a new car aimed at persuading the world that the company was back to stay.

They called in Towns again, by now a freelance, and told him what they wanted for the new Lagonda: Willson's saloon was now outdated. Towns based the styling on a wedge-shaped glass-fibre conversion for the V12 E type Jaguar which he had done for the great Northern enthusiast Jim Thomson. This could well have been the new E type had that car not have been killed by the Americans' concrete blocks in 1974. With another former Aston Martin backroom boy— engineer Mike Loasby, who had been at Triumph for a while—Towns produced the spectacular new Lagonda in record time. It caused such a sensation at the 1976 London Motor Show that it became obvious that the whole structure of the company needed reforming to build the right number of cars and to make a profit: an equation that Aston Martin had never been able to solve before.

Alan Curtis was persuaded to do it and became managing director in 1977. Today's order book is ample justification for the way in which Curtis, Sprague and Minden got their sums right. Like all the other owners before them they have fallen in love with the legend and the people who produce the cars. To quote Sprague: 'We invest our money, they invest their labour.'

Their numbers are smaller now, around 250, and between them they produce six to seven cars a week; this is against more than double that workforce for the same number of cars before. But that's all part of Curtis's equation, an equation that still allows each V8 engine to be assembled by one fitter (he has his name on a plate on the engine now, not just a code with the number); brake assembly to another; hundreds of hours of body and chassis building by others. It's all very old fashioned and reassuring. As reassuring as the Aston Martin V8 they cannot kill. With orders stretching into the 1980s the nose, now bearing a distinct re-semblance to that designed by Feeley for the DB3S; the Vantage engine liberated by Loasby to produce all Marek and Gershon's 460 horses; the suspension clinging to the road with the genius of Beach and the fortitude of Gershon, and the whole thing still looking unmistakeably David Brown, it's no wonder the cars have personality. The latest Lagonda is a fitting memorial for today's men of Newport Pagnell.

XIV

Comparisons with Contemporary Rivals

THE EARLY Aston Martins and Lagondas had a lot of rivals, cars which could match them and sometimes beat them in terms of acceleration, maximum speed and economy, but hardly ever in comfort or roadholding. This was because the DB1 was born of an age when numerous car makers were struggling to regain their feet, or even get started, after the war. Few had researched their market properly, even fewer had the muscle to overcome economic restrictions. One of the nearest rivals was the Frazer-Nash (they adopted the hyphen only after the war) produced from pre-war BMW designs in collaboration with the Bristol aircraft company. Their 2-litre cars were produced in very small quantities in two forms: one, the High Speed model with cycle-type wings and toothpaste tube body and the other, a pretty all-enveloping machine called the Fast Roadster. These cars were aimed at the wealthy gentleman who wanted an all-purpose car (preferably made in Britain) for fast touring, road racing, and even a night out on the town. They were rather more spartan than the Astons, with the exception of the Spa replica, but they were their equals in terms of performance. They were competitors in racing and rallying with their Bristol-built straight-six engines although neither Aston Martin nor Frazer-Nash could produce enough to satisfy their market. Similar comments apply to the Bristol 400 saloon although it was more of a rival for the Lagonda, lacking the Aston Martin's racing reputation. It was at least as well built, if not better, and bore a distinct resemblance to the pre-war German car, but was slightly slower than the Lagonda. A drop-head was built on this 400 chassis, looking very much like the Lagonda which went into production rather later.

The Bristol 401 introduced for 1950 was much better streamlined, having been developed by the aircraft company's aerodynamicists in wind tunnels and along a two-mile runway which had been built for the Brabazon airliner. It took more than thirteen years for Aston Martin to improve on the 401's drag coefficient with the DB4 Vantage. Needless to say, the 401 was about 10 per cent faster than the Lagonda in a straight line and nearly as quick as the lighter DB2; but it was rather more tail-happy, due to its less advanced live rear axle and the overhanging weight of its spare wheel and petrol tank. Fuel consumption was superior, however, at 20 mpg.

One of the DB3S and DBR1's closest rivals was the Jaguar D type.

George Abecassis, who became David Brown's son-in-law, did more than race Aston Martins. He ran Heath, Walton, Motors, who produced a handful of exceptionally competitive Jaguar-engined specials besides selling and servicing Aston Martins, which they do to this day. In the foreground is the ex-Phil Scragg HWM-Jaguar hill-climber and in the background Abecassis's personal HWM-Jaguar fixed-head coupé which bore a remarkable resemblance to an Aston Martin in parts! Had these cars ever been produced in any quantity they would have been a serious rival for Aston Martins, as the few produced proved to be on the track.

The 402 drophead coupé lacked the dowager proportions of the Lagonda soft top and the lithe ability of the DB2; it fell somewhere between and its scuttle shook. The 403 introduced in 1953 had better brakes, improved handling and 100 bhp from its race-developed engine. These cars were at least the equal of the DB2 or DB2/4 on the road although they never quite aspired to the luxurious pre-war image of the Lagonda, appealing to a more austere type of owner.

The later Le Mans Replica, Mille Miglia, Targa Florio and Sebring Frazer-Nashes, all powered by Bristol engines, were serious rivals for the Aston Martins, although their only coupé was a racing model and they were bought primarily for competition. It is significant that John Bolster, one of the most experienced road testers of the time, preferred Astons because of the extreme rigidity and the light weight of their frame, which made the Frazer-Nash seem rather old fashioned by comparison. Their general use of bolt-on wheels did not excite him either.

So far as price was concerned, Frazer-Nash and Bristol always cost more than the DB2 and 2/4; something like twenty-five per cent, depending on the model and specification. Production Ferraris and Maseratis cost twice as much and weighed much more and the extraordinary Spanish Pegaso—produced in the old Hispano-Suiza works—three times as much; about £9000. These were real road-going GT's with 170 bhp twin-overhead-cam V8s, platform chassis, de Dion rear axles and coachbuilt bodies, made for prestige rather than profit by Spain's leading engineering company. Their purpose, even appearance, was rather like the Aston Martin and just went to show what a bargain the British car was! Later Pegasos featured really exotic coachwork, in strange contrast to their general air of howling noise from a highly supercharged V8, and ride as rough as that of a racing Ferrari. The handling of these three cars could border on the horrific, as well.

In terms of price, the Lagonda was beaten by the Alvis, but had far more finesse; it cost only half the price of a Bentley or Rolls, however, so in those terms it could be considered cheap! The Jaguars leaving Coventry in relatively large numbers at around half the price of the Feltham cars were faster and cheaper to run—but they suffered from inferior roadholding and they were far from exclusive.

The XK engine that was to prove to be Aston Martin's most formidable rival in the 1950s and 1960s. Although sharing a similar appearance to Tadek Marek's six-cylinder engine it was of considerably more aged design.

Miller (DB4GT) and MacGregor (DB5 Vantage) in the centre fight it out with two of Aston Martin's rivals, a Maserati Indy on the left and a Jaguar XK140 fixed-head coupé on the right, at Crystal Palace in 1971.

One of the DB2's rivals, although rather costly, was the Spanish Pegaso. This is the Z102B model.

Lancia's 2500GT—developed from a 1700 cc car of 1949—had a similar performance to the Aston but cost a lot more. But it was worth it in many ways. It was a delightful car to drive and the first post-war car other than a DB2 that really deserved the title Gran Turismo. Despite its incredible mechanical specification with 60-degree V6 engine, short fore and aft pushrods, transmission in unit with the final drive, sliding pillar independent front suspension, and independent or de Dion rear suspension, it really was the Italian Aston Martin; beautifully made with a wonderful performance.

Bentley's voluminous Continental really deserved to be called a GT although it never was; this great big four-seater was almost as fast as a DB2, and was much quicker than a Lagonda. Needless to say it was much sought after despite its £8000 price tag; more common Bentleys and Rolls were left wallowing behind Lagondas should they ever be driven with spirit.

As Astons put on weight in the mid-1950s, their rivals changed too. Mercedes and BMW entered the field with their 300SL and 500 series; Ferrari and Maserati started making real road cars such as the 250GT and 3500 GT; Pegaso concen-

One of the cheaper rivals of the mid-1950s was the Jaguar XK140 Special Equipment model, pictured here in its very rare right-hand drive roadster form.

Last, but not least, is Aston Martin's greatest rival over the years, Ferrari. This is the 1972 365 GTC/4 2+2 with a six-carburetter four-overhead-camshaft twelve-cylinder engine producing 340 bhp, giving it a maximum speed of more than 150 mph.

A rival throughout the 1960s was the much cheaper Jaguar E type six cylinder. This is a 'series 1½' 1967 model roadster.

trated on buses and trucks; Frazer-Nash faded, spending most of their energies on selling Porsches (which were rather too small at the time to be considered in the Aston Martin class); Bristol stuck to saloons for normal production; and Jensen made a rather truck-like GT—definitely not an Aston! Jaguars grew heavier in company with Astons and Lancia concentrated on smaller cars. A straight comparison of performance figures would show that many of these cars could outrun a DB Mark II or III; but in a world with few motorways none of them could better them for fast, effortless, travel. The Mercedes Gullwing was a good car providing you were sufficiently skilled to cope with its swing-axle rear suspension; it could be lethal in the hands of the inexperienced. The BMW was rarely seen in sporting circles; Maseratis were rather agricultural and were nothing like their competition models; Jaguars' chassis and rear suspension was dated and machines like the Big Healey, which could match the Feltham cars' performance, were simply not in the same class (and only a fraction of the price in any case); Ferrari, like Mercedes, were faster, but their handling had not caught up.

The Gullwing with its fuel-injected straight-six engine and powerful drum brakes demanded a special driving technique. You entered bends slower than usual, using the tremendous acceleration (0–60 in 7 seconds, standing quarter mile in 15 seconds) to hurtle out of the corner faster than almost anything else other than

One of Aston Martin's most serious rivals from 1967 was the Jensen Interceptor. This is a 1973 series III model.

In the mid-1970s the BMW 3.0 CSL Alpina rivalled Aston Martins.

One of the V8's current rivals is the Porsche. This is a 1977 3.0 Sport model.

a Ferrari. Adopt any other cornering technique, like entering bends fast, and you might not last long enough to reach its maximum of 140 mph (152 mph with special high ratio). Eventually the gullwing doors were virtually outlawed in America as they could prove difficult to open if the car was upside down!

The subsequent redesign necessitated lower frame members to ease entry with a resultant lowering of the rear suspension pivot points and a taming of the mighty Merc.

The first Ferraris that were practical to use on the road were the 250GTs—which were almost as fast as the Mercedes 300SL. These were all 3-litre V12s with coachwork by firms such as Pinin Farina and Boano, and price tags in the region of £6000. They were capable of between 125 and 150 mph depending on gearing; even faster and much more expensive were the very rare 5-litre V12s sold only to a privileged few such as the Shah of Iran. The 250s lacked torque at the bottom end (maximum power was produced at 7000 rpm) although their Colombo-designed engine sounded so good it was a joy to change gear.

On the Lagonda front, Alvis revised their coachwork to look remarkably like the 3-litre and survived a few years longer in the traditional sporting saloon form. They had a similar clientele to Lagonda, notably Prince Philip. Bristol moved further away from their BMW origins with the 404 and 405 and developed such

Rolls-Royce, although producing a totally different car in design to the Aston Martin and Lagonda have always been a serious rival for the attentions of wealthy patrons. This is a 1978-model Corniche.

Rolls-Royce, although producing a totally different car in design to the Aston Martin and Lagonda have always been a serious rival for the attentions of wealthy patrons. This is a 1978-model Corniche.

a distinctive character that they were not really rivals for Lagonda. You either liked the traditional tree-wood Lagonda or you liked the grille-less aircraft-style Bristol; I doubt whether any potential customer ever wavered between the two. Rolls/Bentley moved out of the sporting category with the S series in 1956. Jaguars dominated the lower end of this class (including Alvis and Lagonda) with the Marks VII, VIII and IX saloons.

Aston Martin's breakthrough came with the DB4 in 1959. It had everything: wonderful performance, appearance, handling, braking, not to mention the sheer luxury of it all. For two years the only competitors were Ferrari and Mercedes, and when the DB4GT was introduced it left even the production versions of these exotic rivals behind. Taking the *Autosport* figures as generally the fastest of their day, the DB4GT was capable of 152.5 mph with a 6.4 second 0–60 mph and a 14.2 second mph 0–100; the Ferrari 250GT current in the early 1960s did 136.3 mph, at 7.2 seconds and 20 seconds; the Mercedes 300SL 140.6 mph, 7 seconds and 16.2 seconds (the 152 mph ratio car had much inferior acceleration). The market contracted in 1961 when Jaguars introduced their E type at half the price. It was marginally slower than the DB4GT but a little quicker than the DB4. Its handling was inferior, however, it was nothing near like so luxurious, and it was far from exclusive. The DB4 sacrificed none of Astons' old heritage; its roadholding was as good; it was just as well built and it looked even better. Economy suffered, of course, but performance does not come cheaply and it was comparable with its great rivals. Maseratis fitted fuel injection to their 3.7-litre straight-six twin-overhead-cam twelve-plugged engines (the specification had a familiar ring about it!) giving them comparable performance to the 250GT but not the DB4; besides their suspension still needed revision.

Until 1965, the Jaguar E type, which was a vast improvement over the XKs in that it was fitted with independent rear suspension and a truly modern, beautifully streamlined body, was Astons' chief rival. The Jensen CV8 introduced in 1963 to replace the 4-litre Austin-engined 541 fell somewhere in between at £3300 with rather less performance than either (8.4 seconds 0–60, 131 mph, with only average handling).

A far more desirable, and faster car, using a 5.4-litre Chevrolet engine rather than the Jensen's Chrysler V8, was the Iso Grifo. The body was one of Bertone's masterpieces and the performance was fantastic: It was capable of 163 mph with more than 140 mph in the fourth of its five speeds! It had really good roadholding, but it cost more than £7000, and so few were sold; the same applied to the more exotic Ferraris, such as the Superfast. They were even faster than the Aston but cost the earth and an oil well to buy.

The Porsche 911 series introduced in 1965 was to become a far more serious rival for Aston Martins. The 911S was the quickest of the early 2-litre models, but the 911E was the nicest; you didn't have to row it along on the gearlever at high revs. All were capable of more than 130 mph with a time of 8–9 seconds to 0–60 mph; not so fast as an Aston, but a competitor nevertheless, with much-improved handling over the early models. The demand for Porsches was so high, especially outside Britain, that they obviously restricted Astons' export market.

By the late 1960s, with the introduction of overall speed limits in most countries, style assumed equal importance with performance in the GT stakes. Jensen abandoned their curious CV8 and went to Italy for a proper GT body. Touring, who had designed the DB4, came up with a whole new set of clothes that were to make the Chrysler-engined car a really serious competitor for Aston Martin. The new Jensen was similar to the DBS in conception and certainly speeded up the introduction of that model from Newport Pagnell. The Jensen, voted Car of the Year in 1967, performed pretty well: 132 mph with acceleration in the order of an 8 seconds 0–60 mph. In four-wheel-drive form with anti-lock brakes it was even quicker than an Aston round a corner and it didn't aquaplane; for the first time since the war Aston Martin were involved in a real battle on their home ground. The two-wheel-drive Jensen Interceptor cost a little less than a DB6 and the four-wheel-drive FF a great deal more, and both cars were an immediate success. It is significant that Aston Martin were to struggle financially until Jensens collapsed in 1977 after delving into the small car market; even today the AM V8 convertible has obviously been inspired by the Jensen edition which was introduced late in the West Bromwich car's run.

Jensen aside, Aston Martin's chief rivals in the late 1960s were the Italian trio of Ferrari, Lamborghini and Maserati, Porsche not being quite in the super car class yet and Mercedes sports cars being too much like their contemporary saloons.

The 275 GTB four-cam was typical of the numerous Ferraris produced in the late 1960s; the Lamborghini 400GT was still current and a good comparison with the six-cylinder DBS, although the mid-engined Miura was something else; and Maserati were producing the likes of the Ghibli. Without a doubt the 275 GTB/4 was the fastest from one point to another: it was a pure two-seater that needed driving like a racing car all the time. It had a 3.3-litre V12 engine with six Weber carburetters producing 300 bhp at 8000 rpm; four-wheel independent suspension with transmission at the back for better weight distribution and aggressive no-frills coachwork. Bigger Ferraris such as the 330GT (a two plus two) used first a 4-litre V12 with live rear axle, then changed to a 4.4-litre V12 with independent rear suspension for the 365 GT 2+2. They all had performance in the region of 145–152 mph, and with 7 seconds 0–60 mph, they were obviously ahead of the Aston.

The Lamborghini had curious styling, very pleasing to some, ghastly to others. But everybody agreed it was a supremely civilized car with a superb 4-litre V12 engine and good handling. It was altogether softer than the Ferrari; it was a road car rather than a racing machine, and more like the bigger Ferraris in feel although it had the supreme attraction of being small and dainty.

The Maserati Ghibli looked absolutely marvellous; it was one of the all-time classics and rather like the Aston in appearance. It had a durable 4.7-litre V8 engine giving it performance in the region of 150 mph with a 0–60 mph time of 7 seconds—but its handling imparted by its live rear axle was simply awful. The four-seater version, called the Indy, was slightly slower and handled just as badly.

Like the Lambo, the DBS was a serious attempt to produce a four-seater GT, but it was heavy like the Maserati. The bigger Ferraris felt like the Queen Mary compared to the Aston. The mid-engined Miura was by no stretch of the imagination a GT: driving it was more like riding a wild horse. The Aston might have suffered a little in terms of performance, but its braking and roadholding were second to none and its general finish was markedly superior to that of the Italian super cars.

In automatic form, however, the DBS six-cylinder was decidedly inferior to the Jensen with its American Torqueflite transmission (they produced only sixteen manual Interceptors). Mercifully, the Italians were still shunning automatic boxes on their super cars.

The DBS V8 changed all that, and it found new opposition at home. The Frua-styled AC 428 fitted with a 7-litre Ford V8 engine and automatic transmission as standard was capable of 145 mph with truly astounding acceleration in the sub six-second bracket. This car, endowed with excellent roadholding and a spectacular appearance cost little more than a DBS V8 but went into only limited production; much to Aston Martin's relief!

The clientele were changing, however. As we entered the 1970s the fuel crisis was looming, adding to the restraints of overall speed limits. Soon people began to buy Aston Martins and similar high-performance cars purely for prestige rather than chiefly for performance. Cars such as the Rolls-Royce became competitors. The rear seats became more important and the Aston measured up well here, falling somewhere between the full four-seater Lamborghini Espada and the rather cramped Jensen. Air conditioning became standard (Rolls and Jensen featured it in their cars); automatic gearboxes became more popular (Rolls and Jensen again) and power steering became more acceptable.

Somehow Aston Martin managed to retain much of their old character: the steering stayed heavier than the Rolls or Jensen and imparted more feel. Only Mercedes were comparable with their saloon-like 450SL. The Aston was not so quiet as the Rolls, of course, despite extra sound-proofing, and the customers did not expect it. They still wanted something of the sports car.

The Aston was as good as anything the Italians or Germans could produce with the same sort of accommodation. Only their two-seater super cars were quicker, the Ferrari 365 GTB/4 (commonly, but not officially, called the Daytona) and the Lamborghini Miura SV were substantially faster at 170 mph plus. Better comparisons could be made with the Lamborghini Espada (even bigger inside, and with spaceship styling), the Islero (beautiful handling, old-fashioned styling) and the Jarama (super ride and handling, chunky modern styling); the Ferrari GT4 2+2 (limited leg room, plenty of performance); Porsche Carrera (practical, but rather antiseptic character, go-it-alone styling); and Mercedes 450SL (slow and staid). Then there was the Jaguar/Daimler XJ12. This big saloon set new standards in sophisticated comfort, ride and handling, with near super car performance in extraordinary silence, making it as competitive a Big Cat as ever. Its low price tended to keep it in a different bracket, however.

In the wake of the fuel crisis came today's super cars with the V8 Vantage up among the best, and jealous of its title as the world's fastest-accelerating car. Nevertheless the Lamborghini Countach can probably outrun it but without the luxury. At the time of writing, however, they are nearly extinct. The Jaguar XJS is probably the most sensible super car today. But the whole point of owning and driving a super car is that they don't have to be entirely practical or sensible, so long as they are enjoyable to drive and are right for the image.

Maserati's Khamsin makes nominal concessions to people wanting to sit in the back; the Kyalami is an upmarket version of the de Tomaso Longchamps; the Bora is a mid-engined muscle car with nowhere to put more than one passenger and then only one with rather short legs! The Porsche Turbo has more leg room in the back, but only a little, and the Countach and Berlinetta Boxer 512BB have none at all; Ferrari's 2+2 400 is a good deal slower and even has an optional automatic gearbox; none of them except the Kyalami has the headroom of the Aston. The faster Ferrari, the 512BB, is claimed to be as quick as a Countach at 185 mph plus (not many people have been able to find out); the Aston and Maseratis Khamsin and Bora fall into the 165–170 mph bracket; the Porsche and Jaguar are in the 155 mph zone; the Kyalami and 400 will reach to between 145 and 150 mph.

In terms of silent travel, the Jaguar is best together with the Aston, then the Porsche following. In terms of handling, the Countach comes out on top, with the Bora next, then the Boxer and then the Porsche; the Aston and Maseratis with power steering being the easiest to manoeuvre. The Jaguar is overlight in this department, but this was a concession to the American market. Its ride on the other hand is much better than that of the Aston. The brakes of an Aston, providing you have a strong leg and like vintage-style floor-hinged pedals, are considered to be first class.

So why do people buy Aston Martins? Because they have so many good points, because they are steeped in tradition, and because they are British. The same goes for Lagonda.

XV

The Aston Martin Owners' Club

THE ASTON MARTIN OWNERS' CLUB is one of the most enthusiastic and best organized motoring clubs in the world; its races, concours, even club dinners, are a model in the way they are run. Every member seems to take a positive interest in furthering the interests of the marque. Whenever the companies which have made cars have foundered (as it seems all small motor manufacturers have at one time or another), it has been Aston Martin Owners' Club members who have stepped in to save them.

The club's history in relation to this book coincides well with the subject of post-war Astons and Lagondas, as the Aston Martin Owners' Club (which also caters for the pre-war Aston Martins) was re-formed after the war by Richard Stallebrass and Dudley Coram. Stallebrass, and that other much-revered Aston Martin enthusiast, St John Horsfall, were both killed in accidents soon after the club's re-formation; but their memories live on with trophies and the club's premier race meeting at Silverstone. Dudley Coram was the inspiration behind the Aston Martin Owners' Club until his death in 1976. Today it has twenty branches in the United Kingdom; two in the United States, and representatives in Australia, New Zealand, Sweden, Belgium, South Africa, Spain, France, Switzerland, Japan, the Netherlands, the Republic of Ireland, and Germany. Membership lists extend to Denmark, Norway, Morocco, the Lebanon, Jordan, Kuwait, Kenya, Nigeria, the West Indies, Mexico, Argentina, Brunei and even Iceland. And with Aston Martin Lagonda setting up overseas distributorships in Abu Dhabi, Bahrein, Belgium, Germany, Greece, Hong Kong, Japan, Holland, Oman, Saudi Arabia, Spain, Sweden, the United States and Canada, doubtless there are more to come!

The club has a very active competition programme, having virtually started Snetterton motor racing circuit in 1951 when Oliver Sear, an Aston Martin enthusiast, friend and neighbour of Jock Horsfall, secured permission from the owners of the former aerodrome to run a limited number of motor races.

'This was always provided the RAC Competitions Committee would approve the project [said Dudley Coram in *Aston Martin: The Story of a Sports Car*]. The circuit was duly viewed and passed initial scrutiny with the usual stipulations for the provision of safety measures and other necessary accoutrements,

Part of the line-up for the Aston Martin Owners' Club's display for the Town and Country motoring festival in 1978.

but the controlling body wanted a Speed Trial run that year if they were expected to judge whether the track would be suitable for a full programme of race meetings the following year.

'The club was given exactly six weeks in which to prepare the regulations, scrape together an entry, borrow some prize money, and run the whole show, which was only allowed as a "closed" meeting.

'It says much for the spirit of the club in the way the officials and the entrants turned up on that testing day. The drivers included such people as George Abecassis, Oscar Moore, Don Parker, Dick Jacobs, Duncan Hamilton, Ray Merrick, Ken Wharton and Dennis Poore, the total entry being nearly 100 cars . . . that was the send-off for Snetterton—a circuit that rose to the promotion of many fine national and international meetings.'

I'm glad the Aston Martin Owners' Club succeeded that day: it was the first motor race I saw.

Since then they have gone from strength to strength. They are, for example, the only one-make club to run an international race meeting; the Martini Trophy at Silverstone. Such is the standard of their organization that today, their premier meeting is the St John Horsfall historic sports car meeting at Silverstone where races are organized for all members and anybody else eligible to enter—and there are many. The club pioneered the current brand of historic car racing as long ago as 1967; they virtually started the Cussons Classic Car series in 1971, they ran the last-ever meeting at London's Crystal Palace circuit in 1972 (before moving to Castle Combe) and now they are sponsoring the Thoroughbred racing series in Britain for which marque cars of the 1940s and 1950s, such as Aston Martins and Jaguars, are eligible. It was felt that many of the cars competing in this series were becoming far too specialized, with the result that fields were shrinking as many more standard cars were being rendered less competitive. Race promoters therefore welcomed with open arms the Aston Martin Owners' Club involvement with their record for immaculate organization and hard-line attitudes over eligibility.

Club sprints are organized at Curborough and hill climbs at Wiscombe Park in Devon; the social side is well catered for with two annual concours, an annual

The V8 makes an ideal course car for an Aston Martin Owners' Club meeting.

Needle match against the Ferrari Owners' Club at an Aston Martin Owners' Club meeting.

Aston Martin Owners' Club events encourage the use of standard cars. . . .

ball, cocktail parties, luncheons and dinners, monthly meetings and an award-winning quarterly magazine, *AM*, plus a monthly newsletter that contains a great deal of local news and free advertising for cars and parts. Technical advice is at the highest level and the Aston Martin Register is one of the most detailed publications on any marque; the work that has gone into it over the years is impossible to estimate. The club also has a full-time secretary, registrars for Lionel Martin pre-war cars, Bertelli and 2-litre pre-war cars, post-war cars, technical consultants, a club historian, and a spares and service registrar. A full list of area representatives is included at the end of this chapter.

There is also a separate club for Lagonda owners, The Lagonda Club. It was formed in 1951 by the amalgamation of the Lagonda Car Club and the 2-litre Lagonda Register. The aims of the club are to maintain the traditions of the Lagonda marque and to engage in or promote any motoring activity by which club members may benefit. One of their most recent ventures was the establishment of a fund to provide the financial backing for their book on the history of the marque—a truly worthy effort. The Lagonda Club also organizes competitive and social events for all models, the exchange of technical knowledge and experience, a spare parts service and publishes the quarterly *Lagonda Club Magazine* and regular newsletters. The secretary is Mrs Valerie May, of 68 Savill Road, Lindfield, Haywards Heath, Sussex.

Two of the major markets for Aston Martins and Lagondas are in the United States and Australia, areas in which the Aston Martin Owners' Club are very strong. One of the club's keenest members—still racing a DB4GT—is Rex Woodgate, who until recently was president of Aston Martin's US company. He became Aston Martin's service representative in America in 1961 after years spent working as Stirling Moss's personal mechanic and building DB3Ss, DBR1s and DBR2s at the factory—an ideal man to cope with any owner's problem! During those years Woodgate saw the opportunity to expand Aston Martin sales in America by establishing their own distributorship rather than relying on agents. He persuaded Steve Heggie, who was then managing director, to open the distributorship, Aston Martin Lagonda Incorporated, in 1964, and Woodgate was appointed its first general manager. He became president in 1971 and sales went well until emission regulations made it impossible to import the V8 into America in the early 1970s. The car could have passed the rigorous tests involved, but there just was not the money available for development until the parent company was reorganized in 1975. Woodgate then pressed for the V8 convertible and eventually got it—just as he was recalled to Newport Pagnell to liase sales, marketing and engineering departments! His knowledge of the American market was supported in the most demonstrative way: within weeks US dealers had ordered the entire first year's production of Aston Martin convertibles through the distributorship which continues.

A majority of Aston Martin owners in the United States are members of the club. They have found it necessary to open a number of centres, chiefly because they comprise small groups of highly enthusiastic members scattered over vast distances, a problem shared with the Australians and South Africans. Like the

. . . and non-standard ones, no matter
what the age.

British Aston owners, the Americans and Australians are not only interested in
concours events, but also in racing and competing in all manner of activities.

They keenly support all forms of historic racing in America and organize a
national weekend at Lime Rock, Connecticut, in August, with a slalom for the
more road-going types. Australian Aston Martin activities are similar. Bob Rusk's
story is typical of those who have been loyal Aston Martin and Lagonda enthusiasts for many years. He bought his first Aston Martin when the Kangaroo Stable
publicized the marque in the late 1950s.

'It was a DB Mark III and I may add that it is the only brand new car
that I have ever purchased [said Bob]. I had owned three Bristols and a
2.6 drop-head Lagonda prior to this. The shape of the DB4 when it appeared
on the market really impressed me and I waited until 1962 when I found
one second hand. It was a DB4 series four, purchased for £4250, which, in
those days, was a lot of money. The car had done only 3000 miles and it was
equal to a new car. I drove it for eleven years and I was fortunate in that
I was able to do all the maintenance and mechanical repairs myself, although
I will say that the car gave me very little trouble. The only major problem
that occurred was with the overdrive, which developed a slip, and a vibration
which came in at 3000 revs and only appeared after the clutch had been
overhauled. The clutch has been pulled out three times and balanced and
re-balanced and to this day, that vibration still persists, having baffled the
experts.

'As my everyday car today, I drive a DB6 Mark 2, which I consider to
be the ultimate. The finish on the car is superior, in my opinion, to the
present day cars. It has seating for four and cruises at relatively high speeds
with comfort. It does not have the quick lively feel of the DB4, but it has
many other features to compensate for this. Only a few weekends ago, I drove
1700 miles from Sydney to the Barossa Valley and back for the AMOC
national meeting and the car lived up to my expectations and more.

One of the favourite Aston Martin Owners' Club events is the Wiscombe hill climb.

'I recently purchased a DB4GT, one of the only two in this country, and at the moment I am completely restoring this car in every way. I purchased it from Duncan Bray who raced the car with a reasonable amount of success in Australia and in England and I was fortunate enough to catch him in a weak moment. He purchased the car in England and brought it out to Australia. When his job took him back to England for twelve months [men never like to be parted from their Astons!] he took the car with him, then brought it back again!

'Possibly because we are so far away from the factory, they have not seen us as a potential market in recent years. Since 1970 more cars have come into Australia than ever before, and they have all been second hand, brought in by dealers and private individuals because they were so cheap to buy in England.'

The difficulties in obtaining parts for Aston Martins in Australia were first tackled by Rusk in 1974 when the factory agreed to supply parts direct to him. However, this was found to be a lengthy procedure with orders, prices and cheques going backwards and forwards, and so a credit of $A1000 was raised by club members, allowing parts to be sent on order. Ten per cent was added to the price of each order, to be paid to the Aston Martin Owners' Club of New South Wales. This system, however, had its problems.

'I found that I had created something that was taking far too much of my time with telephone calls, trying to solve owners' problems, telephoned parts orders, trips to Air Cargo, the Post Office, customs and so on [said Rusk]. I thought of giving it up but decided that too many people now relied on me for parts and, as I personally was the only Member with the time to put into it, I decided to do something about it on a professional basis. As a result I visited the factory in 1978.

'The three weeks spent there were a joy. I was made to feel part of the establishment. So much so, that after a few days I felt that I had worked there for years. The enthusiasm shown by all the staff towards Aston Martins and Lagondas, as well as their jobs, was most impressive.'

As a result Rusk set up Tickford Distributors in New South Wales to ship in bulk orders of parts—saving a lot of money in air freight—with the object of being able to supply most parts off the shelf and employing service agents in a similar manner to the organization set up by Woodgate in America years before.

In this way the Aston Martin Owners' Club has gone far beyond the role of most marque clubs in supporting their favourite car. British and international representatives are:

SW London and Surrey: Mrs J. Creed, 35 Vincent Road, Stoke d'Abernon, Surrey; Northern Ireland: Geoffrey McCrea, Ballycraig, 333 Belmont Road, Belfast; Leics, Notts, Derby, Lincs: Peter and John Stafford, Tudor Lodge, Melton Road, Edwalton, Notts; Glos, Somerset and Wilts: Keith Ashcroft, Stonedge House, Chew Stoke, near Bristol and Gary Dickens, Five Elms, Hamp Avenue, Bridgwater, Somerset; Staffs, Worcs, Warwick, Shrops and Hereford: Don Aylett (club chairman), Balscote House, Balscote, near Banbury, Oxon; Yorkshire: Kenneth Birch, Glengarth, Bracken Bed Lane, Halifax; SE London and Kent: Roy Chambers, The Beeches, Temple Ewell, near Dover; Durham and Northumberland: W. H. Symons, Birkhill, Otterburn, Northumberland; Lancs, Cheshire and Cumbria: Peter Grant, Dubthorn, Astbury, Congleton, Cheshire; Bucks, Berks and Oxon: Trever Brinsden, 120 Tilehurst Road, Reading, Berks; NE London and Essex: Paul and Pauline Dobson, 122 Lodge Crescent, Waltham Cross, Herts; NW London, Herts and Middlesex: Colin Bishop, 2 Alden Road, 14 The Avenue, Hatch End, Middlesex; Hampshire and Dorset: Terence Brook, 3 Bugle Street, Southampton; Norfolk, Suffolk and Cambridgeshire: J. Norrington, Little Choppins Stud, Coddenham, Suffolk; Beds, Northants and Huntingdon: John Palmer, 28/30 Queensberry Road, Kettering, Northants; Sussex: Colin Simmonds, Forthings, Newick Lane, Mayfield, Sussex; North Wales: Ian Sheppard, Bankside, Truemans Way, Hawarden, Deeside; South Wales: David Limbrey, 11 Linden Way, Danycraig, Porthcawl; Scotland: Bob Clare, 56 Airlie Street, Hyndland, Glasgow; Devon and Cornwall: David Ettridge, Oakleigh, Elmway, Sidford, Devon.

United States of America: Charles L. Turner, 195 Mount Paran Road NW, Atlanta, Georgia 30327; Richard F. Green, 7440 Amarillo Road, Dublin, California 94566.
Australia: Charles Williams, 24 Arnold Road, East Brighton, Vic 3187; Bob Rusk, 20 McCarrs Creek Road, Church Point 2105, New South Wales.
Sweden: Tommy Blank, 4968 Oxbacksgaten 8, 15133 Sodertalje, Sweden.
Belgium: Raymond Dierick, Kleensgraat 66, B-9180 Belsele, Belgium.
South Africa: Ron Newman, c/o IBM, PO Box 1419, Johannesburg 2000.
Spain: Alberto Foch, Avda. Pearson 44, Barcelona 17.
France: Jacques Bertin, 4 Rue Robert Turquan, 75016 Paris.
Switzerland: Jean Ruegger-Deschenaux, Dufour Strasse 65, 8702 Zollikon,

Switzerland.

Japan: Y. Shimazaki, 2-10-2 Nagato-cho, Chiyoda-ku, Tokyo.

Holland: John Hugenholtz, Bloemendaalsweg 250, Overveen.

Ireland: Dr Kevin Healy, 45 Fitzwilliam Square, Dublin.

Germany: Peter Groh, Stadbgrabenstrasse 22, 703 Boblingen, West Germany.

New Zealand: Roger Boyd, 191 Queens Street, Pukekohe, New Zealand.

XVI

The Future

I AM THANKFUL that I am writing this book in 1978. Three years ago Aston Martin had very little future and Lagonda none at all. Now with the first year of Alan Curtis's five-year programme passed, the future looks bright. Orders stretch into the 1980s for new Aston Martins and Lagondas; they could make a dozen cars a week but they feel better insulated against possible market fluctuations by producing only six or seven. The company is self-supporting at last—a historic achievement for an Aston Martin or Lagonda proprietor—so they are in a good position to think of the future.

They have produced a big saloon years ahead of everybody else with the Lagonda and the obvious rivals in the field, Rolls-Royce, swear that their new car won't be ready till 1980. They have a two-plus-two that can leave anything behind for the next few years in the Aston Martin Vantage and a detuned version for strangled areas such as California. But they haven't had a two-seater since an ill-fated DBS prototype in 1966. Two-seaters, by tradition, ought to be a lot faster than two-plus-twos—and a de-toxed two-seater could hardly be expected to out-drag the no-holds-barred Vantage. So how should the extra power be found? One possible solution is to increase the engine's capacity and Aston Martin have already experimented with a 5.8-litre V8. But the fuel consumption is heavy enough already, so it seems unlikely that this will prove to be the answer. A popular alternative could be turbocharging. Rex Woodgate has already experimented with it and there are two turbocharged V8s racing quite successfully in Britain. Porsche have also found this form of extracting more power to be highly successful on their 911 series and we have the engineering expertise in Britain: the truck world is full of turbocharged V8s. There is not much point in changing the basic Aston Martin engine: it is the newest V8 in current production, some of the others dating back to the time David Brown was talking about a V8 as he experimented with the Lagonda V12! So it seems likely that the fourth generation of Aston Martins will be turbocharged. It is the only practical way of extracting more power today.

Another factor influencing the fourth generation is the tantalizing position of Lamborghini. In 1978 they were in a similar financial position to that of Aston Martin in 1975. They had some wonderful cars without the money to make them. BMW came near to snapping up the company until their financial father figures black-marked the lire. But the present proprietors at Newport Pagnell were ready to put their money where their mouths were when it came to the crunch with Aston Martin in 1975 and they have certainly been investigating the possibilities at Sant'Agata during 1978.

It is an open secret as I write this book that a new Aston Martin is intended soon. But it will not be a Lamborghini, nor a Lamborghini Lagonda. It will be pure Aston Martin. It was to have been introduced at the Birmingham Motor Show in October 1978 but obviously Aston Martin Lagonda didn't want a repeat performance of the embarrassing delay between the show Lagonda of 1976 and the production reality of 1978. They have enough orders in hand, so they do not need to startle the world all over again.

So what will be the fourth generation of post-war Aston Martins? Add up the essential elements and it has to be a mid-engined two-seater with a turbocharged V8 produced at the exclusive rate of half a dozen a year with a high price tag. Panther have already explored the £40,000 region with a totally impractical six-wheeler. Such an Aston would have to be mid-engined because it would be good for the magic 200 mph, a figure they have been dreaming of since Gershon's day. The two Lola T70 111Bs that were modified for road use went really well if you were brave enough and they are very similar to the ill-fated Surtees Aston Martin of 1967. So the suspension know-how is there and so are the aerodynamics.

It seems certain that William Towns will have done the styling. And as he has recently finished a convertible for Jim Thomson, perhaps he is thinking about that possibility too. To work out if anybody could keep a soft top on at that speed is a problem, but it could be done with a Porsche-style Targa top.

With these three cars: the mid-engined 200 mph two-seater, the current two-plus-two and the Lagonda four-door, that adds up to six or seven cars a week. What else can they make that makes sense? What are the other gaps to fill?

They could safely sell more if they had a bigger factory, or another one that could make engines. So what about Lamborghini? What else could Aston Martin Lagonda make to use their capacity and strengthen their range still further? Smaller versions of their current cars, using less petrol, is the answer. And Lamborghinis have some super ones with engines of their very own, a feature dear to Aston Martin Lagonda's heart. They still abhor big American V8s as much as Gershon. With Towns's styling them and a 3- or 4-litre Lamborghini engine Ferrari would really have strong competition right across the range.

XVII

Your Aston Martin and Lagonda Log Book

THE PRODUCTION life of a majority of sporting cars can be condensed to a surprising degree. Once the format has been established through prototypes, the pattern changes only occasionally. With Aston Martin and Lagonda it is totally different. There have been nearly thirty basic models since the war, some, such as the DB4 and the V8 with five distinct series. And because of the personal requirements of first owners, eternal problems with component supplies for such small production runs, and constant development, hardly any two cars are exactly alike. The same goes for colour schemes: almost anything goes for an Aston Martin or Lagonda provided it looks elegant. Although basic colours such as red, blue, green and white feature to a large degree, there's no colour scheme that can be described as non-standard. However, establishing the original colour scheme of an Aston Martin or Lagonda is hardly ever the problem it is with cheaper sporting vehicles: Astons and Lagondas were painted and trimmed so well that they have frequently kept their original livery, and thanks to the Aston Martin Owners' Club Register, and records kept by the factory and specialists, it can be surprisingly easy to establish the original specification. Therefore it is pointless to try to list all the colours here. The basic mechanical specification can be a useful reference, however:

Aston Martin Two-Litre (later called the DB1)

Fifteen built between September 1948 and May 1950. Chassis numbers AMC/48/1 to AMC/50/15.

Engine

Four cylinders; CUBIC CAPACITY 1970 cc; BORE AND STROKE 82.55 mm × 92 mm; MAX. POWER 90 bhp (gross) at 4750 rpm; COMPRESSION RATIO 7.25:1 (alternative 8.5:1 giving 95 bhp); CARBURETTERS twin 1.5-inch SU; CLUTCH Borg and Beck single dry plate.

Chassis

WEIGHT (dry) with alloy drop-head coupé bodywork, 2523 lb (one fitted with saloon body); WHEELBASE 9 ft; FRONT TRACK 4 ft 6 ins; REAR TRACK 4 ft 6 ins; LENGTH (with drop-head body) 14 ft 8 ins; WIDTH 5 ft 7.5 ins; HEIGHT 4 ft 7.5 ins; TURNING CIRCLE 35 ft; FRONT SUSPENSION coil springs and trailing arms; REAR SUSPENSION coil springs and parallel arms with Panhard rod; BRAKES 12-inch drum all round; GEARBOX David Brown four forward, one reverse; (ratios) 1st 12, 2nd 7.7, 3rd 5.17, 4th 4.1, reverse 12, with standard 4.1 axle ratio (3.9 alternative); REAR AXLE hypoid beval; STEERING Marles box; TYRES AND WHEELS Dunlop 5.75 ins × 16 ins.

Lagonda 2½-litre

Approximately 550 made between September 1948 and October 1953. Chassis numbers LAG/48/1 on.

Engine

Six cylinders; CUBIC CAPACITY 2580 cc; BORE AND STROKE 78 mm × 90 mm; MAX. POWER 105 bhp at 5000 rpm; COMPRESSION RATIO 6.5:1; CARBURETTERS twin SU 1.5-inch H4; CLUTCH Borg and Beck 9-inch single dry plate.

Chassis

WEIGHT (dry) 3584 lb (saloon body); WHEELBASE 9 ft 5.5 ins; FRONT TRACK 4 ft 8.75 ins; REAR TRACK 4 ft 8.75 ins; LENGTH 15 ft 8 ins; WIDTH 5 ft 8 ins; height 5 ft 4 ins; TURNING CIRCLE 38 ft; FRONT SUSPENSION independent wishbone and coil; REAR SUSPENSION independent wishbone and torsion bar; BRAKES 12-inch drum all round; GEARBOX David Brown four forward, one reverse (ratios) 1st 11.03, 2nd 7.48, 3rd 5.02, 4th 3.77, reverse 11.03, with 3.77 rear axle ratio; REAR AXLE hypoid beval; TYRES AND WHEELS Dunlop 6 ins × 16 ins.

Aston Martin DB2

407 made between May 1950 and May 1953. Chassis numbers LML/50/10 to LML/50/460 and LML/50/X1 to LML/50/X5, plus team cars.

Engine

Six cylinders; CUBIC CAPACITY 2580 cc; BORE AND STROKE 78 mm × 90 mm; MAX. POWER (standard form) 105 bhp at 5000 rpm; COMPRESSION RATIO (standard form) 6.5:1; CARBURETTERS (standard form) twin SU 1.5-inch H4; MAX. POWER (early special engine) 116 bhp at 5000 rpm; COMPRESSION RATIO (early special engine) 7.5:1; CARBURETTERS (early special engine) twin SU 1.75-inch HV6; MAX. POWER (later Vantage engine 123 bhp at 5000 rpm; COMPRESSION RATIO (Vantage) 8.16:1; CARBURETTERS (Vantage) twin SU 1.75-inch HV6; CLUTCH Borg and Beck 9-inch single dry plate.

Chassis

WEIGHT (dry) with alloy saloon body, 2430 lb; WHEELBASE 8 ft 3 ins; FRONT TRACK 4 ft 6 ins; REAR TRACK 4 ft 6 ins; LENGTH 13 ft 6.5 ins; WIDTH 5 ft 5 ins; HEIGHT 4 ft 5.5 ins; TURNING CIRCLE 35 ft; FRONT SUSPENSION coil springs and trailing arms; REAR SUSPENSION coil springs and parallel arms with Panhard rod; BRAKES 12-inch drum all round; GEARBOX David Brown four forward, one reverse; (ratios) 1st 11.03, 2nd 7.05, 3rd 4.75, 4th 3.77, reverse 11.03, with 3.77 rear axle ratio (3.5, 3.67, 4.1 alternatives); OPTIONAL GEAR RATIOS 1st 11.03, 2nd 7.48, 3rd 5.02, 4th 3.77 with 3.77 rear axle ratio; REAR AXLE hypoid bevel; STEERING Marles box; TYRES AND WHEELS Dunlop 6.00 ins × 16 ins.

Aston Martin DB3

Ten made between September 1951 and May 1953. Chassis numbers DB3/1–DB3/10.

Engine

Initially as DB2 Vantage with triple Weber 36DCF5 or 35DCO carburetters, giving 140 bhp at 5300 rpm. Later, from 1952, with 3-litre engine (bore increased to 83 mm), capacity 2922 cc, producing 163 bhp at 5500 rpm; CLUTCH Borg and Beck 9-inch single dry plate.

Chassis

WEIGHT (dry) with standard open alloy body, 2010 lb; WHEELBASE 7 ft 9 ins; FRONT TRACK 4 ft 3 ins; REAR TRACK 4 ft 3 ins; LENGTH 13 ft 2.5 ins; WIDTH 5 ft 1.5 ins; HEIGHT 3 ft 4 ins; TURNING CIRCLE 32 ft; FRONT SUSPENSION trailing arms and torsion bars; REAR SUSPENSION trailing arms and torsion bars with Panhard rod; BRAKES drums all round, 13-inch front, 11-inch rear; GEARBOX (1951) David Brown five forward, one reverse; (ratios) 1st 11.91, 2nd 7.76, 3rd 5.24, 4th 4.11, 5th 3.41, reverse 8.63; (early 1952) 1st 11.91, 2nd 7.76, 3rd 5.24, 4th 4.11, 5th 3.64; (late 1952 and 1953) David Brown four forward, one reverse; (ratios) 1st 11.97, 2nd 7.67, 3rd 5.16, 4th 4.11, reverse 11.97, all with 4.11 rear axle ratio; REAR AXLE hypoid bevel; STEERING rack and pinion; TYRES AND WHEELS Dunlop 6.00 × 16 ins.

Aston Martin DB3S

Thirty made between May 1953 and October 1956 (first production cars October 1955). Chassis numbers DB3S/1–DB3S/11 (team cars) and DB3S/101–DB3S/120 except for DB3S/109 (production cars).

Engine

As 3-litre DB3 developed to produce 182 bhp at 5500 rpm, later 225 bhp and 236 bhp at 6000 rpm on team cars. Production cars produced 180 bhp at 5500 rpm with compression ratio of 8.68:1 and three Weber 40DCO3 carburetters; some developed to 210 bhp at 6000 rpm; some fitted with 84-mm bore engine giving 2992 cc; CLUTCH 9-inch single dry plate (triple plate clutch on team cars from 1954).

Chassis

WEIGHT (dry) with open alloy body, 1960 lb; WHEELBASE 7 ft 3 ins; FRONT TRACK 4 ft 1 in; REAR TRACK 4 ft 1 in; LENGTH 12 ft 10 ins; WIDTH 4 ft 11 ins; HEIGHT (including screen) 3 ft 5 ins; TURNING CIRCLE 30 ft; FRONT SUSPENSION trailing arms and torsion bars; REAR SUSPENSION trailing arms and torsion bars with de Dion tube and central slide; BRAKES (production and early team cars) drums all round, 13 ins front, 11 ins rear (later team cars) discs all round 11.5 ins with option of 12.5 ins front; GEARBOX David Brown four forward, one reverse; (ratios) 1st 10.88, 2nd 6.97, 3rd 4.69, 4th 3.73, reverse 10.88 with 3.73 rear axle ratio (3.27, 3.54, 3.91 alternatives); REAR AXLE spiral bevel; STEERING rack and pinion; TYRES AND WHEELS Dunlop 6.00 ins × 16 ins with drum brakes, Borrani wheels with disc brakes.

Aston Martin DB2/4 (later called Mark I)

565 made between October 1953 and October 1955. Chassis numbers LML/501–LML/1065.

Engine

As DB2 Vantage until April 1954 for drop-head, August 1954 for saloon. Then 3-litre engine as Lagonda, with 83-mm bore. Standard compression ratio of 8.16:1 gave 140 bhp at 5000 rpm; CLUTCH Borg and Beck 9-inch dry single plate.

Chassis

WEIGHT (dry) 2632 lb with alloy saloon body; WHEELBASE 8 ft 3 ins; FRONT TRACK 4 ft 6 ins; REAR TRACK 4 ft 6 ins; LENGTH 14 ft 1.5 in; WIDTH 5 ft 5 ins; HEIGHT 4 ft 5.5 ins; TURNING CIRCLE 35 ft; FRONT SUSPENSION coil springs and trailing arms; REAR SUSPENSION coil springs and parallel arms with Panhard rod; BRAKES 12-inch drum all round; GEARBOX David Brown four forward, one reverse; (ratios) 1st 10.9, 2nd 7.38, 3rd 4.96, 4th 3.73, reverse 10.9 with 3.73 rear axle ratio; REAR AXLE hypoid bevel; STEERING Marles box; TYRES AND WHEELS Dunlop 6.00 ins × 16 ins.

Lagonda 3-litre

430 made between October 1953 and October 1957. Chassis numbers LB290 on.

Engine

As earlier Lagonda saloon and drop-head.

Chassis

WEIGHT (dry) 3808 lb with alloy saloon body; WHEELBASE 9 ft 5.5 ins; FRONT TRACK 4 ft 8.75 ins; REAR TRACK 4 ft 8.75 ins; LENGTH 16 ft 4 ins; WIDTH 5 ft 9.5 ins; HEIGHT 5 ft 2 ins; TURNING CIRCLE 38 ft; FRONT SUSPENSION independent wishbone and coil; REAR SUSPENSION independent wishbone and torsion bar; BRAKES 12-inch drums all round; GEARBOX David Brown four forward, one reverse; (ratios) 1st 11.03, 2nd 7.48, 3rd 5.02, 4th 3.77, reverse 11.03 with 3.77 rear axle ratio; REAR AXLE hypoid bevel; TYRES AND WHEELS Dunlop 6.00 ins × 16 ins.

Aston Martin DB 2/4 Mark II

199 made between October 1955 and October 1957. Chassis numbers AM300/1101–AM300/1299.

Engine

As DB 2/4 Mark I.

Chassis

As DB 2/4 Mark I except 14 ft 3.5 ins long and 4 ft 6.75 ins high with saloon body; drop-head and Tickford fixed-head bodies optional.

Aston Martin DB Mark III

551 made between March 1957 and July 1959. Chassis numbers AM300/3A/1300–AM300/3/1850.

Engine

As DB 2/4 Mark II except further developed to produce 162 bhp at 5500 rpm; 178 bhp at 5500 rpm with twin exhausts; 195 bhp at 5500 rpm with triple 35DCO Webers; 214 bhp with triple 45DCO Webers; with alternative 180 bhp with two or three SU carburetters; CLUTCH Borg and Beck 9-inch dry single plate.

Chassis

As DB2/4 Mark II except: WEIGHT (dry) 2800 lb with alloy saloon body; LENGTH 14 ft 3.5 ins; HEIGHT 4 ft 6.25 ins; BRAKES drums all round on first 100 with option of discs at front, discs at front standardized after that; GEARBOX David Brown four forward, one reverse; (ratios) 1st 11, 2nd 7.45, 3rd 5.01, 4th 3.77, reverse 11, with 3.77 rear axle ratio; optional 1st 11, 2nd 6.39, 3rd 4.75, 4th 3.77, reverse 11; optional overdrive giving 2.93 fifth ratio; optional axle ratios 3.27, 3.5 or 4.09; optional Borg Warner automatic transmission.

Aston Martin DB4

1100 made between October 1958 and June 1963. Chassis numbers DB4/101/R–DB4/995/R, DB4/1001/L–DB4/1215/L; series one October 1958–February 1960, series two January 1960–April 1961, series three April 1961–September 1961, series four September 1961–October 1962, series five September 1962–June 1963.

Engine

Six cylinders; CUBIC CAPACITY 3670 cc; BORE AND STROKE 92 mm; MAX. POWER 240 bhp, at 5500 rpm; COMPRESSION RATIO 8.25:1; CARBURETTERS twin SU 2-inch HD8; optional Vantage engine from series four with triple SU HD8 carburetters, 9:1 compression; optional GT engine from series three (specification as Aston Martin DB4GT); CLUTCH Borg and Beck 10-inch single dry plate, twin plate 9-inch clutch from series four.

Chassis

WEIGHT (dry) with alloy saloon body 2983 lb, drop-head body optional; WHEELBASE 8 ft 2 ins; FRONT TRACK 4 ft 6 ins; REAR TRACK 4 ft 5.5 ins; LENGTH 14 ft 8.375 ins; WIDTH 5 ft 6 ins; HEIGHT 4 ft 4 ins; TURNING CIRCLE 34 ft; FRONT SUSPENSION wishbones and coil; REAR SUSPENSION trailing links and coils with Watt linkage; BRAKES discs all round; GEARBOX David Brown four forward, one reverse; (ratios) 1st 8.82, 2nd 6.16, 3rd 4.42, 4th 3.54, reverse 8.92 with 3.54 axle ratio; optional ZF five-speed (ratios as DB5) on late-model series five; alternative axle ratios of 3.31 and 2.93 with series one; overdrive optional from series two with 3.77 axle; 4.09 axle optional from series three (only with overdrive); 3.54 and 3.77 alternative axle ratios from series four; Borg Warner automatic transmission optional from series five; REAR AXLE hypoid bevel; STEERING rack and pinion; TYRES AND WHEELS Dunlop 6.00 ins × 16 ins; 6.00 ins × 15 ins from series five.

Aston Martin DB4GT

100 made between September 1959 and June 1963. Some fitted with lightweight Zagato bodies. Chassis numbers DB4GT/0101/L–DB4GT/0201/L (except 0192 and 0194–0198).

Engine

As DB4 except developed to produce 302 bhp at 6000 rpm with 9:1 compression ratio and triple 45DCOE Weber carburetters; some cars fitted with 93-mm bore engines giving 3749 cc and 314 bhp with Zagato and 9.7:1 compression ratio; CLUTCH Borg and Beck 9-inch twin-plate.

Chassis

As DB4 except: WEIGHT (dry) 2815 lb (some lighter still), optional Zagato body weight (dry) 2665 lb; WHEELBASE 7 ft 9 ins; LENGTH 14 ft 3.375 ins; GEARBOX

David Brown four forward, one reverse; 1st 8.82, 2nd 6.16, 3rd 4.42, 4th 3.54, reverse 8.58 with 3.54 rear axle ratio; alternative axle ratios 2.93, 3.31, 3.77, 4.09 until October 1961; alternative axle ratios 2.93, 3.31, 3.77 only available from October 1961; alternative gearbox, David Brown four forward, one reverse, from October 1961, 1st 10.3, 2nd 6.5, 3rd 4.42, 4th 3.54, reverse 8.92 with 3.54 axle; REAR AXLE hypoid bevel with limited slip differential; TYRES AND WHEELS Dunlop 6.00 ins × 16 ins Borrani.

Lagonda Rapide

55 made between May 1961 and October 1964. Chassis numbers LR0101–0155.

Engine

As DB4 with 96 mm stroke giving 3995 cc; max. power 236 bhp at 5000 rpm with two twin-choke Solex carburetters; DB4 Vantage engine optional.

Chassis

As DB4 except: WEIGHT (dry) 3848 lb; WHEELBASE 9 ft 6 ins; LENGTH 16 ft 3.5 ins; TURNING CIRCLE 41 ft; REAR SUSPENSION independent torsion bars and radius arms with de Dion tube; GEARBOX Borg Warner automatic with 3.77 or 3.54 rear axle ratio; David Brown manual gearbox optional; TYRES AND WHEELS Dunlop 7.10 ins × 15 ins.

Aston Martin DB5

1018 made between July 1963 and September 1965. Chassis numbers DB5/1215/R–DB5/2275/L (except 2124 and 2125).

Engine

As Lagonda Rapide except: MAX. POWER 240 bhp at 5000 rpm with triple SU HD8 carburetters; Vantage engine with triple Weber 45DCOE carburetters optional from September 1964 with max. power 300 bhp at 5750 rpm; CLUTCH 10-inch Laycock diaphragm.

Chassis

As series five DB4 except: WEIGHT (dry) 3233 lb convertible body optional; LENGTH 15 ft; GEARBOX ZF standard from manual chassis 1340 except 1641 and 1643; (ratios) 1st 10.18, 2nd 6.64, 3rd 4.64, 4th 3.77, 5th 3.14, reverse 12.48, with 3.77 rear axle ratio; Borg Warner automatic gearbox optional.

Aston Martin DB6

1330 made between October 1965 and July 1969. Chassis numbers DB6/2351/R–DB6/3599/L and DB6/4001–DB6/4081.

Engine

As DB5 except Vantage engine developed to give 325 bhp at 5750 rpm with 9.4 : 1 compression ratio; later cars fitted with 9.5 diaphragm clutch.

Chassis

As DB5 except: WEIGHT (dry) 3250 lb convertible body optional; WHEELBASE 8 ft 5.75 ins; LENGTH 15 ft 2 ins; HEIGHT 4 ft 5.5 ins; GEARBOX ZF five forward, one reverse; (ratios) 1st 10.07, 2nd 6.34, 3rd 4.59, 4th 3.73, 5th 3.11, reverse 12.34 with 3.73 rear axle ratio; 3.54 ratio optional with automatic transmission; STEERING rack and pinion (power assistance optional).

Aston Martin DB6 Mark 2

245 made between July 1969 and November 1970. Chassis numbers DB6Mk2/ 4101/R–DB6Mk2/4345/R (except 4162 and 4252).

Engine

As DB6 except AE Brico fuel injection optional; CLUTCH 10-inch diaphragm.

Chassis

As DB6 except: WEIGHT (dry) 3300 lb convertible body optional; REAR TRACK 4 ft 6 ins; WIDTH 5 ft 8 ins; GEARBOX ZF five forward, one reverse; (ratios) 1st 11.07, 2nd 6.34, 3rd 4.59, 4th 3.73, 5th 3.11, reverse 12.34 with 3.73 rear axle ratio; POWER STEERING standard; TYRES AND WHEELS 8.15 ins × 15 ins.

Aston Martin DBS

800 built between October 1967 and May 1972; 70 similar Aston Martin Vantage built between May 1972 and July 1973. Chassis numbers DBS/5001/R–DBS/5829/RC, AM/6001/RA–AM/6070/R.

Engine

As DB6 Mark 2; all Aston Martin Vantages fitted with Vantage engine.

Chassis

WEIGHT (dry) 3500 lb; WHEELBASE 8 ft 6.75 ins; FRONT TRACK 4 ft 11 ins; REAR TRACK 4 ft 11 ins; LENGTH 15 ft 0.5 ins; WIDTH 6 ft; HEIGHT 4 ft 4.25 ins; TURNING CIRCLE 36 ft; FRONT SUSPENSION wishbone and coil; REAR SUSPENSION radius arms and coil springs with de Dion tube and Watt linkage; BRAKES discs all round 11.5-inch front, 10.8-inch rear; GEARBOX ZF five forward, one reverse; (ratios) 1st 11.07, 2nd 6.56, 3rd 4.58, 4th 3.73, 5th 3.09 with 3.73 rear axle ratio; 3.54 ratio with optional Borg Warner automatic gearbox; REAR AXLE hypoid bevel; STEERING power-assisted rack and pinion; TYRES AND WHEELS Dunlop 8.15 ins × 15 ins.

A.M.—Q

Aston Martin DBSV8

405 made between September 1969 and April 1972. Chassis numbers DBSV8/10001/R–DBSV8/10405/RCA.

(V8 series one September 1969 to (approx) June 1972; series two June 1972–August 1973; series three August 1973–May 1975; series four May 1975–January 1977; series five February 1977–December 1978 and later.)

Engine

Eight cylinders; CUBIC CAPACITY 5340 cc; BORE AND STROKE 100 mm × 85 mm; MAX. POWER 345 bhp at 6200 rpm; COMPRESSION RATIO 9:1; FUEL INJECTION Bosch mechanical; CLUTCH Borg and Beck 10.5-inch single dry plate.

Chassis

As DBS (six-cylinder) except: WEIGHT (dry) 3584 lb; GEARBOX ZF five forward, one reverse; (ratios) 1st 10.27, 2nd 6.3, 3rd 4.31, 4th 3.54, 5th 2.99, reverse 9.31 with 3.54 rear axle ratio; Chrysler Torqueflite automatic transmission optional (with 3.33 rear axle); 3.33 alternative axle ratios for manual cars, and 2.88 for automatic; TYRES AND WHEELS 7 ins × 15 ins.

Aston Martin V8

1350 (factory estimate) made between May 1972 and December 1978. Chassis numbers V8/10501/RCA–V8/10789, V8/11001/R.

Engine

As DBSV8 until chassis number V8/11001/R when fitted with carburetters four Weber 42 DCNF; developed to produce maximum power 397 bhp from series five.

Chassis

As DBSV8 except: WEIGHT (dry) 3808 lb convertible body optional from late 1978; LENGTH 15 ft 3.75 ins; optional rear axle ratios of 3.07 from series three; 8.3 optional compression ratio from series four.

Aston Martin Vantage

100 (factory estimate) produced between February 1977 and December 1978. Chassis numbers V8/11000/V on.

Engine

As Aston Martin V8 except developed to produce MAX. POWER 485 bhp; CARBURETTERS four Weber 48 IDF.

Chassis

As Aston Martin V8.

Aston Martin Lagonda

Seven made between November 1974 and May 1975. Chassis numbers L/12001/RAC.

Engine

As Aston Martin V8 series three.

Chassis

As Aston Martin V8 except: WEIGHT (dry) 4400 lb; WHEELBASE 9 ft 6.75 ins; LENGTH 16 ft 2 ins; HEIGHT 4 ft 5.25 ins; TURNING CIRCLE 44 ft 6 ins.

Lagonda

Eighteen (factory estimate) made between September 1976 and December 1978. Chassis numbers L/12001 on.

Engine

As Aston Martin V8 series five.

Chassis

As Aston Martin V8 except: WEIGHT (dry) 4450 lb; WHEELBASE 9 ft 6.75 ins; LENGTH 17 ft 4 ins; WIDTH 5 ft 11.5 ins; FRONT TRACK 4 ft 11 ins; REAR TRACK 4 ft 11 ins; HEIGHT 4 ft 3.25 ins; TURNING CIRCLE 38 ft.

Index

Index of Illustrations

Picture Acknowledgements

The author is grateful for permission to reproduce illustration material:

Alexander, Ron, 76 top
Associated Press, 142
Aston Martin-Lagonda, **plates 9, 10, 14, 15, 17, 18, 19, 20**; pages 3, 4, 5 top, 6, 11 left and right, 12 bottom, 14 right, 21 bottom, 22 top and bottom, 25 top and bottom, 28 top, 32 bottom, 33 top left, 38 bottom, 39 top and bottom, 42 top and bottom right, 49 left and right, 56 right, 58 bottom, 89 bottom, 90, 91, 94 bottom left and right, 95 left and right, 96 top and bottom, 97 top and bottom, 100 middle and bottom, 164 middle, 201, 205
Autocar (The), 16, 17, 23, 33 middle and bottom, 35 top, bottom left and right, 47 bottom, 48, 54 top, middle and bottom, 55, 58 top, 63 left, 65, 67, 76 bottom left and right, 82, 85, 86, 101 middle, 102, 103 top and bottom, 105 top and bottom, 109, 110, 111, 113, 116, 118 top and bottom, 119, 124 bottom, 126 top and bottom, 127, 128, 129 top, middle and bottom, 130, 131, 135, 136 bottom, 139, 140 top, middle and bottom, 143, 144, 145, 146 middle and bottom, 163 left and right, 181 right, 182 bottom

Baker, Harold, 157 bottom
Barnes, Owen, **plate 11**, 211 bottom, 212–14
Blank, Tommy, **plate 6**

Chapman, Ronald A., 63 right
Courtaulds, 164 top, 182 top left

Dray, John and Bill, 2, 10 top
Dudley Studios, 12 top

Foster, Pete, Collection, 154 bottom

Holder, Tim, 195

Jaguar Cars, 210 left
Jilian, 68 bottom, 101 top right
Joscelyne, Brian, **plate 1**; 154 top

Kellett, H., and Son, 223
Klementaski, Louis, 14 left, 15, 41, 42 bottom left, 56 left, 101 bottom, 124 top
Kunkel, Paul, **plates 2, 12, 13**

Light Car, The, 10 bottom

Magee, Shaun, 28 bottom
Marsh Plant Hire, 190–2
Morris, Robert, Collection, 188–9

Motor (The), cover, **plates 21, 22, 25**; 3, 5 bottom, 26 left and right, 31, 33 top right, 38 top and middle, 45, 47 top, 71, 72, 89 top, 93, 94 top, 124 middle, 151 top and bottom, 162 right, 203, 204 left and right, 211 top right
Motor Cycling, 9

Ottway, Dr Michael, 112

Perkins, John, *CAR* magazine, **plate 23**
Phillips, George, *Autosport*, 182 top right

Skilleter, Paul, **plates 3, 4, 7, 16, 24, 26**; 13, 108 bottom, 117, 157 top, 164 bottom, 166, 167–78, 181 left, 183 left and right, 210 right, 211 top left, 220 top, middle and bottom, 222
Skilleter, Paul, *Motor*, 32 top, 79
Skilleter, Paul, *Thoroughbred and Classic Cars*, **plate 5**; 108 top

Temple Press, 44, 60, 61, 68 top, 100 top left, 105 middle, 114, 136 top, 146 top, 150 top, middle and bottom, 162 left, 198, 199, 219
Thoroughbred and Classic Cars, **plate 8**

Ware, A. C. K., 21 top, 62